William Sylvester Walker

From The Land Of The Wombat

William Sylvester Walker

From The Land Of The Wombat

ISBN/EAN: 9783741153600

Manufactured in Europe, USA, Canada, Australia, Japa

Cover: Foto ©Andreas Hilbeck / pixelio.de

Manufactured and distributed by brebook publishing software (www.brebook.com)

William Sylvester Walker

From The Land Of The Wombat

From the Land of the Wombat

BY THE SAME AUTHOR

WHEN THE MOPOKE CALLS

Uniform in size and price with this volume, and illustrated with 22 full-page drawings by Simon H. Vedder.

Spectator.—"A brightly-written volume of the trials and humours of Colonial life some thirty years or more back. 'Midnight,' the story of a bushranger who for a while evaded suspicion by successfully impersonating a captain of police, is a favourable specimen of Mr. Walker's powers. He, too, we are glad to see, has a kind word for the blacks. Mr. Vedder's pictures are good."

World.—"Mr. William S. Walker is steeped in the traditions of Australian bushlore, and his collection of tales contain the experiences of a career spent amid what was in those days a wild and unsettled region. They are full of the sound of the vagrant's song of freedom, and are particularly fresh and unhackneyed."

Times.—"A collection of Australian stories, giving a capital idea of life on the remote out-stations of the eastern colonies in the last generation. Not the least attractive chapter is the first, describing the sea voyage, when the passenger by sailing ship had to furnish his own cabin. There is humour in the lamentable tribulation of the jackeroo, or tenderfoot; there is romance in the legend of the haunted gully, and in the tale of the dead digger's Christmas box to his comrades; and there is the height of sensation in the fighting of the flood, when the bursting of waterspouts, after a prolonged drought, threatens to engulf a station with its beleaguered occupants."

Literary World.—"The stories are particularly rich in local colour, and the very full descriptions of the characteristic scenery amid which the incidents take place will be read with interest. The good stories that it unquestionably contains."

London Review.—"It is a varied collection, and the author seems to have met all kind of men and lived through some curious experiences and incidents. The stories are often exciting, and are relieved by a good deal of humour and real sentiment. They are, without exception, unquestionably well told, and all have the stamp of reality upon them."

Bookseller.—"Mr. Walker has succeeded in conveying to the reader a very clear and realistic impression of Australian life and character. We are introduced to the eccentricities of the 'jackeroo,' or 'new chum'. We are taken behind the scenes of up-country racecourses and we see how the 'Squatters' Plate' is unexpectedly won by an unconsidered competitor. We have speaking likenesses of the Chinese workman, of the worn-out old negro, or of the rough hutkeeper, and other characteristic dwellers in the lands 'down under'. Bushranging experiences are not overlooked, and altogether many of the incidents and scenes here described are set forth with a picturesque power which makes the author a worthy relative of 'Rolf Boldrewood,' that popular Australian writer, who is Mr. Walker's uncle. The illustrations have been drawn by Mr. S. H. Vedder, and, as our readers can judge, are distinctly good."

Bookman.—"Capital tales of sketches of Australian life."

Weekly Sun.—"There is no more interesting writer about Australia than Mr. William S. Walker, the well-known 'Coo-ee'. His new book gives a new interest to Colonial life. We get something more than its roughness and ruggedness; we get its humour and human interest. No other writer on antipodean subjects writes with so much dramatic power as Mr. Walker."

Manchester Courier.—"There is not a single story that will not repay perusal, while some are singularly interesting and several most pathetic."

JOHN LONG, PUBLISHER, LONDON

"WE CAME ACROSS A GIRL ALMOST WHITE."

From the Land of the Wombat.

Page 21.
Frontispiece.

From the Land of the Wombat

By
William Sylvester Walker
("Coo-ee")
Author of "When the Mopoke Calls"

With Illustrations by J. Ayton Symington

London
John Long
6 Chandos Street, Strand
1899

"Her hearth is wide to every wind
    That makes the white-ash spin,
And tide and tide, and 'tween the tides,
    Her sons go out and in.

"And some return by failing light,
    And some in waking dream ;
For she hears the heels of the dripping ghosts
    That ride the rough roof beam."

—KIPLING.

TO

"ROLF BOLDREWOOD"

FROM

W. S. W.

1898.

PROLOGUE

To the Spirit in the Australian "Native" Rose.

Thy first children, sporting lightly, found thee sweet and
    coloured brightly
  By Sydney's rocklands, seawards, long ago.
Thy rich crimson more than vying with the day in radiance
    dying,
  Thy soft green a set-off to thy glow.

And they, forthwith, called thee "Native" Rose of Austral
    correlative
  To thy flower and serried leaves—you *bore* no thorn.
And from out thy bush-land wildness, spoke thy Spirit in its
    mildness,
  "Welcome, Home and Haven, to the Native-born".

Land thy native-born so cherish, that they dream that never
    blemish
  Will come near it. Spirit guard them aye!
Keep them in their time of trouble, make their passing care
    a bubble,
  Floating, gleaming, with the prisms of the day.

So thy pioneers of past days, looking back from happy last
    days,
  Bless thee for the hopes which cheer them yet,
That Australia's guide to progress never yet was grey grim
    ogress,
  But a spirit pure as that on Olivet.

And from thy pink petals dancing, comes that perfume so entrancing
  That the bush exhales its very self.
Scents of every gum and flower, herb and leaf, thy Southern dower,
  Thou hast made Australia's woods thine own sweet pelf.

So thy scent of far-off wildwood, haunting spirit of my childhood,
  Brings thy form and beauty into sight o'er sea,
And I gradually see clearly, thy nobility so nearly,
  Dearest *eidolon*, now bright on shore and lea.

Comes my stately, gracious maiden, radiant, with her bush-flowers laden,
  And they lie enwreathed about her hair and breast.
Thy *one* flower supreme expressing all Australia's fragrant blessing ;
  As Australia's Spirit stands at last—confest.

CONTENTS

	PAGE
PROLOGUE: TO THE SPIRIT IN THE AUSTRALIAN "NATIVE" ROSE	vii
LA REVANCHE	1
A MAD SOMNAMBULIST	11
LALOR OF CORINGA	18
A VOICE FROM THE DEAD	46
AN UP-COUNTRY RACE MEETING	58
WADDYGĀLO	67
THE WRAITH OF TOM IMRIE	84
A RABBIT STATION	102
THE CHASE OF THE WHITE KANGAROO	124
A FREE SELECTOR	144
FATHER'S "FORTUN'"	182
ON THE LEAD	200
MUZZLEM'S	217
L'ENVOI	219

LIST OF ILLUSTRATIONS

Facing page

LALOR OF CORINGA.
    We came across a girl almost white . *frontispiece*

LA REVANCHE.
    I gave her a violent push instead, which sent her reeling some yards 6

A MAD SOMNAMBULIST.
    Then we formed up and proceeded to the skillion bedroom 16

A VOICE FROM THE DEAD.
    He is there now 49

AN UP-COUNTRY RACE MEETING.
    Right into forty feet of Gunyahgo river water 64

WADDYGALO.
    A white man 78

THE WRAITH OF TOM IMRIE.
    Tom Imrie sitting on his roan horse . . . 99

LIST OF ILLUSTRATIONS

Facing page

A RABBIT STATION.
    I gave her the usual "nip" necessary on these occasions 115

THE CHASE OF THE WHITE KANGAROO.
    I struggled to get my revolver free . . . 139

A FREE SELECTOR.
    Come in, wid yez 152
    The Hon. Josiah Barnes in the lower branches of a gum tree 178

FATHER'S "FORTUN'".
    She had fallen near a number of moss-grown boulders 197

ON THE LEAD.
    Albeit she had to hold her pretty arms and hands behind her, because of the soap suds . . 208

LA REVANCHE

There is no grief like the grief which does not speak.—Proverb.

I WAS sitting on my favourite seat in the beautiful and wonderful botanical gardens in Sydney, wonderful in their tropic glory, and production of many a clime and country, beautiful in their scenery and situation.

The seat I affected was a little back from the boomerang-like sweep of the sea walk near the front wall, over the many side walks and lawns to where the turn locates the last agglomerate of sandstone rocks in that part of the gardens: until you go out by the gate at the top of the rising ground above into the precincts of the domain. Rock lilies and specimens of the beautiful pittosporums with their fragile shiny black upper stems, were growing in the crannies over my head and a faint perfume from many blossoms lingered in the air. I was thinking over old times, old scenes and old episodes, when I had rowed, sailed, and explored, every part of the beautiful blue waters in front of me, clambered almost every crag, and travelled far along the sea-capes. My eyes wandered over "Farm Cove" below the stately pile of "Government House" to where the *Wolverene* lay at anchor. The *Sandfly*, one of our stinging marine insect men-of-war, had just anchored much nearer inshore, after a cruise to the South Seas, where she had been to suppress "black-birding".

As I pondered, a familiar step broke the absorption and interest of my retrospect. It was Inspector Brodribb.

"Look here," he said, "I know you fellows from the bush like to get into these quiet spots now and then, to 'squat,' as it were, away from the ken of your fellow-men. There's no assignation, is there; no lady expected?"

"No, sir," replied I, after the fashion of a harassed Minister. "I left word at the club where I should be found if any one called, and I suppose my message has brought you on here."

"You are right," responded the inspector. "But I really have something of importance to tell you, and it was *not* merely idle curiosity that made me search for you. Do you remember a man named Thompson—Jim Thompson? He was shepherding for you once on the Nardoo. At least he says so, and as he is dying at the hospital, he has eased his mind by making a confession of something very like murder, although he did not actually murder the man himself. And a trail of circumstances, only accountable for by the 'wages of sin' conclusion has, from the consequences of the first act, wiped out three other people who were at one time friends, and who seemed to live and act but for each other. All these people therefore being dead, and Thompson himself far on the way to another Court of Justice, there can be no one for me to secure, so I must perforce make the best of tangible evidence, and for that purpose I wish you to accompany me to the hospital to identify the man. Come up now, and see him. He told me to tell you that he has something of importance to give you."

We departed, and by the sick bed I knew the man at once. He *had* been a shepherd of ours at one time, and I remembered all the circumstances connected with him.

He had worked fairly well for a year, and beyond being a bit "scary" about the "warrigal" blacks, quite satisfied my partners and myself, until he went to Adelaide with our travelling sheep and disappeared. He had been a well set up good-looking fellow, much out of the style of the usual shepherd, when I last saw him, but now looked fearfully emaciated. A galloping consumption had apparently set its seal upon him; and he was positively ghastly. "Will you take this, sir," he croaked almost in a whisper, "and read it? Publish it in the papers after my death if it is wished. I've written down pretty well the story of my life since I left Auburn six years ago." He handed me a thick roll of paper, evidently manuscript, and signed to us to go.

"I won't say any more about it now," remarked Brodribb afterwards, "I know all the main facts of the case, but I will call down at your club to-night and talk it over. Perhaps, as you are so fond of reading your own works out loud to your rather bored friends, you might read Thompson's confession to me. It will be a change, and will have the merit of being original, which is more than you ever *can* be."

"I will, with pleasure," said I. "Good-bye, infidel, and come and dine with me as a favour on your part."

On getting back to the club I adjourned to my bedroom, and in the privacy of that apartment, glanced at the manuscript.

Thompson had always been fond of writing, as I knew. He was also addicted to the composition of poetry, and received a very large correspondence for a shepherd. The scroll was headed thus :—

"CONFESSIONS OF A PENITENT MAN.

"I'm the last of the four. It had to be so, so that I'd get my full share of the punishment. But I never thought it would be my hand and my will that would be the means to lay Jack Stedman in his lonely bush grave—no.

"When I left Auburn, sir, as you know, I went to Adelaide with the sheep. Well, my pockets were full of money, and Jack Stedman, an old mate of mine, was in Adelaide too. He'd done well on the diggings and was doing well still. He was at Broken Hill at the silver mines. He'd come away for a 'spell'. He was on wages, not working on his own hook, and he asked me to come too, for times were good. After a week or so we started, and we both got on together for day work at one of the proprietary claims. Silverton wasn't as big then as it is now, and times were real good for a man who was worth his salt. The town was growing steadily, all hands seemed pretty flush, and what drinking saloons and hotel bars there were, were doing a roaring trade. A shilling a nobbler all round and help yourself out of the bottle. Well, there was a saloon that me and Jack used to spend a lot of time and money at, worse luck, both at the bar and billiard-room and in the back parlour too when we got to be favourites. What a good-looking fellow Jack Stedman was! I often used to think so when I seen him talking to one or both of the girls at that bar. Women always seemed to like to talk to Jack Stedman. The two girls there kept the place. They were sisters, and the eldest was clean gone on Jack. But, my word, wasn't the youngest one a beauty! Skin like milk and roses, white teeth and beautiful flossy hair. I fell in love with her, head over heels, straight off. But she didn't cotton to me much, and that made me all the more madly in love with her. Her name was Lucy—Lucy Devenish—and her sister's name was Laura. Well, as I said, these two Devenish girls took up a lot of our time and thought, the two of us.

"I'd catch myself thinking of Lucy in the mine, and once I nearly fell down the shaft with thinking about her, instead of keeping my eyes and senses clear. Jack was dead set on Lucy too, but he used to talk a lot with Laura. I never could make that Laura out quite to my satisfaction. She wasn't pretty, and she used to look like a she-devil sometimes, but there was something about her which attracted men. I think it must have been the vitality in her. I always thought *that* so strong, that she might have been a cat instead of a woman. And she had the lissomness of a snake too, with the stony look of it in her eyes sometimes. It used to make me shudder. Speak to her on any subject which didn't please her or about any one she didn't care for, and you would soon see that look come into her brown eyes, with a sort of yellow glare behind it. But speak about *Jack*, and—well, there.

"I never saw anything like it. Her eyes would first lighten and soften, and a look of tenderness come into them. She would become animated, and the yellow light in her eyes would be more lively. But there was a funny *living* expression in them *always*. That woman would love a man like a madwoman, I have often thought. And she would stick you like a pig if you didn't love *her*, was my next idea.

"Well, things went on. Our tent was about 200 yards from the shaft we worked in. One day Jack twisted his ankle badly through doubling over on top of it when using the pick in an awkward drive. That necessitated Lucy's presence now and then at our 'digs,' for let me tell you that those two girls had pretty nigh claimed Jack and me as their property by this time, and yet for all that, up to now, there had been no proposals for tying our lives together. We had not settled who was to be joined to who, and we did not know whether any fixed union would be satisfactory to all the parties concerned.

"Now, about this time, this was how I fixed it. Laura was passionately in love with Jack, with a passion nothing would break or stop. Whatever came before that passion would be swept away as if it never had been. And the restraint she had hitherto kept upon herself made those wonderful eyes smoulder like a volcano about to burst out again. And Jack was strangely influenced by Laura. He was drawn to her by her stronger will. I'm blest if I didn't think sometimes that she hypnotised him. And he *loved* Lucy, and she loved him. And I loved Lucy more than all the earth put together. We used to go out riding on Sundays and any half-holiday we got, the whole lot of us sometimes, sometimes by twos. Stedman was a good all round man. He could build a house, fence, break a colt, sink a shaft, and timber it too. And was a good judge of sheep and cattle. It is very often the best all round men who take to mining in the end. That's my experience anyway, and Jack was native born too. He had broken in a nice colt for a lady's horse. Laura could ride above a bit; Lucy was a bit timid. But Lord bless you, Laura wasn't afraid of anything, and she rode it very well. Somehow one Sunday, when Jack was laid up with his accident, Laura and I found ourselves jogging along some miles from the town, on a bush track, and we turned our horses out in hobbles for a spell, and sat down on a fallen log.

"I had in fact, lately, got very jealous of Jack, for I could see that Lucy didn't care the snap of a finger for me, and Jack seemed more to her than ever since the accident. The way she would coddle him up, or stop and read to him, or bring him any dainty, riled me, and Laura had noticed it.

"Well, we sat on that fallen log, in that bush solitude, among the gum trees, with the parrots feeding on the blossoms and the sun shining here and there through the branches, making regular patterns on the grass.

"Sudden like, Laura says, ' Jim, what a fool you are. Why do you care for Lucy so much?' ' 'Cause I *am* a fool, I suppose,' says I. ' Well,' says she, ' I suppose no other woman would satisfy you now, eh?' And she took my hand and looked me in the face. And what, with the effect of her wonderful eyes and the curious attraction of herself, I felt I could not stand against her wiles. And she said, ' Ah, Jim, I can give you love such as that chit cannot give to a man'.

And she fairly drew my soul out of me. I don't know even now whether I loved or hated her most; but I became her slave from that very day. And when we got up to go, Laura nearly put her foot on a big black snake that was coiled up by a branch in some tufted grass just where I was going to give her a lift to put her up into her saddle again as she came forward to me. I gave her a violent push instead, which sent her reeling aside some yards; and she fell down flat. I had my knife out in a minute, cut a stick and killed the brute. Then the horses broke away with the flurry of it all, and off they went back to the camp. So we had to walk home.

"When she got up from where I had pushed her to, she was quite white, as she thought I had suddenly gone mad, until she seen me kill the snake. Ah, that walk! Shall I ever forget it? She clung round my neck and kissed me, and said I had saved her life.

"She was a bad woman and I was a fool; but I'd go the same way yet if I had to go over my life again.

"There was something magnetic about her. It couldn't have been exactly love, because I didn't feel like what I felt towards Lucy; but it was as if I was compelled to her against my will.

"And I believe, as a dying man, that when I held her in my arms that day, felt her heart beat against me, and kissed her over and over again, that I'd have given up twenty Lucys in the mad passion I felt for her at the moment, aye, and afterwards. I didn't know it was in me. 'You needn't tell them we've been doing any sweethearting, Jim,' says Laura when we got near the township, and were a matter of wonder to some of the people we met, being on foot, and she in her riding habit. But horses breaking away in the bush is common enough, and the nags were all right with their mob near our place, letting us catch them and take their bridles and saddles off. Of course, Lucy comes down when she got the chance and, my word, I caught the look in Laura's eyes when she and Jack kissed each other. Baffled rage and fury was in it, and nothing else.

"I minded the old saying about 'a woman scorned,' but if ever battle, murder and sudden death came out of any woman's eyes, they came out of Laura's then.

"I GAVE HER A VIOLENT PUSH INSTEAD, WHICH SENT HER REELING SOME YARDS."

From the Land of the Wombat.

"But it soon passed off, quick as thought, and she began chaffing them for a pair of ninnies, and telling them to do their love-making in private next time. 'I don't care,' says Stedman, 'who sees us. We're going to be married in a fortnight.' Oh, my, Laura's eyes! They frightened me. 'Am I to be a bridesmaid?' says she, turning to Stedman. 'I'm the best qualified.'

"And she gave him such a look that he turned pale. But this fit of anger also passed off, and the two were married. The wedding was a grand affair, and they went away for a month. When they came back I was head over ears in Laura's toils. She could do what she liked with me, and just fairly maddened me. But she wouldn't marry me; and at last she told me how she loved Jack, and how he had deceived her. But though she professed that she had been treated badly, she gammoned me she had got over it, and that she now loved me. Well, Laura being all in all to me now, I was that mad with Jack, with his underhandedness and his slyness all round, that I felt I could have killed him.

"He was the stronger man of the two of us, and in a fair stand-up fight I thought he would get the best of it; and I was no slouch either with my hands.

"Somehow I brooded on it night and day, and when a man does that he nourishes devils. I had loved Lucy beyond everything, and Jack had taken her from me. I used to think if there had been no Jack Stedman, Lucy would have been mine right enough. But that wasn't all, for whether it was Laura's stronger will over my thoughts, or my getting to fancy it was, I got to hate that Jack Stedman with such a bitter hate that my devils began to shape my thoughts into action. 'Why don't you get rid of him and be revenged? He has worked you enough harm. There's ways of getting rid of a man without the rest of the world knowing. There must be. Think it out.' These were the thoughts my whispering devils brought me.

"Laura breathed in my ear one day after he had been kissing Lucy before us. It was after they went. They had a separate tent now, and Jack and she had fixed it up beautiful. 'Jim,' whispers Laura, 'I *hate* him.' And the thought in my heart kept growing, and I let it grow.

"One day Jack and Lucy began chaffing us, and asking

why we didn't get spliced. We told them there was no hurry. But that night during a walk home with Laura, she said: 'Isn't it all very fine for Stedman to talk, seeing he made love to me first, your girl, Jim, and then threw me aside like an old shoe? Oh, I wish I was a man. I wouldn't let him laugh in his sleeve. I wish he was dead, and I was dead, and the whole lot of us were dead, I do.'

"Well, I felt mean and baulked, somehow, and I felt cowardly too. It isn't nice when your girl says these sort of things to you. I should have liked to have given Stedman a good hiding, a right down A1 copper-fastened father of a hiding, for my heart was burning in me, but he was just too good for me for a fair thing. And the whispering devils told me of the unfair thing.

"'Rest easy, my lass,' said I, 'I'll give him such a hiding some of these days when I get a fair chance that he won't want another. He's a heavier weight than I am, but I'll down him, I promise you. I've licked a better man than myself before through a little science, and I'll do it again.'

"'How will you do it? Jim,' says she, 'if you do I'll give you myself.' And the light in her eyes was like a devil's and an angel's mixed.

"And I felt that strange, strange, drawn-out-of-myself feeling I always felt when she caressed me. And my devils' thoughts came for more nourishing and pampering; it was the *look* she gave me. She wouldn't care if he *was* dead. And there was always before us both his handsome, sneering face, as if nothing in the world was too good for him, and men and women too must cast themselves down at his feet just to please him.

"About a week or so after this there was a rush for a new diggings, about fifty miles off, and Jack and I were to club our money, and go in on our own hook. And the girls were going to invest in it too, they had plenty, both of 'em. Well, about this new rush. The prospectors had struck it real rich. But it wasn't gold or silver I wanted.

"I wanted my thought worked out. It was never away from me, and I dreamed it, such black dreams that I was glad to be awake again.

"We started, and I'm blessed if we didn't pass the very log where Laura and I had sat that Sunday we took the ride together. And there was the place where I had killed the black snake!

"The devils stood by me *then*, quick and sudden, and says they, 'Why don't you do it?' And all the jealousy I had felt and concealed, which made my hate the fiercer, was because of late I had noticed that Laura, who could so influence my passion for *her*—I won't call it love—still showed that she *really* loved Jack. And he had begun to turn to her, for she lured him on, in the way she could lure a man on. But she loved him, still loved him, I could see it in her eyes, in her manner. And she only *influenced* me; *I* didn't see that love-light in her eyes which I had caught in them for Jack. *What was she driving at?*

"The devils were very close. 'Which way will you have it?' says they. 'Let Jack get tired of Lucy, and take away the only woman you have now?'

"'Wife or no wife, she'll go to him.' And I believe she would have done so. Though she *hated* Stedman with all the strength of her nature for marrying Lucy, she would give herself to him principle or no principle if he but held up a finger. And Stedman wasn't all true to Lucy. He was getting shaken. We camped that night near a fine, rocky waterhole, with good grass and plenty of trees growing about it; we turned out early, as we meant to start at daybreak, for it would be sundown before we got to the new rush next day, and this camp divided the stages of good water and feed, and was the best stopping place on the road. I left Jack to hobble the horses, and get the fire under way, saying I was going to look round to see if the creek where we were showed the 'colour'.

"It was a warm afternoon about four o'clock by the sun. There was a black snake on the rocks, a quarter of a mile up the creek. There were two of them, but one got away. I broke the back of the last one, but didn't finish him, and got him into a bag I'd brought for specimens.

"When I got back I shook him down amongst the ration bags, and told Jack to get the tea and sugar, as the 'billy,' was 'on the boil'.

"He had his back turned, looking out on the plain.

"Off he went whistling; and as soon as he reached for the tea-bag, careless-like, the snake bit him.

"He shook it off as I rushed up. A snake with his spine broke *can* bite proper, but I finished it with a stick and threw it into the blazing fire.

"'By Jove, Jim,' says he, 'I'm done for.' 'Not you,' says I. 'Drink this brandy, and keep walking about. I'll get the horses quick, and we'll go back to the doctor. You'll be all right. Likely he mayn't have much poison this time of the year.' But I *knew* well enough. He was a dead man before we had gone ten miles!

"Lucy went clean out of her mind, and died within a month of the news.

"Laura kept her promise and married me, but Jack stood by our bed every night, and my sweet fruit turned into bitter Dead Sea apples.

"Everything we put our hands to failed, and there was that understanding between us, though I didn't tell her, and never told her, which brought a strong look of horror into her eyes every time I looked at her, and made us miserable outcasts to each other. Laura got thrown from her horse and killed, not far from where poor Stedman's bones lie, and I'm here, dying, but I couldn't go until I had eased my guilty mind with a full confession.

"JAMES THOMPSON."

. . . .

Brodribb turned up for dinner and I read him Thompson's manuscript afterwards. He said nothing, and we both remained in silence for a minute, during which a waiter entered with a telegram which Brodribb read. "No answer," said he. When the waiter left the room he handed the telegram to me. It contained but two words. They were "Thompson's dead!" Like lightning the same words in a nigger minstrel comedy flashed into my mind.

"Perhaps it's just as well!" we remarked simultaneously.

A MAD SOMNAMBULIST

This is the very witching hour of night
When churchyards yawn and graves give up their dead.
—*Shakespeare.*

I DO not know the term which learned doctors would give it. But in this particular case I daresay they would trace its origin to some disturbance of the brain, which makes a body do all sorts of things without knowledge of action. It wasn't fair sleep-walking. There was something else in it. Therefore I shall not attempt any scientific explanation. I prefer to leave that to the "faculty". The brain did not belong to me, so I do not hold myself responsible for its actions. Nevertheless, that particular brain and the body belonging to it made things generally extremely unpleasant to a number of sensible people; and caused them to act after the fashion of fools or escaped lunatics, forcing them to perpetrate actions during the whole of one night, which they would have blushed to do in the light of the sun. They did not behave themselves in a seemly manner, and the memory of it makes me laugh yet, though at the time I was quite as scared as the rest of them, if not more so.

I was a "new chum" or "jackeroo" at the time, getting my experience of bushland and station life, but I never bargained for such a drilling as I got on that particular occasion. And I wasn't the worst off in the crowd either; I observed *with* others from a comparatively safe position.

I will tell the story, however, as actual experience dictates, and my readers can judge for themselves.

. . . .

"There were four of us that night at the home station. Another new chum and myself were representatives of the 'firm'. The 'boss' was away, luckily for ourselves. The other two were friends who were in search of new country and who were 'spelling' to rest their horses.

"We had had tea, smoked our pipes, had indulged in several rounds with the gloves, violently aided and abetted by 'Spang' and 'Woppits,' two youthful fox terriers, and finally settled down to a game of chess, two playing, and two looking on and advising, when all of a sudden 'old Wallace,' a grim, scarred old blue brindle kangaroo dog, now very stiff on his legs from long running and fights with warrigals and tame dogs, growled and then gave a solitary bark.

"A stranger on horseback rode up. He turned his horse out, and we proceeded to make him as comfortable as possible, and got him a substantial supper which O'Shea, the general factotum from the kitchen, brought in, stayed as long as he dared, to hear the news and gossip, and then took his departure. O'Shea was a rather touchy Irishman, and Mrs. O'Shea did our cooking and washing. The other new chum, my companion, was also an Irishman, and he and O'Shea were eternally at daggers drawn. My chum's name was Kilpatrick. He and I inhabited the bedroom 'skillion' at the end of the verandah, and for that night I gave up my bed to the stranger and 'dossed' down with my two friends in the big room, where they had the two bunks. We all slipped into dreamland. I was in the middle of a cattle-muster dream, performing prodigies of riding and stock-whip cracking, when I was suddenly alive to a hoarse, strained voice, and a sort of knowledge of another agonised tone, exclaiming: 'For God's sake don't'. I sat up, scared and anxious, trying hard to collect my scattered wits. My two friends were doing the same. 'What is it?' whispered I, seeing their alarmed faces. 'I believe that fiend is murdering poor Kilpatrick,' said the elder Brett. Sure enough, I heard a choking gurgle!

"The next room to us, the 'boss's' room, was self-contained and had a ceiling. The skillion bedroom, as I have already stated, was outside at the end of the verandah. It was from thence the noises came, where the stranger and Kilpatrick were. We stared in horror, and we all got on to our legs.

"'The wages of sin are death.'

"'Repeat that, or ——'

"'T—the w—wages of s—sin are d—death,' replied a palsied voice, which I instantly recognised as Kilpatrick's.

A MAD SOMNAMBULIST

"'Great Scott what are they up to?' we all gasped.

"'But—oh—beloved—brethren,' went on the first voice in a dreamy, far away tone, changing to a fierce whisper.

"'Repeat it.'

"'B—b—u—t, o—o—o—h—h, b—b—e—l—o—v—ed b—breth—r—e—n,' came the response (Kilpatrick's).

"'If we sin—we—do—so—knowingly. We should repent.' 'D—d—a—m' (*not* Kilpatrick's). 'W—w—e s—s—h—ould r—repent' (unmistakably Kilpatrick!).

"'Come on, you fellows,' whispered the eldest and strongest Brett, 'let's see what they are doing.' I seized the poker and we stole round in scanty apparel to the 'skillion' window. There was no light, but the moon shone in upon Kilpatrick in a reduced garment, kneeling on the floor with uplifted and clasped hands, as if engaged in a devotional exercise, whilst above him towered the form of the last arrival, brandishing an American axe, his face livid and ghastly, his lips rapidly moving, his eyes staring. It was an awful apparition.

"The window was a large one, not more than three feet from the ground, and we could see distinctly. 'Oh, Lord,' said Brett. 'The man's mad. He'll kill him, sure. Let's get O'Shea, and then we'll all rush him. We slipped softly away, rushed into O'Shea's bedroom and told him quite regardless of his better half and our own scandalous costumes. Brett was always a good sort of fellow to break any news, especially if it was bad news. He never troubled about any one's feelings; but when he told O'Shea that the stranger had gone raving mad and was killing Kilpatrick, the only thing O'Shea said was :—

"'Arrah, by Jasus, is it kilt I'll be?' and both he and Mrs. O'Shea tore out into the night and made for the 'lignum' at the end of the paddock.

"Some one, I think it was myself, suggested that we should go back to the house and procure the gun we used for 'killing,' also some powder and projectiles for it. I had lost the poker in the 'scurry'. But who would venture? Not one of us, either *en masse* or singly. I blush to own it, but we couldn't raise a blush between us then. None of us seemed to have any blood. We were all anæmic. But we were men of action, for we carefully barricaded ourselves in, and waited in terror.

"In about ten minutes there was an awful yell. 'He's done for him now, boys,' said Brett. 'The poor beggar's spiflicated. It'll be our turn soon.' But there was another yell, and we became aware of footsteps flying past the door. There were two people running. There was no doubt of that. Patter, patter, went the bare feet. Then the sound died away in the distance towards the 'lignum'. 'He'll finish Kilpatrick before he gets to the paddock fence and then he'll exterminate the O'Sheas,' said Brett. 'Let's see if we can get something to kill him with when he comes for us. We *must* get something, an axe is long odds against a Crimean shirt and no trousers, and it's so precious cold too about one's legs. Fancy a sweep of that axe against them.' We rummaged in every conceivable hole and corner throughout the kitchen, we ransacked the O'Sheas' bedroom, and explored boxes and mattresses, but the only available weapons were saucepans, the big frying pan and a wooden poker. The younger Brett suggested the carving knives and forks. 'No good,' said Brett, 'he'd kill three of us while the other was trying to stick him, and kill him afterwards. I want something long and sharp and heavy.' Whilst madly hunting for something defensive, again we heard a quick patter outside, a gasping choke, a scuffle and a thumping, and Kilpatrick fell down the bark chimney into the fireplace! 'Oh, Lord, boys,' he groaned, 'what are we to do? The fellow's raving mad. He was going to kill me, and made me say my prayers or something, but the moment he got his eyes off me, I bolted out of the window. Lord save us, and the holy Virgin save us. He's gone blithering down through the bally lignum in his shirt. Where he got the axe from, the devil only knows. He must have got it from the woodheap while I was asleep. Oh, the brute!'

"'Well, he'll bag the O'Sheas if he's gone that way. They are in the "lignum". They are all dressed up to date. I say, Kilpatrick, don't you think you could make a rush over to the house and get the gun and some powder and shot—the biggest shot you can find? We'll stay here and look out for you. You'll have plenty of time while he's killing the O'Sheas, for the old woman will give you lots of warning—*she* won't die quietly.' 'No fear,' said Kilpatrick. 'Go yourself; I've done all the work up to now and it's lucky I came down the

chimney. I knew you fellows would barricade the door.'
After an hour there was a timid knock. On looking through
a chink, we could discern the O'Sheas, trembling with cold
and nearly dead with fright; they did not have much clothing
either. It wasn't a dress rehearsal. They came in by means
of the chimney, as Brett said it wouldn't be prudent to remove
the barricade. How they did it I don't know, but they did.
And Mrs. O'Shea did a 'lightning change,' with her hands
before her face from the fireplace into her bed. She then
freely wept in the sanctity of her nuptial couch. O'Shea
himself, trembling with wrath, alarm and cold, only wished he
hadn't left the crimson meat axe at the blanky chopping
blocks.

"'Look here, O'Shea,' authoritatively said Brett, 'you go
and get the meat axe, come back here, and then we'll "rush"
him when he comes. You down him with the meat axe and we'll
hold him.' 'Is it me?' said the Irishman, 'sure I'm that
frozen that me jints wouldn't hould it. I'll get into me bid.'
'Be a man,' said Brett, 'have you got a revolver anywhere?'
'The divil a pishtol have I got, but if I had that gory
mate axe I'd have something better to foight with than nothing
at all whativer. If I only had a shillelah now. But that
divil's got an axe, an' he's prancin' about in the lignum seekin'
whom he may devour. Howly saints and angils, did ye ever
hear the like? S—s—h!'

"A steady step went past the door, and an inexpressive,
incurious, and abstracted voice said loudly: 'Hold up the
corners of the world, O Lord, so that when our feet essay to
walk they shall not slip'. O'Shea vanished with great rapidity
and silence, and got under his wife's bed, whilst the voice
grew indistinct again. 'I'll see if the beggar's got the axe,'
whispered Kilpatrick, and climbed up the chimney. He soon
came back. 'He's coming again, boys! Lord, if I only had
that gun!' Again went the step past the door and the im-
passive voice chanted: 'The wages of sin! The wages of sin!
The wages of sin are—death! death! death!' O'Shea was
looking out from under the bed, with a face of absolutely idiotic
terror. 'Oh, Lord,' he whispered, 'he'll make cowld mate of the
lot of us!' Mrs. O'Shea was shaking under the clothes. The
voice muttered on, dying away in the distance again. 'May
the Lord have mercy on me sinful sowl,' mopped and gibbered

O'Shea. 'I'd give a pound of Barrett's twist if I could get the laste taste of the handle of that crimson blanketty mate axe.' Mrs. O'Shea sobbed aloud, and said four Ave Marias and six Paternosters.

"The step did not return again, but we passed the rest of that night in abject misery, varied by excursions up the chimney to reconnoitre. We looked like mad sweeps, and there was not an atom of self-respect left among us except Mrs. O'Shea, who kept under the bedclothes *all* the time.

"O'Shea did not come out till daylight, when he got out of his bedroom window, stole softly round the corner, and appropriated the meat axe. He then got into his trousers. Brett, after a deliberate, stealthy stalk, got possession of the gun and loaded both barrels with swan shot. O'Shea then presented him with his best Sunday go-to-meeting pants, 'so as not to scandalise the missus,' he said. He had no more, and the rest of us unlucky beggars had to go without. I made a sort of petticoat out of the kitchen tablecloth, for decency's sake, and precious dirty it was too, with a mustard plaster on it at one end —O'Shea's end I should think. The others got old bags, cut off the bottoms, and tied them round their waists. Then I got a crowbar outside, young Brett appropriated an adze, Kilpatrick an auger from the toolhouse, and the army started. We found the axe in the verandah. Mrs. O'Shea, who now joined us in an elegant flannel combination, appropriated that. She looked exactly like a pudding about to be boiled. Then we formed up and proceeded to the skillion bedroom. Our plans had been carefully gone over. Brett in the middle, with the gun ready cocked, was to shoot the madman dead the instant he came out, and we others stood by to make mincemeat of him. But we never did. For a deep-toned snore broke the early morning stillness, and looking through the window we saw our enemy peacefully asleep. O'Shea wished Brett to start operations immediately, but he refused, and then a light broke gradually in upon us, revealing the situation. There had been a constantly-recurring rumour from up the river about a certain person who used to go on in an extraordinary way after other people were asleep. Most of us had heard of it, at muster camp fires, and several people besides ourselves had wished to shoot the offender. 'Oh, Lord,' said Brett senior, 'it's that brute Jenkins. I've heard of him.' There was a whispered

"THEN WE FORMED UP AND PROCEEDED TO THE SKILLION BEDROOM."

From the Land of the Wombat.

consultation and we all stole away. We all knew him, or rather knew *of* him. Even Mrs. O'Shea had heard of his peculiar ways a hundred times from stockmen and other waifs and strays, who 'made' the station at sundown.

"He was the son of a clergyman, and a certain sermon his father had preached in his young days had obtained a powerful lien on his mind. Thus he made the victim of his somnambulistic tendencies repeat that awful sermon. It had been a nightmare to several individuals. They had to repeat it word for word, under threat of brain cleavage. Personally, of course, none of us had had the advantage of a former introduction to this Mr. Jenkins. We bathed, dressed and breakfasted. Mrs. O'Shea brought the breakfast in. It was a genuine success. We had steak, poached eggs, tea, toast, scones and fresh butter.

"'I hope you slept well,' said I to our guest. 'Very fairly,' replied Jenkins, 'the air's good here, and I was rather tired after the last stage from Wyadra.' 'I didn't sleep well at all,' said Brett senior; 'I was dreaming about accidents, and was disturbed till morning.' Kilpatrick, the ill-used, remarked: 'Mind you let us know when you are coming again, will you, old fellow, then we'll give you a better time, and we shall be better prepared all round to receive you properly. So awkward your turning up so late, you know.'

"'I'll lasso him next time, and tie him up at night,' said Brett *sotto voce*. And after O'Shea had brought his horse round, held his stirrup, and received half-a-crown, he grinned, and remarked when our guest was out of hearing: 'And I'll plant that blanky mate axe handy'."

LALOR OF CORINGA

> And often, through the purple night,
> Below the starry clusters bright,
> Some bearded meteor, trailing light,
> Moves over still Shalott.
> —*Tennyson.*

THERE used to be a peculiar sleeping place in the Sydney Domain, used only by those "in the swim"—"deadbeats" of a respectable class. I believe it is still there. To the inquiring speculator I would suggest that it is not far distant from "Lady Macquarrie's Chair," the carved stone seat at the point. But I will not divulge the exact spot, because I have a sort of lingering regard for the place, as such a very unique and undiscoverable refuge for a man who is not in funds, has a doubt as to where he will get a breakfast in the morning, and is, in fact, in his attire, general appearance and insolvency, the counterpart and equal of a starved out "deadbeat," or a poor broken devil of a beach-comber, a beggar, but not a professional one, a man who *will* work if Fortune smiles upon him. To such a one, this sleeping hole is a perfect refuge, policeman proof, and rainproof. Therefore, I leave it alone, unknown, except to those who use it, who will bear me out that there *is* such a place, and who will sympathise with me for my unwillingness to disclose its exact locality.

To me the memory of this refuge always recalls a night of beauty and calm, but not exactly of perfect repose and perfect silence, for there were the sounds of oars on the moonlit waters, the thud of racing paddles and screws, and many red, green and mast-head lights of ferry steamers scintillating all over the beautiful harbour. As the moon rose too I remember how, as it outlined the spars, hull, blocks and ropes of a large French old fashioned frigate over there in connection with the Sydney Exhibition, the crew burst forth into a song from some opera with thrilling effect. On such a night then, I was sitting on one of the flat-topped sandstone rocks in the said Domain thinking of various things and enjoying the rapidly cooling air of the Australian night, always so delightful after the close of a warm summer day. How I pine for those perfect days and nights sometimes now, in another clime, after a harassing three weeks or a month of rain, drizzly or heavy, but rain, and rain always, damp cold weather, without a trace of that revivifying factor of our health and happiness—the sun. My feet rested on the couch grass, and I lit my pipe. Suddenly one of my ankles was touched. I sprang off the rock, and sideways, thinking it might be a deadly brown snake, common enough even now about the rocks and bush of Sydney harbour. I looked down, and saw a hand, and part of an arm, protruding from under the rock I had been sitting upon. The owner of that hand and arm came out. "Beg y' pard'n, sir, I'm expectin' two mates o' mine to join me directly. I saw you as you come up the hill, and we're not bushrangers or spielers. I couldn't help showing *you* the place, sir, as my mates don't know it, and it's time for me to come out and wait for them. I was having a bit of a spell. It's the best home in Sydney, for the landlord don't charge anything for your 'doss'. Here come my two mates, sir." The look on the man's face did not alarm me. He looked like a broken-down man, of course, but there was something about him which spoke of better days. His two "mates," as he called them, were young men, much younger than himself, but apparently quite as destitute. "This gent's all right," he called out to them. "He won't disturb us or inform. Would you like to look in, sir?"

I got down on my knees on the couch grass, and, looking under the base of the rock, saw a regular, hollowed-out chamber. It was three feet or more down a slope to the floor. The rock above was hollowed like a dome. One apparently had to get in by lying at full length and rolling down the slope. There was just room to do that. I didn't try. The vault would hold from three to four "deadbeats". It smelt of them, and also of bad tobacco, chiefly cigar ends.

This refuge hollow was well off the track, though for the matter of that hundreds of respectable citizens might have traversed a road almost against the rock itself without discovering the chamber.

Bottle-brush or honeysuckle trees grew about it, and even the couch grass at the mouth of the place rustled up into position after being disturbed. Unless you got down on your hands and knees to verify the fact that a sleeping place existed there, you would have been unable to prove it. I called the first man aside and looked at him more closely. He seemed to be about fifty-five years of age, with an irredeemable expression of sadness on his face. Impelled by curiosity I asked him to come with me to the hotel at the bottom of Woolloomoolloo, adjacent to the Domain. I invited him to a private room and a drink, and asked him to tell me what he knew about the cave. He told me, and more besides. He told me a story of his previous life, a very strange one. We had a few drinks as he proceeded, and he took a little money from me, under protest, to get something to eat on the morrow. I provided him at once with some cold meat and bread, also two bottles of beer to take with him to share with his mates. And when he left I parted from him sorrowfully, reflecting how time and misfortune leaves its mark upon some of us, whilst others, less deserving, live in comfort and happiness. My "deadbeat's" story ran as follows :—

"During one summer, well back in the sixties, I was exploring in Northern Queensland, with a black boy, looking for new country. My previous geographical knowledge carried me as far as Barkly's Tableland, and thence we struck about south-west, into the northern territory of South Australia. We chanced after long travel upon a fine piece of country near a large lake. There was no river in the vicinity that I could see, but the lake seemed to be fed by a polygonum swamp, which extended far and wide at the head of it, over a patch of ground which embraced many thousands of acres. I intended to select country suitable for breeding stations for either sheep or cattle, 'take up' the ground, and sell it to pioneer squatters, whereby I calculated I should reap a very handsome profit. To pay a comparatively small rent to Government for a large mileage of land, and to sell this for thousands, meant money. The risks, and these were many, I took upon myself, and as these risks of danger in travelling over unknown country affected myself only, I included them in the price. I calculated that when my work was done I should have earned my profit. Our provisions were running short, but we had guns and ammunition with us, also some fine kangaroo dogs, which were of great help to us in securing game, and giving timely warning of blacks.

"But on arrival at the lake, we found abundance of wild fowl of all descriptions, whilst small armies of the slate-grey coloured 'native companions' stalked around it. Kangaroo and emu were seen round the borders and out on the plains, which stretched away to the westward endlessly to the vision. We had eight well-seasoned horses, riding one each, and using others alternately for saddle and pack. The horses were in fair condition, spite of the long travel, but they were poor and wanted rest. 'Spell oh' was the word. We couldn't have got a better halting-ground, and I saw also the country I wanted, ready to my hand. Our horses with the packs, by this time, with constant repetition of the day's experience, didn't want driving. They either ran ahead or followed. Horses have a horror of being left behind in a new country, and often had I seen detached horses following a party in a buggy along a bush road, or other ridden horses, as in our case now. They also found time to snatch mouthfuls of feed as they went along.

"My black boy was an old and tried servant. None were equal to him in bush-lore, and he was much attached to me personally. Without further circumlocution as to myself and antecedents, I may mention that I was about twenty-five years of age, an Australian native, brought up to and reared in bush-life, and had drifted to a small settlement on the coast, which is now Burketown, in the company of several other adventurers, in search of anything that 'might turn up,' like Mr. Micawber. I had been fairly educated, and was strong and active, enjoying the inestimable blessing of perfect health. We had seen but few natives *en route*, but at Lake Hope, as I had at once christened the good country we had found, we came across a girl almost white, but starving and completely exhausted.

"My black boy, Eacharn, did not understand her language;

but he made out a word here and there, which enabled him to derive some sort of sense out of her speech.

"This is what she said to him, as per his translation:—

"'Missa Will, she say you father belonging to her. My word, Missa Will, I no think you married. Where wife belongin' to you?' 'Don't you see, you idiot,' I said, 'what she means? She wants to make us understand that her father is a white man. How could I be her father? The girl is about sixteen years old?' I went over to the poor thing, who, by the way, bore traces of remarkable beauty, albeit wildly terrified, and broken down by pain and suffering. Eacharn and I soon made a nice shady 'gunyah' for her, and I gave her my blankets and fed her slowly. This girl was an octoroon, a marvellous sight to me. Where had she come from? What on earth could she be doing here? Half-caste blacks are often good-looking. Even pure blacks when young are very passable, but here was something beyond them altogether. We carefully nursed this young girl, so curiously thrown upon our hands, and in a few days she began to get about, thanks to the nourishing broth and tit-bits I made for her. Then a few blacks put in an appearance, and with the exception of the chief, a copper-coloured old man with snow-white hair, evidently of the 'Combo' tribe, they seemed absolutely terrified by her appearance. The chief questioned her—in a language which Eacharn apparently knew nothing about—to his great amazement, as evinced by his upheld hands, rolling eyes and gaping mouth.

"The girl answered the "Combo" man evidently to his satisfaction, and they all went away. We now built a capital substantial large 'gunyah,' more after the European model, with a fire-place and bark chimney, bark roof, and sides of uprights, dabbed with mud between the cracks. Owing to the abundance of game, we lived in clover; it being only necessary to take a horse and a couple of dogs out for an hour or so to get kangaroo or emu. And we snared pigeons with horse-hair loops, and with a couple of shots and judicious cover could get a lot of ducks in the lake at sundown. On a previous occasion, during Eacharn's absence, to my great amazement, my fair charge addressed me in English. She said her name was 'Louise,' that she came from her home 'over there,' pointing in a south-west direction, repeating the fact that her father was a white man, that she had two other sisters and a brother, and that there were other white people where she had come from. She had run away, why she did not tell me, only that she thought she hadn't been properly treated. She stated that she had lived on lizards, grubs, and an occasional bird, but how caught or killed she did not say. She had come a long way, and had at last reached Lake Hope, so utterly done up that she thought she would soon die, when we came up and found her. She began to pick up daily, and helped us with our building, and my heart warmed to the poor thing. Here she was, a pretty, utterly unprotected maiden, thrown suddenly upon two strangers, and my heart beat high with the hope that some day I might be the means of restoring her to her friends. But on mentioning this she seemed anything but pleased and hung her head, whilst her eloquent dark eyes flashed disapproval. A day or two after this disclosure, Louise, who now spoke to us both in English, started Eacharn off on a botanising expedition to get something called 'ninda'. After an hour or so he brought back a big load of a sort of vetch, which seemed to please her. These small beans were pounded in an old 'coolamon' we had found, and she afterwards made cakes of them. They had previously been mixed with water, and supplemented our scanty stock of flour, but a little of that was also mixed with them. Eacharn very soon began to stand in great awe of her, puzzled by her colour, hair and eyes. He would have been much easier had she been only a half-caste, for he was used to them, but this strange being was now to him 'white-gin,' pure and simple. The subsequent unearthing of chrysalids and large grubs, through her knowledge of the country, in places where even he would not have thought of finding them, raised her still more in his estimation. She showed him how and where to find them, and he had a regular jubilee gorge.

"They also caught geckoes, iguanas and other hideous reptiles, rushing together with great vigour all over the place in pursuit. They unearthed them from small cottonbush mounds and from tree bases and roasted them at the fire. Thus about a fortnight passed away since we had been the means of rescuing 'Louise' from her then position of complete exhaustion. She would have managed to get on somehow, I do believe, even if we had not found her. Her chief want had been water, and I gathered that the last two days of her journey had been without it! But she had reached Lake Hope, 'Elinabra' *she* called it. Her knowledge of the blacks' ways, who will live easily where a white man will starve, was something marvellous. She could make fire come from a bit of wood and a sort of bow, for which she used kangaroo sinew. The bow was of hard wood, the fire-producing wood was soft, and she revolved the bow on one of the points so rapidly that she got fire apparently with little trouble, and not very long over it either. The way she got a coolamon full of ants' eggs was also curious. If we had killed a kangaroo she got a good bunch of the entrails fastened on to a long, straight, strong stick. Eacharn by her orders had made her a sort of spear spade out of hard wood. She then took the entrails and pushed them violently about on the surface of the ant bed. The ants attacked it furiously. When they were all out, and three-quarters of their thousands were attacking and fastening on the moving mass, she drew it off and flung it aside with a conglomerate of desperate ants on it. Then she dug into the ant bed and got her eggs by the million! These eggs she mixed in handfuls with the pounded ninda beans, and they gave her cakes a consistency, and, I expect, made them more nourishing. She was now looking well and hearty, kept herself perfectly clean, and was as particular about her dress as she could be considering her limited wardrobe. One day as we were getting breakfast, at which Louise now always presided, a man came up on horseback from the westward riding one horse and leading another with a side-saddle upon it. He stayed of course; and spoke to 'Louise' the moment he saw her, in the untranslatable language. I gathered from the pantomimic action of the two that he was very angry, and the girl apologetic, though defending herself. After a meal of which he partook, in intervals between further conversation with Miss 'Louise,' he addressed himself to me in English. 'Mr. Elliott' (I had informed him of my name when he first came), 'I live beyond you, and have only lately been informed of your arrival here. We get messages fairly quickly hereabouts—at least *I* do. My place is about 160 miles from here, and though we have neither telegraph lines, roads nor railways at present, at any rate from east to west, I *hear* all the same. Louise tells me you have acted most kindly to her; my name is Lalor, and she is my sister. Shake hands. I suppose you intend to take up this country, and fancy you are the only white man who ever saw it.' 'Not now,' said I, 'although I thought so at first.' 'Well, never mind,' replied he, 'I am not going to disturb you. I have lived beyond you all my life, I was born where I live, and but for this foolish girl's action, which I will explain in due course, I should not have been here now, but should have been sure to have come across you later on.

"'You will get plenty of water at various places, both north and south, from where you are now, but out to the westward you won't get a drop. Here you can see the hoofmarks of your horses. You can travel westward and leave *no* trace. It is over the other side of that waterless, trackless region where my home is.' I explained that as yet I had explored neither north nor south, being perfectly contented to 'spell' my horses as long as I could, but that as I intended to take the country up, I had meant to do so, making my present camp my basis of operations. 'Well,' resumed Lalor, 'if you wish to take up any country here, it is a long way back to Burketown. Do you know any one there who is going to back you?' I explained that I had a partner in the venture, a man who would do all I required. 'Well,' said Lalor, 'you had better send him a letter and inform him about this country, giving him instructions to take it up from the Government.' Observing my look of blank astonishment he proceeded : 'It is a good deal simpler than you think. Write your letter and give the details of the country you want taken up. I should recommend four five-mile blocks at present, north and south from this place. The blacks call it " Elinabra ".' 'I call it " Lake Hope," ' said I. 'A good name,' responded Lalor. 'I will engage to send your letter in an hour from now.' He then drew a peculiar instrument about four or five inches long from his pocket, of carved wood apparently, and blew into it. It made a noise like a foghorn, but so startling and strange were the notes, three, with variations, that the sudden and unexpected sound sent our horses scampering all over the place in hobbles; frightened all the 'gallars,' cockatoos, kangaroos, emus, and all living creatures anywhere near us into fits, and such a quacking, snorting, screaming and flapping took place that Lake Hope seemed a perfect pandemonium of alarm and confusion for the time being. When all had quietened down I wrote my letter, pretty Louise smiling at the expression on my face as I concluded. And well she might smile. I was thinking who or what this extraordinary man Lalor was. How could he communicate with a mysterious postal delivery? By her directions, in fact with her guidance, the letter was stuck into a cleft stick, and just as it was ready two stalwart black fellows stood before us in full fighting rig, fillets and feathers in hair, a waistband of emu skin apiece, and they were also armed with a couple of light throwing spears and a tomahawk which each carried. Lalor said one word which I did not catch and they vanished. 'Your letter will be in Burketown in about five days,' said he. 'They will pass it on to the next tribe and fresh runners will go from there. There's a signal to meet others!' A smoke fire rose from a distant ridge. 'Our system of communication is perfect, but I may as well give you an outline of my present plans and a bit of my past life as well. Had it not been for this girl here I might have left you alone, but your exceeding goodness to her has made me think whether I do not owe you some return for your kindness, and perhaps you will be of my way of thinking before I finish.'

"Quite nonplussed by the suddenness of all the passing events and the extraordinary method of communication with the wild tribes, I waited in breathless silence until he resumed. 'As I said, I am a native of this part of the country, but not anything like a full-blooded one. I have more of the white blood in my veins. My father was a man who lived with the blacks—lived among them for some years. He married a quadroon. So far for my parentage. My father educated us, and educated our mother also. He taught many in his time. My mother was, of course, the offspring of a white man, united to a half-caste, who came among the tribes earlier. I shall have to take my sister back. Will you come with us?' A side look from Louise settled *that* question. For days past I had been thinking that it would be hard to lose her. I think any man knows if a girl likes him. And Louise had shown me that in many ways. She was very pretty, and though half wild sometimes, had a way of coming close to me whenever she got a chance, as if she wanted protection and love. And my feelings met hers more than half way, I can assure you. 'I have a reason for wishing you to come,' went on Lalor; 'I have something to tell you, and when I *do* tell you, you will think that the telling has been better for you, and will be glad that you accepted my offer.' I kept my *own* reason, but that was quite sufficient for me. 'And I will tell you another thing,' he went on. 'Take each of you, you and your black boy, but one horse each. You need not fear that the others will stray. And everything else you leave behind you here will be taken care of.'

"And he produced his strange sound-making apparatus and tapped it significantly. 'Will you trust me and come?' 'Well, I will,' I replied. 'I will come and see this unknown land of yours, and my horses are quite fresh again.' 'Nevertheless, take the best you have,' rejoined Lalor; 'you will need them. I have always looked forward to the advent of a decent white man to this part of the world, but only one whom I can make a friend of, and if you will trust me and be guided by my advice you will find that your eventual possession of Lake Hope and the adjoining country will be to our mutual advantage, and instead of selling it, you might be induced to settle there!' I had not the remotest intention of settling there when I came, but certain circumstances alter cases, and I began to see my way to it. I had no home ties. My father and mother were dead. Anyway, with my growing love for Louise, it made me think, and think deeply. I said nothing, however, and Lalor continued: 'Look here, Mr. Elliott, it must be plain to you, that beyond your claim on my goodwill from your goodness to my sister, I need not enlarge upon my own circumstances to you at all, but I am going to take you into my confidence partly, as you will eventually find out, and beyond this hint, now twice repeated, I shall say nothing more till the occasion arises. Let us get our things ready and we will start to-morrow. I am anxious to get back.'

"And we did, the four of us. Miss Louise rode in her side saddle well and fearlessly, though her skirts were short and she wore no boots. But she didn't seem to care for appearances, and in that far away interior neither did we. We jogged off at daylight, Lalor sounding his extraordinary apparatus twice with a variation of the three foghorn notes. We saw no signs of any blacks, but he said they had got their orders by the sounds.

"Once out beyond the margin of the lake country, say ten miles, our surroundings changed entirely, and we were riding over a sandy desert of open plains with very scant vegetation. Then came a region of stones, small waterworn pebbles, but no sand. About two miles of this, and we were on the sand again. It seemed peculiarly fine and light. There were hillocks too in every direction, then rolling, undulating country, but still all sand, and the silence of our transit, as the footfalls of the horses were inaudible, was remarkable, and the utter absence of anything in the way of animals, birds or even insects, was stupefying, absolutely stupefying! Our horses, Eacharn's and mine, didn't seem to know what to make of it, and kept snorting and staring about, as if they didn't half like it. Only for the companionship of the other two, who seemed perfectly used to it, I believe they would have turned back. *I should, I know, before I had got half the distance if I had been alone.* But for the sun, there were no landmarks for a stranger, and I can imagine that any one lost in this appalling place would go mad in a very short time. Absolute silence, broken only by our conversation, the jingle of bits, the creak of the saddles, and the occasional snort of a horse! *Our horses' hoofs made no sound whatever!* According to Lalor's particular request we had filled our water-bags at Lake Hope. We carried eight altogether, two on each horse, and these had been made, our four at least, considerably larger than before. Louise had helped with these, and used the needle very deftly.

"Lalor expatiated much on the waterless condition of to-day's journey and to-morrow's, but said that it was as good as a fence for any stock, as they wouldn't attempt to stray out in his direction, nor would his stray my way. As we progressed, to my horror, after pulling up for a drink out of my water-bag, just a mouthful, I saw that the marks where my horse's feet were lifted from began to fill up instantly! The sand was like the sand in an ant lion's pit, and moved on touch! Also like the sand in an hour-glass. A *trackless* waste verily! It made me shiver! Where we had come through, a cavalcade of four ridden horses, with sixteen hoof marks, deep indented, not a mark would be seen a quarter of an hour after we had passed any spot. And this sort of sand wouldn't hold water, for it wouldn't turn to mud. Rain would go through it very quickly, and the sun would evaporate the moisture.

The shifting, sliding, *moving* particles would go on obliterating everything on its surface. And the slightest breath of air set it all moving, rolling and glittering. All those quadrillions of quadrillions of tiny globules of sand were as shifty and slippery as diamonds, and as hard. A Metallic Desert! We held a course of about due west by south as I could tell by the compass and the sun. Lalor said he could go without either, and I quite believed him, though I did not know how he did it until he said 'it was by the motion of the sand itself. It travelled from the south to the north, even when you could hardly perceive any wind. Therefore, knowing the direction it travelled in one could define east and west.' His opinion was that the sand was magnetic! We travelled on all day, giving the horses a drink at noon and in the evening, reserving some for the morning, for the next day at noon we were to come on the water-line. There were some sand hummocks where we camped, and, for the first time since we left, we saw a little vegetation, some scrubby hard bushes, which, strange to say, the horses devoured eagerly, as if they liked them. Then there were a number of small water melons scattered about, which were pulpy and full of juice. These also were greedily devoured. On examining these hummocks I saw the sand move and slide down the whole depth of the hummock if I came within five yards of them! We slept on the bare sand with a blanket around us. The next day was a hot day. We gave the horses the remnant of the water saved for the morning, but they didn't take it all, to my surprise. They were satisfied, and were apparently quite fresh when mounted. There was virtue then in the scrubby bushes and water melons. We steered as aforesaid by the sun, but Lalor had other landmarks, as the country became a little more rugged, with the scrubby bushes and water melons getting thicker, but even here, looking for Lalor's journey tracks to Lake Hope, I failed to see any. I mentioned to him the absence of any, in fact the utter obliteration of tracks which I expected to see, as the ground was changing. 'Yes,' he replied, 'even here tracks disappear very rapidly. The least puff of wind obliterates them. This sand is light and easily blown, but it is not always on the move like the other we have passed. Do you see that cloud?'—pointing about due south, where a small one was rising, and advancing rapidly. 'There will be a puff of wind when that fellow gets overhead which will make our tracks disappear.' This remark was soon verified. As the cloud passed overhead there was a fierce puff of wind, and several whirlwinds passed in rolling columns over the plain, ahead of us, behind us, and all around us!

"In the storm of dust which arose our tracks were swept out of existence in a moment! 'What an awful country to get lost in,' I thought presently. When all was calm again I saw the expected water, the water we counted upon at noon. A lovely lake. I could see green vegetation and trees, and the very ripple of the waters with the sun making the tiny waves glitter. Lalor and Louise were watching me. 'There's the water,' said I. 'There's no water there,' replied Lalor, 'that's only the desert *mirage*.' Sure enough it went backward as we came on. After a little it vanished altogether, a mocking phantom, a grisly practical joke. They both smiled. Eacharn was taken in as well as I was, and I thought of the lines, and the frequent death of bushmen who see this sight:—

"But what is this? A vision sweet!
Green trees, a rippling flow
Of tossing wavelets at his feet,
A glorious pool below.

"Beware! the Thirst Fiend of the Plain
But mocks his fervid gaze,
And backward flits the spectre vain
Into the flickering haze.

"Lured by the ghastly 'mirage dance,'
The silver, glittering wave
To madness turns his straining glance—
He finds a bushman's grave.

"And bones lie bleaching on the sod
'Out-back' on desert grim,
Where almost seems the wrath of God
To have o'ertaken him.

"Very shortly after this we came in sight of three trees in a clump, right ahead of us. Lalor's horses whinnied, and ours understanding them whinnied also. 'Water,' thought I. As we approached these trees we saw other clumps of four to six to a dozen. 'Now, Mr. Elliott,' said Lalor, 'we are now coming on the water-line. Where those trees stand is water. I reckon the distance from here to Lake Hope at about seventy-five miles. This is the end of the belt, the impassable belt, but no man could live here even unless he possessed the knowledge that the dwellers in these parts do. We shall have these trees with us all the way home now. We mustn't take too much, and we shall willingly economise, for these trees are valuable. They form the connecting link between us and the outer world, and without them we should never reach that outer world or *our* inner world in either direction anyway.' We got to the third clump, and I was anxiously looking everywhere for water but not a drop could I see, no depression, no place to hold the sparkling fluid, nothing but sand and trees. Was the mirage the reflection of some beautiful lake that we should soon burst suddenly upon? Would there be a rift in the earth filled with a rushing river? We pulled up by the third clump. I thought he (Lalor) was going to rest and light his pipe as he got off his horse, so I got off too, saying : ' No wonder you see the necessity for economising, Mr. Lalor. There doesn't seem to be much water anywhere since we left Lake Hope.' Lalor gave his horse to Eacharn to hold, got down on his hands and knees, drew his sheath knife, dug and scraped away at the base of the tree about three feet outwards, found a root and dug away till he had bared six feet or so. It was long, straight and supple, about two inches in diameter but tapering towards the end, and ran straight out not more than six inches from the top soil. He cut this root straight through and held his end up in the air as high as his chest, then he called Louise. She sprang off her horse, took Lalor's knife and wormed away to the end of the root, which she drew out of the ground. She then let it trail. Lalor still kept his end well up. 'Now, Mr. Elliott,' said he, 'would you like a drink?' I got my pannikin, and he let a red-coloured liquid run into it. It tasted a little bitter, and perhaps a trifle astringent, but it was water right enough. We all had a drink and got a quart each for the horses, which they drank from a canvas bucket.

"Lalor carried the root some distance away from the tree and hurled it as far away as he could, remarking that the sand would soon cover it. 'For reasons of my own I don't want to leave any traces behind me at present,' he remarked.

"A momentary suspicion flashed across my brain. What if Lalor had some treacherous thought lurking about myself and Eacharn? Might he not also wish *us* to be out of the way?

"But a look at his frank, open face dispelled my surmise, and I determined to see the matter through. He resumed: 'My father got this secret of the water trees from the blacks when he first came here years ago. He always impressed the need of secrecy about them upon me, but why I could never make out until quite lately. But you will see for yourself later on.' Now, I thought, why on earth was Lalor always hinting at some hidden knowledge of which I had not yet been informed?

"I began to feel quite excited, and pursued my journey a prey to all sorts of wild ideas, and began to feel very curious about this mysterious home of his. On the evening of the fourth day from Lake Hope we came in sight of a town. As I thought, it was Lalor's place at last. I was quite unprepared for anything like that which met my view. There was a large creek or river ahead, ridgy country all about covered with trees, but the home station was a perfect paradise, a very fairyland in this unknown interior. Several, as many as twenty, low, verandahed, white-washed houses, covered with grape-vines and festooned with passion fruit, met my view as we drew nearer. Flowers and vegetable gardens about the houses, calves and cows about the stockyards. From a mile back indeed, as we rode through the horse paddock, which was fenced with a good bush fence, regular post and rail, Lalor had blown his sound producer, and the citizens of this paradise were out to meet us. As we rode up there was a score of collies and kangaroo dogs, which gave our dogs a rather warm welcome in the way of barking, growling, showing teeth, and bristle erecting, but it all ended in tail wagging, to our mutual satisfaction. From the house we stopped at, the biggest in the place, came forth two attractive girls, one about twelve the other fourteen years, dressed in European fashion. They ran eagerly to welcome Lalor and Louise, but were much wonderstruck at my appearance and that of my black boy, Eacharn. I noticed several other heads of women peeping from other houses. It *was* a small town!

"'Welcome to Coringa!' said Lalor. 'Allow me to introduce

you to my wife.' And a handsome girl, also an octoroon, and a young mother, came up with a well-grown boy in her arms, the image of Lalor himself.

"Lalor now sounded a low note on his sound maker and two quadroon lads appeared. 'Take Mr. Elliott's horses and ours, my lads, and look after Eacharn. Take him to your house. Remember he is your mate now.' And he said something to them in the unknown tongue we had both noticed. They nodded; took off all the horses' saddles, placed them in the rack in the verandah, and disappeared with Eacharn towards the river.

"'Now, Mr. Elliott, perhaps you would like to wash and dress as well as you can. Don't be too particular; an explorer away from his base of supplies doesn't carry his house and property about with him as I do here.'

"I was shown into as nice a bedroom as ever any man saw. For myself, after the months of knocking about I had experienced, I felt completely nonplussed as I gazed around me on clean sheets and bedlinen, washhand-stand, etc., etc., and caught a glimpse of my shock of hair and sun-tanned face in the mirror by the window.

"A passion-flower creeper, also a vine, showed their graceful fronds and clinging tendrils about the verandah posts and side.

"I finished my toilet, and went to look abroad upon the comfortable scene of Coringa station or town—this oasis of the interior. The neat verandah-surrounded houses were shingled, the population—for there were many people, men, women, girls and boys moving about—seemed contented and happy. Everything about me spoke of prosperity and comfort, and the absolute reality of everything forced itself upon me. Lalor broke in upon my reverie with an abrupt 'Come to dinner, man '.

"I followed him into a large, substantially-furnished room. Everything seemed to be home-made. Mrs. Lalor was at one end of a snowy tablecloth, Louise and the two girls were in different places, and my vacant seat was next to Louise. She was neatly and plainly dressed in a black skirt, with a blue blouse, and had a ribbon or two about her neck and rich dark hair. She also wore neat boots, as I observed afterwards. I thought she looked charming.

"I might give the *menu*, as I considered it remarkable at the time :—

"' Kangaroo tail soup.

"' Silver bream and parsley sauce.

"' Shoulder of mutton.

"' Vegetables of different sorts.

"' Quondong tartlets with cream.
"' Cheese and salad.

"'Two wines, white and red, and some excellent home-brewed ale and sugar beer.'

"I think that was pretty good for a bush interior, and what was very pleasant also was the conversation of Mrs. Lalor and the girls.

"Louise did not look the least tired, and was quite mistress of herself and her knife and fork.

"I observed, generally, that Lalor should be happy in his present surroundings and certainly didn't ever deserve to be if he was not. 'Yes, I am,' replied he with a glance at Louise, 'mostly always I am, except when certain circumstances forbid.'

"And I fancied that Louise's colour heightened.

"I forebore to press the subject and reverted to our journey, concluding by making remarks about the houses and general appearance of prosperity about the station.

"'We are a self-supporting community here,' said Lalor. 'Some of us are nearly related. But I hinted that I would tell you all about it, and I may as well commence now in the presence of my wife and sisters, so that you may form some sort of idea about ourselves and our belongings. You have noticed the obedience which the true blacks give to me on account of my peculiar whistle?'

"I acquiesced, and he went on :—

"'I must refer in the first place to the difference of our castes. They reverence us all here as if we were higher beings, as I suppose we are, but they reverence the memory of my father more than any one who ever came among them, and it is owing to his influence and their own superstition that they give the homage to us now.

"'The particular tribe that used to live here, "Combo," the king, or ruling tribe, are obliterated. The white blood has blotted them out in the course of years by marriage. We are all either quadroons or octoroons, and the pure blacks won't live with us. The descendants of that once numerous tribe which had its "tauri" on this river are now only to be seen about Lake Hope, where I found you and Louise,'—with another curious glance at her.

"'Long, long ago, this tribe of blacks, migrating backwards and forwards by various routes to this place, Lake Hope and the coast, had a knowledge which no white man had, namely, how to get over the waterless tract to the westward and back again; for you must know that there are several routes here, known only to ourselves. One is by a line of native wells; one by a line of rough ground where water can be got by digging, if you know where to dig. There is a spring route, and the tree track. And another by following the flight of pigeons. They one and all can only be used at certain seasons, not all at once, but singly, and any one without this requisite knowledge would be absolutely certain to stray, and perish miserably for want of water. Therefore there is an almost impassable barricade between us and any civilisation from the coast. From the westward I do not think any one will come very far from the old explorer's line, or from the telegraph route.

"'That is how I wish it to be. I do not covet attention from the outside world. An influx of pure white people would break up our small community. We have our own laws and usages.' And Lalor looked anxious and troubled.

"After a pause he went on: 'I have our own family tree from the first white man who came amongst these blacks up to the present day. The first founder of our race married a wife, or rather several. He had been lost and the blacks took pity on him. How he came to be at Lake Hope he couldn't tell. He called himself "Die-dog-Dick". He did die long ago, leaving several half-caste children behind him. Then the blacks say he came again, in another form, still a white man, but different. This man married or took as wives some of the half-caste girls he found in the tribe, and *they* left families, quadroons. He disappeared altogether. I think he was killed in some disturbance. Years went on, and part of this tribe were then nearer the coast, when a man, a powerful, handsome man, rode in amongst them, driving horses. He stayed and went on to Lake Hope, finally coming out here with the blacks. He rather overawed them, but they were subject to his influence, as one of their old men had foretold that old "Die-dog-Dick" would appear in many forms, until the whole tribe were white! This last man was an escaped bushranger, and gave the name of "Nightfall," which was the time he first appeared among them. He entered the plural matrimonial state and has now a numerous progeny about here. All these men became attached to their children (even old "Die-dog-Dick"), and taught them many things. Old "Die-dog-Dick" taught the girls to sew and cook better, and make some sort of dress of skins. He had been a whaler in his time. And they kept learning, and the next generation learnt more and taught more and so on. "Nightfall" had been everything. My father said he had been a gentleman. Before my father knew anything about "Nightfall" he was in Burketown, and one day was accosted by a man who gave him a mason's sign and expressed a wish to converse with him privately. So they adjourned, after taking a drink together, to a remote place along the shore, where the man, who said he had been a bushranger, told him that he wished to share a secret with him, and he should judge if it was worth sharing.

"'My father was young and ready to go in for almost anything, and the offer was nothing but a proposal to go into partnership together over a certain speculation. He consented, and the two disappeared, only to come back at long intervals to Burketown. They came to Coringa, and here they both died, and their bodies are in the graveyard yonder in the hop ridge. No other white man ever came, and the blacks say we are the white race ordained from the first to live at Coringa. They come here sometimes with messages, or on a visit, in small parties, but to them we are a cherished race. So far so good. I have more to tell you, but I will conclude at a more fitting season. Come out in the verandah and have a pipe, and I will show you over our possessions to-morrow.' Mrs. Lalor and the girls joined us, and we sat and smoked, chatting

pleasantly, and listening to that intensely soothing chirp of
the tree crickets, militant everywhere at that time of night
and so well known in Australia. On saying good-night, there
was no mistake about Louise's hand-shake. There was a warm
pressure which tingled in all my veins, and gave me something
to think about for a restless hour or so before I fell asleep.
As for herself, when she was sensible of my returning pressure
she flushed all over. Ah, 'Love's young dream!' how pleasant
it was, and that night I wandered hand in hand with Louise;
my dear Louise, through many changing scenes of the 'Land
of Nod'. Next morning I woke to three distinct long-drawn-
out signals from Lalor's foghorn whistle sounding in my ears.
At breakfast (after prayers, to my great astonishment and
edification) we had a nice fish from the river, eggs, a cold
turkey of the plains, and all sorts of other nice things, including
quondong jelly, a speciality. Mrs. Lalor and the girls did all
they could to put me at my ease and make things pleasant.
And they succeeded. Then Lalor took me for a stroll round
the place, introduced me to the father of the family next door
but one, and got him to trim my hair and beard, which he did
very well. This man whom he called Peter Neil, a descendant
of old 'Die-dog-Dick,' had several children from a baby to a
six-year-old, and Mrs. Neil, a quadroon, was a bright, happy-
looking mother. All about the houses and gardens were
beautifully kept. Vegetables grew in profusion, especially
cabbages and melons. There were apparati down at the river
for irrigation, and the water was carried all over the place by
shoots, runnels and trenches. I now had got beyond surprise,
and viewed with calmness corn and maize growing, orchards,
hay-fields, paddocks containing cattle, sheep, horses and even
camels, of which I saw twenty in a large paddock! Where
they were was a huge sort of brush-covered shed, for shelter
I thought. 'Our transport,' smiled Lalor. 'For that desert,
waterless except for our knowledge, we require them sometimes. There will be a transport team going out when you
go back, and I and Peter are going to take charge of them:
also some more of us. You will likely have a stampede with
your horses, but I will send word over to Lake Hope, so as
to prevent them smashing their hobbles, or bolting to "king-
dom come" when the camels arrive. Your two horses here
will soon get used to the smell of them, for I will have them

led past them often with ours, which don't mind them. You must remember that our colony here has been a self-supporting go-ahead community for many years now. We have a regular system of communication with the coast, but only one or two of us show up there, and they don't know of our existence in such numbers. To tell you the truth, there are very few, even if they did, who would ever find us. The desert would stop them. The blacks would mislead them, and the poison plant would settle them. But these difficulties will be overcome some day, in the natural course of things, I am afraid'—and he changed colour, turning quite pale.

"'The fact is, Mr. Elliott, that I have been here all my life, and my people and kindred with me; and I *dread* the advent of the pure white race. Then our happy community will be broken up and scattered to the winds; and why *should* we be? We live here happy and comfortably. We don't want money. There is still some left to pay for luxuries, but we grow our own flour now, and maize, and our milling is good enough for us. We have cattle and sheep, and there is plenty of game and fish. No, I dread the advent of strangers, and we keep in the dark as much as we can.' I inspected the flour mill. It was worked by the wind, on the orthodox plan, and though the appliances were rough, they were very ingenious, and I doubted not their ability to supply the whole community, which numbered, all told, about 250 souls. I was informed that there were two other settlements up the Yeril, with about fifty people in each. I include them with the total population. Coringa people numbered 150. 'Coringa is our capital,' said Lalor; 'all the head men of the different places have my mystic whistle. It was an invention of my father's, and the pure blacks obey it anywhere, as you have seen. And now I will give you an idea of the secret I have shied off from, but cannot tell you yet. It is a haunting terror to me night and day, but some time or other I may have to take you into my confidence. I merely hint at it again now, so that if ever you see me look worried or sad, don't take any notice.' And he sighed deeply. What could it be, thought I. It was not the first time he had thrown out hints, and he evidently *wished* to tell me. Well, it was not my business. I would await his own good time. Ah, my Louise, she now was always in my thoughts; if Lalor possessed some dread secret I would be near her to take care of her anyway.

"Next day Lalor and I visited Mintheringie, the next station of this nearly white race, about twenty miles above Coringa on the Yeril. Here too the principal man was a quadroon, a single man. He eyed me, I thought, rather suspiciously. He seemed to be about twenty-five years old. We stayed there that night and went on to Oodalba the next day, about fifteen miles farther north. Both places bore the same signs of prosperity and progress as Coringa did.

"Lalor had a long conversation with the quadroon 'boss' at Mintheringie, but of course I gathered nothing from the unknown language. When we arrived back at Coringa, Mrs. Lalor and the girls met us. Lalor said something to Louise, which seemed to make her angry, and I saw little of her for the rest of that day. Lalor had looked much upset all the way home, but I said nothing, remembering our conversation. You must recollect that Louise had been under my care when we camped at Lake Hope. I had watched her recover, and I *now* knew that if I saw her hurt or annoyed in anyway it hurt me too. I felt it, and resented it. The girl was beautiful, and lovable—to me at least. I was only a young fellow, about Lalor's own age, and I did not like his manner to his sister. Though nothing had been said, I knew from the look in Louise's eyes when they met mine what *she* thought, and I knew my own feelings too. They had developed into love, deep happy love. I would have done anything for the girl.

"That evening Lalor and his wife got into a heated discussion about something or other, which I guessed had some reference to Louise. So I left them, and strolled down the river. Louise joined me, and there were tears in her eyes. One look was enough. I took her into my arms, and in that moment I knew she was all mine. Oh, the happiness of those few moments! Warm, passionate, impulsive and affectionate, she told me brokenly of her trials.

"'You saw that man, Ned Nightfall, at Mintheringie?' said she. I said I didn't know his name, but that I noticed her brother called him 'Ned'. 'Well, dear,' said Louise, 'I will tell you all about him. I *hate* him. He wants to marry me. And my brother wants me to marry him. Sophie (Lalor's wife) doesn't. She knows I hate him. But my brother is very determined. And we had such a time here before you came. That's why I ran away, or rather rode away. But I lost my horse a day's journey from Lake Hope. And it took me three days to get there on foot. Oh, Mr. Elliott, when are you going back? You mustn't leave me here.' Leave her! Not I indeed. 'And, indeed, Mr. Elliott, if you did,' said she, 'I should kill myself. I *hate* him. There's something about him which makes me shudder; and as to being his wife, I'd sooner be dead. But here comes my brother.' We walked straight up to Lalor, who was looking grave and stern.

"He saw how it was at once before I told him, and, merely turning to my sweetheart, said, 'Louise, go up to Sophie. Tell her I have something very private to talk to Mr. Elliott about. Ask Sophie to go over to Peter's and take you and the girls with her. What I have to say must be heard by no one but Mr. Elliott and myself. You can all come back in an hour.' He preceded me to the house, and the women-folk going out, we took seats in his private room.

"When all was quiet he began: 'Mr. Elliott, I have told you our family history up to now, but there are dissensions among us; dissensions which I cannot stop or hinder, and it is here, on this one point, and another, that my family skeleton troubles me. I had hoped, by marrying Louise to one of Nightfall's descendants, to prevent any more jarring notes of discord, to amalgamate our interests and stave off what I dread. And now *you* step in. What am I to do? Of course, you really love my sister. But for you the foolish girl might be dead.' 'Do you call her foolish?' exclaimed I. 'Do you think it right and just to compel her to marry a man she dislikes with every fibre of her being, every pulse in her body? Of *course*, I love her.'

"He considered for a bit, and then said: 'And are you quite willing to make her your wife as long as you live? Matrimony among us now is as sacred as among you whites. Since my father's day, laws have been made and our observance of them is very strict. There are no more plural marriages. But I dread the time coming. Perhaps it is selfish on my part, but I hoped to keep our race separate, to found a community working together for their mutual benefit. And for that, and with that goal as a fixed purpose, I have striven all my life. Your marriage with Louise may hinder that end, unless you accept my decision and consent to become one of ourselves and never go back to civilisation.' Here was a staggerer! I was not ashamed to take Louise anywhere. Civilising influences, manners, dress, etc., she had already learned. She would only improve if further civilised.

"But on speaking to her afterwards it was with her brother's own intense dislike that she spoke of removal. She simply said: 'Mr. Elliott, I love you, and I shall die if you go away, but I cannot go among your people. When I ran away from here it was not to the whites I went but to the blacks, though I wanted my brother to think I had gone to the whites,' she whispered, with a glimmer of mischief in her eyes. 'And now I *really* have gone to one white, anyhow. My brother would *never* have brought you here had you not found me and saved my life. But he loves me and I love him, though he is severe with me sometimes. But I don't care now.'

"So I resolved to stay where I was. And we were married and I lived in Paradise. Just before we were married Lalor, I and some others, including Peter and Ned Nightfall, had come back from the coast, where we had been with the transport train. On the way out Nightfall had been inclined to be insolent to me, but I walked up to him and gave him to understand that on the slightest hint from him I should give him a good hiding. And he saw I meant what I said. But a black, vindictive look crept into his eyes all the same. And a sinister, well-pleased expression lurked about his face on the way home for some reason or other. The camels were well packed. Lalor's signals to all the black tribes had been marvellous, and we had hundreds to help us. We left a camel here and a camel there, and my six extra horses were utilised from Lake Hope on our journey in. Only two of us, Lalor and myself, appeared together the first time and loaded our purchases on horses. We represented ourselves as Lalor had done before as getting these things for a distant station. Peter and young Nightfall appeared from quite a different direction and got more things. I don't know how they worked the affair, but my impression was that Lalor had a secret agent or two in the town. I know he got money and that he paid for stores. Anyhow I made no inquiries. Our party never came together again till Lalor and I had reached Lake Hope. We had separated 100 miles from the coast on our way in. Blacks carried stores and parcels for miles in all directions. At Lake Hope the camels were utilised, Lalor and I and Peter going back with them. The horses went home by another route altogether. Even here the party split up into small numbers. We got water when we wanted it, and arrived safely at home, leaving no tracks behind us. And our marriage was very happy. And I helped to build a nice house for Louise and myself, making many friends among my cheerful willing helpers. Ah! that time, the pure unalloyed happiness of it! I shall never forget it, never! The only pure unalloyed happiness of my whole lifetime! But the change was coming.

"One night, six months after our marriage, Lalor came and sat with me, motioning Louise to go over to Sophie. His face was overcast, he was trembling and could hardly speak. 'Elliott,' he said at last, 'what I feared is coming true. I have been betrayed. I hear that a large body of people have left Burketown and are coming out here. Of course, at *last* they *might* have found us out, but, if my suspicions are right, they will be *guided* out. Were it not that there is a traitor among us the outside world would have never found us. They would never get over the drought belt. Mark my words, we shall all be wanderers on the face of the earth soon, and within another six months, if I don't mistake. Don't tell Louise, for God's sake; it would kill her. It will kill us all, I fear, sooner or later.

"'I know who has done it, and he shall pay for it when his time comes. I have only to speak the word, and he would never be heard of again! Man!' he suddenly exclaimed, in a low strained voice, his body trembling and his hands shaking with passion and excitement, 'we are ruined. *Do you know that we are living, actually living, on* GOLD? Gold is beneath our feet and gold is all around us.' I was certain he had gone mad. Why should we be ruined? But I soon saw his drift. 'My father's warning, my father's warning,' resumed he. 'Before he died, he told me that the discovery of gold was Nightfall's first secret. Only those two knew it, and they came to the conclusion that it would not be possible to work it without attracting a vast population to the spot. And Nightfall was not anxious to be where there were many people—for reasons of his own. If it became known, nothing would prevent the white races from devastating the whole country. No physical difficulty, no formation of nature, nothing, would daunt or stop them once this treasure was revealed!

"'And those two, Nightfall and my father, were so worked upon by the thought of it all, that they decided not to say anything about it. They were happy with their wives and coming children, and my father proposed and carried out a plan of supply for the place. They got grain and seeds and began to cultivate. They both had money, and they used this year by year. There was plenty of labour from the two former generations, and bit by bit they schemed, and managed, with the help of the blacks, to get supplies out. Gradually they got some stock. There is a south route always open, where they managed to get stock out in small quantities, but it is a long way round. The camels were strays; the herd now is the offspring of two, and they have bred up and worked for our benefit. We all have worked for years. Now, this is my skeleton, my secret, my family ghost. Nightfall sometimes drank, especially when his children were able to understand. The blacks brought him liquor, only once or twice though, for my father put a stop to it as much as he could. But afterwards Nightfall made liquor himself. What he said I don't know, but the Nightfalls all know about the gold. It *leaked* out. Now, there is no other could have done this evil to me but Ned Nightfall, curse him! Not another soul here either wants the gold *or* the white people. It was the knowledge that he might do something underhand which made me wish to propitiate him with my sister.'

"'But why not make as much as ever you can before any one comes out, and stick to your share and as much ground as ever you can?' said I. 'It will make a city of Coringa, and you ought to become enormously wealthy.' 'Elliott, my father's dying words were: "Seek not riches if you wish to be really happy. Seek not to go into the world. Beware of riches. Beware of drink."'

"I could see that there was not the least use of my talking to Lalor. His mind and nature were fixed, and I couldn't help him. His will had grown to his teaching. That night the old black chief came in from Lake Hope. He and Lalor spoke together in the unknown tongue for upwards of two hours. Next morning he was gone. Lalor's later words kept ringing in my head: 'Mark my words, Elliott, if we are found out, Coringa will disappear. The blacks reverence us. They think we are the spirits of their departed fathers and grandfathers come back to live with them. They will spirit us away I don't know where.'

"I thought over these words, and worked myself up into a frenzy. And the next day I rode over to Mintheringie and laid young Nightfall up for a week, after a stormy altercation. I remembered his devilish glee on our return from the coast with the transport train, and I felt sure he had taken specimens of gold in the quartz with him, and 'blown' the whole affair. Anyway, I gave him something to remember *me* by. But I never breathed a word to Louise.

"A month after Lalor's dreadful disclosure, Coringa was surrounded suddenly at night by hundreds of armed blacks. There was no fighting, but I heard Lalor's foghorn whistle sound several times. What happened then I don't know, for in the confusion I lost Louise, and all became blank to me. I came to myself in the hospital at Burketown, and how I got there I don't know. I suspect I was taken there, as I partly remembered travelling on a camel, but I couldn't tell for certain. The doctor said it was sunstroke, but that I would get well. It appears that I had been raving for a fortnight. I got well, quite well, at last, and went out with a party of diggers who were going to a new rush. We didn't go the way I first went, and I didn't know the place. I never saw Eacharn again. I was always expecting Louise to turn up. But she never did. What became of her and the rest of them I never knew. And the diggings wasn't Coringa. Only a wretched digging town, growing bigger every day, and hundreds coming night and morning from all parts.

"There wasn't a single person who wasn't *pure* black, pure white, pure yellow or pure brown amongst the thousands that worked there. That's what gets me.

"And I sometimes sleep under that rock in the Domain. I've met some queer chaps there, I can tell you, coves who've travelled a deal, and chaps who've come down in the world like me, through the booze. And some of 'em have had a good education, a ' 'varsity' education, only you wouldn't think it to look at 'em.

"Yes, sir, thank you, I'll have another whisky. I don't

often get 'em now. But I don't care for money, sir. The half-crown you gave me will keep me for a bit. And I'm *not* always out of work, sir. I get a good billet here and there now and again."

We passed out, and I left him, bound back up the hill to his "mates". They were considerably "younger in the horn" than he was, and I could not help thinking that he could put them up to many wrinkles.

As I lit my pipe, I wondered if he would tell them the same story he had just told me, and the look of perplexity on my face, lit up by the match, must have induced a stalwart policeman who was passing at the time to say, "I see you've been speaking to 'old Jimmy,' sir. He's not near as bad as they make some of them, sir. He's not a regular loafer. He's all right, is old Jimmy. But I daresay he's been spinning you his yarn, sir. He kept me and a mate alive here, one night, watching for a bad case. (Thank you, sir.) Gave us important information, did old Jimmy. And we copped the man we was watching for. But not till old Jimmy had spun his yarn out. He's rare entertaining. Started out to colonise a desert island with a lot of camels and half-castes, and such truck, he did. And he would have done it, only there was a gold reef in the way. Old Jimmy? He's all right! Good night, sir." And I wended my way homewards.

A VOICE FROM THE DEAD

> And bones lie bleaching on the sod
> "Out-back" on desert grim,
> Where almost seems the Wrath of God
> To have o'ertaken him.
> —*Coo-ee.*

LATITUDE and longitude about 41 S. and E. respectively.

A stately clipper ship is racing through the water, exhibiting her gleaming copper sides as she drives before the gale and soars aloft and plunges deep amidst the mighty billows of the "roaring forties".

On the weather side of the poop are two men, opposite types of ordinary manhood. Mentally, they are dissimilar. One is educated, the other is not. Their avocations are also different, for one is an A.B., the other a passenger.

The latter has a wide and varied knowledge of the "world and all that therein is," for he has travelled in many climes and gathered his experience. He has been a writer of varied fame, an author, writing often for magazines. He has been a reporter, and even a war correspondent. The two do not keep their respective positions very long, for the sailor, with a grateful look at the passenger, says, "Thank ye, sir," and a very sharp observer might have observed something suspiciously like a tear in the corner of his eye as he stooped to coil away a rope, and he was shortly afterwards called away to another part of the ship.

"Curious," muttered John Boyd, "*bon ami* Boyd," as he was called among his friends and associates. "Old Sheila, our Highland nurse, would declare that Tom Trevittick was 'fey'. I noticed the same look in poor Adair's eyes the night before he fell, leading his men in that last desperate charge of theirs. I wonder greatly what he can have to tell me?"

. . . .

A VOICE FROM THE DEAD

The watch had been set. Sails "alow and aloft" were tugging and straining. Silvery moonbeams traced each rope, yard, spar and block clearly against the luminous, grey, fleecy sky.

The wind was well out on the quarter, and though the big seas came racing after the noble vessel with apparent vindictiveness, they but lifted her and drove her forward as if in sport, and as she raised her figurehead aloft, after it had been buried in the foaming, roaring, hissing surges about her flying cutwater, the very stars twinkled through the whirling scud aloft with delight and satisfaction, as if they witnessed one of the noblest sights in the universe: a clipper ship running free before a stiff gale of wind in the open ocean: where sea and sky meet.

Tom Trevittick's face was very pale and drawn-looking as he faced Boyd in the moonlight across the main-deck capstan, and the wash and surge of the sea, and the hum of the freshening gale as it tore through the shrouds, and the sounding ropes and backstays, formed a style of accompaniment to poor Tom's earnest words that his hearer, as he leaned with his arms on the solid mass between them, and his legs apart and firmly planted upon the uneasy deck, never forgot.

"You may think, sir," said Tom, "that it's something like cheek on my part spinning you a long yarn about my troubles, but you've got a kind look in your face, sir, and you've been main good to us rough chaps ever since we left Greenwich.

"You see, it's this way, sir. I've got a notion in my head that this is my last cruise. I know you won't go against a man, sir, but if I am not drowned or killed this voyage I shall be on the next. So" (sinking his voice to a whisper) "I mean to leave this ship at Melbourne and try my luck on the diggings, if I ever get there. I had a little money saved before I sailed from England this trip, but I left it all with my poor old mother, and if my cruise is shorter, and poor Tom goes under sooner than he knows now, I thought, maybe, sir, that you would write my poor mother a line or two, just telling her that I did my duty while aboard the ship, for I am not much of a scholar, and could go aloft and stow the main-royal much easier than I could write a letter. So I made bold to ask you to write mother's address in your notebook, as I see you often use one, if you don't mind, sir" (as

Boyd produced it). "It is 'Mrs. Trevittick, 10 Cliff Row, Penzance, Cornwall,' sir."

When Boyd had duly entered the address Tom gave a great sigh of relief, and resumed: "And so, sir, I'd better heave ahead. I don't feel so anxious like now you've got that address. I've been at sea all my life, pretty well—man and boy—and I've got this notion that my time is coming to an end; and though I've heard my mates sing in the fo'c'stle o' nights as how 'there's a sweet little cherub as sits up aloft to look after the life of poor Jack,' I believe as how he has folded his wings and is waiting for the end of my voyage, for my flag is half-mast high already."

"But why do you take this despondent view of things?" said Boyd, almost sternly. "It's your duty not to give way to such feelings."

And then, noticing a half-sad, yet utterly convinced expression upon Tom's face, he added: "Cheer up, man; either you're not well or you have allowed this strange fancy to prey upon your mind until your morbid ideas have got the better of your common-sense."

"So I've said to myself often, sir," said Tom, "but I haven't told a living soul on board, except Jem Drake, what I'm agoin' to tell you of now.

"You remember when we first picked up our nor'-east trades, this trip, what bright warm nights we had for a week or so? Well, sir, one night me and Jem Drake, the captain of the fore-top, it being our watch below, goes to sleep on the forecastle, being too warm for our liking in the bunks.

"That night, shortly after 'two bells,' I was woke up all of a suddint, by feeling as if my blanket was bein' twitched off my legs, and I stirred Jem up and accused him of playin' off some of his jokes upon me.

"As I'd had a hard day's work, I felt cross-like at bein' disturbed out of a sound sleep. Jem denied it, growlin' at me for wakin' him. It was very bright, and I could see the rail athwart the poop, under the lift of the foresail, and the second mate sitting on the hencoop quite plain. Well, I soon dropped off to sleep again, and the same feeling, as if the blanket had been pulled off me, came over me again, and woke me.

i.

"HE IS THERE NOW."

From the Land of the Wombat. *Page 49.*

"I turned sharp round thinking to catch Jem Drake this time, but he was sound asleep, and his face was calm and quiet. I felt then as if some power I could not withstand was drawing my head round so as to look under the foresail towards the break of the poop again. The second mate was leaning on the poop rail this time, but, Lord in heaven, as sure as I'm a living sinner, alongside of him was my old father, in heavy sea-boots and sailor's togs, just as I saw him lying ashore drowned—trying to make Penzance in his lugger in a storm—and the moon shone down so clear on his white head and face that he looked as if he had come from the other world to warn me. But," continued Tom in low earnest tones, "the strangest thing of all was that he held a tin pannikin in his hand, for all the world like the one I use in my mess, and he pointed to it and then looked at me.

"I rubbed my eyes hard, thinking I must be dreaming, woke Jem up, and pointed the ghost out, but he told me I was a fool, as he could see the second mate plain enough but nothing else. Well, sir, as I looked the figure seemed to melt away, but all I know is, that I then saw my father there as plain as ever I saw anything in my life. *And may the Lord be merciful to me,*" screamed Trevittick, "*but he is there now!*"

And he fell at Boyd's feet in a fit! In a moment John Boyd was supporting the unfortunate man, and in an almost equally short time the two were surrounded by an excited group of crew and passengers, all anxious to know what was the matter. The surgeon, Dr. Arthur, having been hastily summoned, gave orders for Tom to be carried to his berth and applied the usual remedies.

In about a quarter of an hour the patient came to himself, and, after staring wildly on those around him, said to Boyd: "You see, sir, there was no mistake. What I told you was quite true!"

When he became tranquil he was left in charge of his mate, Jem Drake, who was greatly concerned with regard to his sudden seizure, and, despite Boyd's futile attempts to argue him out of the belief that it could have been anything else but pure hallucination, shook his head with a gesture of dissent, and remarked that Tom Trevittick wasn't given to making mistakes, and that he had heard his messmates talk of many a strange story in which old sailors had been warned of their approaching death in visions and dreams.

In the conversation which afterwards took place between Boyd and Dr. Arthur, the latter attributed Trevittick's sudden seizure as the first symptom of a constitutional break up, but, despite his sinister auguries, Tom rapidly recovered, and was soon able to go about his duties again, to all appearance none the worse for his attack.

The rest of the voyage was devoid of incident of any great moment, except that in future conversation nothing could shake Trevittick's belief in his approaching death, and the certainty of having seen his father on two occasions.

On arrival in Melbourne, Boyd heard casually from the doctor that Trevittick had carried out his intention of leaving the ship, and it was believed that he had, like many other seamen, gone to the diggings. Three months afterwards, Boyd himself started on what our American relations would designate a "pasear," striking up the Quondong River *en route* for a new "rush," wishing to see a new gold-field in its inception. It had been reported through the newspapers and by hearsay that payable gold had been found in the Quondong "back-country," and the *locale* was at the base of a certain Mount Roto. Boyd was well used to long rides, and in his desire to notify facts personally, had taken the simple yet excellent means of doing so by purchasing two good serviceable horses in excellent condition, and he was now using one alternately as packhorse, and jogging along the up-river road, making a station each night.

He had passed great numbers of swagmen, all "on the wallaby," as it is called in bush parlance, all going the same way, and with but two salient ideas in their collective heads: the first being to get to Mount Roto as soon as possible, and that once there they would soon "make their piles".

Diggers are proverbially sanguine on their way to a new "rush," but, as a rule, the nearer they get to their "El Dorado" the more discouraging are the reports. Distance lends the proverbial enchantment; and the reports of large "finds," whether true or the reverse, are dazzling enough to unhinge men's calm judgment and make them forget at the outset the dangers and difficulties that must be surmounted to ensure success.

Though these ideas of perfect security and easy transit seemed to be so general amongst the travellers, Boyd met with one exception, a grizzled old shepherd, who was plodding sturdily along with two well-bred collie dogs running at his heels. From him Boyd gathered the following description of the country to be traversed :—

"Them greenhorns and them chaps that stick to the river, and make a station every night, may talk very big about their bushmanship and all that, but their tongues won't wag so fast when they strike out on to the '*back-country*' and leave the *water* behind. They'll be craning their necks over some beautiful blue pool in the blazing hot sun some day out there, and they'll see the rippling waves come breaking in among the yellow yam flowers at their feet, but they can never reach it, for it just goes back and back through the haze the farther they advance!

"There's *death* in that sight, sir, and the crows, with the steely glare in their eyes, they know where they lie—so still so still—poor fellers.

"You see, sir, I know this terrible 'back-country'. I've shepherded on it for years, and I tell you as a friend, if ever your head begins to turn, and the awful feeling begins to creep upon you that you're *lost*, don't give way to it, sir, for it ends in *madness;* but *follow your 'back-tracks,' inch by inch, step by step, back to the last water you left*, or your bones will lie bleaching in the sun, and nothing will remain to tell the tale of your fate but a metal button or two, your 'jack-shay,' knife, or pannikin. I've seen many a skeleton lying out there on the hot, dry 'salt-bush' plains, and no one the wiser!"

And the shepherd lit his pipe and trudged on, vouchsafing no other words.

On arrival at the last "township" on the northern waters of the Quondong—from which point he would have to diverge across the dreaded plains—Boyd found a number of men liquoring and carousing, but reluctant to start for the mountain, on account of the scarcity of water. All kinds of wild tales were current. Men had been lost; no one knew how many men were on the diggings. Some said only the prospectors, who had a track of their own; others said there were plenty of diggers there. A legend existed that the road, which was well-defined and easy for a day and a half from the township, had disappeared at this point; that there was a great fissure in the earth which nobody could cross, that all traces of a road at all were swallowed up in endless miles of burning sand. And, as there was plenty of whisky and brandy in the township, they elected to stay where they were.

One thing was certain, according to some, that there could be no communication with the diggers except by a well-mounted man, who could make ample provision, and the mystery of the vanished road had settled all the swagmen. One unhappy individual had appeared in the township in a dreadful state, having cut his body with a knife in order to drink his own blood, so as to assuage the awful thirst madness that had come upon him. And *his* statement corroborated the theory of the lost road.

Boyd was not a man to be daunted by tales of this description, and though there was no doubt that some unfortunate foot-travellers had perished, he determined to start, and as it was three days' (mounted) journey to Roto across the "back-country," he left the township well supplied for emergencies, carrying large canvas water-bags on the pack-horses, besides two large canteens, resolving to husband this supply to the uttermost. He also made up his mind to ride through the greater part of the night and early morning, to avoid the heat. Knowing that Roto lay to the north, and being provided with a reliable pocket compass, he did not trouble himself much about the lost road.

On the evening of the second day he came upon the place where the road had disappeared, and after riding straight on for a considerable distance, found it again; the cause of its vanishing being apparently due to a succession of whirlwind and dust storms which had obliterated all tracks.

On the third evening he could see Mount Roto plainly enough, a blue pinnacle in the distance. His horses had carried him well so far, and he still had a little water left. His plan of avoiding the hot, toilsome hours of the day and travelling in the cool night and morning had answered well. Travelling from sunset till a couple of hours later, he determined on a three hours' spell, and turning out his horses in hobbles, lay down with his saddle for a pillow, watching the Southern Cross glittering overhead.

He had just dozed off when something startled his horses, and shortly afterwards he heard them both galloping furiously in hobbles. Jumping up and seizing the bridles, he set off full speed, but he had a smart run of a quarter of a mile before he headed them, which he managed to do by a small clump of myall trees, one of many scattered about the plain.

As he was leading them back, he noticed that they were very uneasy, and kept snorting with fright, and it then struck him that they had exhibited this same nervousness more or less since he had turned them out. As he came back on his tracks the horses became worse, in fact almost unmanageable, and it was with difficulty that he could steady and soothe them enough to saddle up and mount.

Once in the saddle again, however, he determined to find out the mystery by taking a circuit round the camp.

He had hardly ridden 200 yards when they both shied violently at a dead body, quite unrecognisable because of the wild dogs and crows. He had noticed three or four of the former sneaking about when he first rode up.

The bones of the legs and arms were pretty well denuded of flesh, and shone grim and ghastly in the moonlight, and the clothes on the corpse were very much torn and frayed, as if it had been dragged about a great deal. Something glittering on the sand at his feet attracted his attention. Dismounting, and soothing his terrified horses, he managed to get hold of this glittering article, which he slipped into one of his saddle-bags. It was a tin pannikin which he took with him. When daylight came and he dismounted again for breakfast, on re-examining the pannikin he became aware that some rude letters were scratched on the bottom of it; and, after puzzling over them for some time, at last to his horror deciphered the following message from the dead:—

"Tom Trevittick,
A.B., Ship *Waratah*,
Warned of his death at Sea.
To him as finds this panikin.
Hed of Devils Guly,
Six steps from Gumb-tree,
Mark T, due noarth,
Dig."

Much troubled and grieved Boyd pushed on. Having given the remainder of his water to the horses, about a mouthful apiece, reserving a very small portion in case of emergency, determining if possible to get assistance at Roto, and to return and bury the dead body, obtaining further evidence if possible.

As his horses were now uncommonly thirsty, he was glad when he heard them both whinny, and as Roto was now looming high over his head, he picked his way through the scrub and big loose boulders at the base of the mountain, and shortly afterwards saw the smoke of a digger's fire. Two rough-looking men came up, apparently astonished to see a stranger.

"Well, boss," said the spokesman, "so you've found us out. Them's good horses or you wouldn't have got over the 'Never Never' country so easy. I guess we shan't have a rush out here until after the rains. Them plains frightens every one but 'back-blockers' and old shepherds. But come along and have a bite and a pannikin o' billy tea. Me and my mate were just gettin' a snack as you came along."

Thankfully accepting their hospitality, after a few minutes' conversation, Boyd told them of the dead body, but reserved all the history connected with it.

"Well, he's not the first by long chalks, but we can't afford to go aburyin' of it just now. We've lost about six men from this here camp agoin' philanderin' back to the township with jest as much knowledge of the bush as a Methody missionaryin' cove 'off his chump'. By the way, there was a sailor chap up here, runned away from his ship in port, he said. 'Tom,' we chaps called him. He hasn't turned up for some time. He *was* a chap for prospectin'. Swore there was a big reef here, only he never could find it. Said he knew somethin' about minin' in Cornwall."

All the more convinced, Boyd kept his own counsel, resolving to penetrate the meaning of poor Tom's message by hook or by crook, and, after a day's rest, persuaded two of the diggers to return with him and bury the body. They accomplished this after two days' absence. Additional proof was found in some shreds of clothing, the blue pilot cloth such as any sailor wears for his best, a button or two, marked "Jarvis, Marine Outfitter, Penzance"; and all combined to make Boyd sure that the mutilated remains had in life been Tom Trevittick. Boyd, after due consideration, resolved to make a clean breast of it to the digger who had first accosted him on arrival at Roto, and related the whole story from beginning to end.

The digger, whose name was "Swanhill Jack," as he informed Boyd—"leastaways, that's what they all call me about here, and as to my other name, why, it don't matter"—seemed to be a decent sort of fellow, and Boyd at length showed him the writing on the pannikin.

"I must tell my mate, sir," said he, "and if there's any luck in it, we'll go third shares apiece. Depend upon it, it's a 'golden hole,' or he's buried any nuggets he's got to keep 'em dark." A consultation was held, in which Swanhill Jack's mate took part, and an agreement was entered into in black and white, to this effect:—

"I, John Boyd, being in receipt of a message from a dead man, hold myself responsible to carry out his wishes".

The next part of this document, as dictated by Swanhill Jack, who insisted upon his own words being put down—"for what I ses I sticks to, like grim death to a dead nigger," said he—ran thus:—

"Me and my mate, Bob, swears to help the 'boss,' good or bad, to carry out the dead man's wish.

"(Signed)   J. BOYD.
(„   )   SWANHILL JACK.
(„   )   BOB."

"Where is the 'Devil's Gully?'" asked Boyd.

"It's about a day's walk from here, along the base of Roto," replied Jack; "but as there's only the one lagoon as I knows on, we'll have to carry water with us."

A day later they left the camp, taking Boyd's two horses with them, and a goodly supply of necessaries, and in answer to questions from other diggers, Jack said they "were goin' prospectin'".

Towards night they camped on the far side of Roto, near to a deep ravine, the bottom of which was covered with boulders of rock and sand.

Strange to say, after clambering about next morning in almost inaccessible spots, they found a native well, which they would never have noticed but that a number of "squatter" and "bronzewing" pigeons flew up from near it. Water there was to their astonishment, collected from the last rains, in a narrow deep hole, which shot in under an overhanging rock at an angle of forty-five degrees, and by crawling in and lowering the "billy" with a strap, they were able to fill it. On procuring a lengthy sapling they ascertained that there was six feet of water in the well.

A solitary white gum tree, sure sign of water, and the only one among the rocks, grew close by.

"That tree has its taproot in water," said Jack, "but you might come here many a time in this danged thick scrub, and not get perched on this ledge, on this of the gully, as we are now."

After carefully examining the tree, Boyd found a big letter T, cut in the white bark, as marked on the pannikin, and taking his compass, strode six steps to the north. At this point they commenced to dig.

"It's been dug before!" exclaimed Jack. "Now that I look close, I can see the darned stuff's all loose." Not three feet from the surface Jack's spade struck something hard, which being uncovered, they found to be the cap of a quartz-reef, honeycombed and studded with gold! Trembling with excitement, they uncovered it a good deal further, when Jack, turning white as a sheet, choked out: "Peg out a claim, Bob, this is the richest reef ever I see!"

Three claims were promptly pegged out and bits of paper, with their names on them, were fastened to three of the pegs, whilst the three men, thus strangely brought together in such a big venture, shook hands and had a long serious discussion far into the night.

The next day at dawn Jack rose, shook himself, lit his pipe, and then swore solemnly for five minutes, for three more men were sitting quietly on the other side of the gully, waiting for the prospectors to commence operations!

Their decision was rapid, for in less than twenty minutes' time three more claims were pegged out north along the line of the reef. These six men worked like demons for six days, and at the end of that time every claim was abandoned on the old diggings and every digger was located on the new one at Devil's Gully. But it took time with the reef, for though they could pile up plenty of stuff to be crushed, there were no appliances. But, locally treated by simple means, the stone was rich enough to give every man the wildest ideas of riches. Rain now fell in abundance, and a river went swirling by the gorge below the now busy mining camp.

Boyd had always attended well to his horses, which had

good feeding out on the plains by the small lagoon Jack had mentioned, but they very soon had plenty of mates, for an influx of 200 men, some on foot and others mounted, came pouring into the district. Then drays came lumbering up, and bullocks were to be seen pasturing. After that a hundred or so of men arrived weekly, and the reef was "prospected" along, far from the first prospectors. Stores became abundant, and water was conserved in every direction by digging large tanks. Machinery at last began to arrive; and things looked as if a city was arising, but at the end of three months Boyd sold out of the "Dead Man's Reef," at a very decent price, leaving Jack and Bob to follow their luck to the end (they were wealthy men now, even if they sold out entirely), started for Melbourne and home. On arrival in the old country, he found out Tom Trevittick's mother, and told her gently all the story. When she recovered from her grief, she said she had dreamed of her son lying out in the desert, with strange creatures like wolves prowling about him. " But I didn't think he was dead," said the old lady simply, " I only thought he was sleeping."

Boyd purchased a comfortable cottage for her, and allowed the poor old thing a most handsome annuity, paying her also a visit from time to time whenever his stirring adventurous life permitted him.

The pannikin he keeps himself as a relic, and to this day the wind never rises suddenly, or he hears it moaning, but the scene on board ship, the stormy wash of the waves, the freshening hum of the gale, and poor Tom Trevittick's pale, set face rise up before him, seeming to remind him over and over again of the Message from the Dead.

AN UP-COUNTRY RACE-MEETING

> We've drunk as much as we're able,
>   And the Cross swings low for the morn;
> Last toast—and a foot on the table!—
>   A health to the native-born!
>
> —*Kipling.*

THE great annual races were to be held at Brandyville, on the Gunyahgo River. We had about 100 miles to ride from Auburn. We were running two horses, one for the flat, and one for the steeplechase. These were our trained horses, and had been sent on a week before.

After making "hay," considerable "hay," at Hooligan's, which constituted our first stage, we made still more "hay" at Bylo, where there was a public-house of a very ordinary sort, where a shepherd or a shearer, after "knocking down his cheque," could calculate with certainty and precision for an extra dose of the "horrors," accompanied by "jim-jams," on account of the awful character of the liquor supplied. At Bylo we were assisted in our hay-making festivity by several other travellers, and some atrocious sherry, the only vendible alcoholic mixture on the place at the time. We finished it to the dregs, and found about three-quarters of a pound of plug sheep-dip tobacco at the bottom of the cask. Beyond a casual headache or two amongst our crowd in the morning, there were not many complaints. We were all pretty tough, and our constitutions were strong, or the results might have been different. Beyond a yearly flare-up or so, we had not as yet injured them. And now, having gone so far in the way of introduction to my readers, I may state that I am going to drop the personal pronoun in the singular number as much as possible, as I do not wish to get mixed up too much in the

AN UP-COUNTRY RACE-MEETING 59

events which happened at these races, for it could not possibly be supposed that I both originated and performed the various antics herein portrayed, of which I am the truthful chronicler. So I take shelter under the plural "we". And really the plural "we" had more to do with events than "I". There were many shoulders among the "we" implicated stronger to bear the burden of blame for anything unseemly than the mere two possessed by myself or "I".

Our party consisted of two much-esteemed friends who were staying with us, our three selves, better known in the district as Kirley Brothers & Vandyke. That was the brand on our wool-bales, and our own trade-mark. We were Kirleys, my brother and I, naturally, in the common sequence of things, and Vandyke—was Vandyke. He was one of the biggest men in Australia, and stood six feet seven in his bare pelt. With his boots and tall Queensland hat on he measured a bit over a foot more.

The best heavy-weight boxer or fighter—he wasn't particular, and you could get either event on. It depended upon the humour he was in.

One of the best swimmers in Victoria, a crack shot, rifle or gun, a very good jumper for his great height and weight, and a man who could drive or ride any blessed thing. I was always thankful that I wasn't his journey hack or stock horse, and comforted myself considerably with the after idea that I was only one of two Kirleys, and not much good at that. With regard to our firm—of which I confess I was very proud when I saw it first gazetted—a friend of ours camped one night on the Gunyahgo River in a shepherd's hut and told us the following yarn: Two swagmen were there discussing the merits of the different squatter firms in the district. Number one swagman gave Number two the following advice: "If you come across those blanky Kirley Brothers & Vandyke, you look out. If you say a word to either of those crimson blanketty Kirleys, you have to go outside and get a punchin', and if *they* can't do it that (native phraseology) Vandyke will give yer the blankiest scupperin' yer ever had inside of 'arf a minute, you bet your bally boots on *that !* "

I considered our reputation had been made; and we always strove to act up to it, both before and after this expression of public opinion. I also am of opinion that our hitherto consistent conduct raised the price of our wool and stock in the market considerably.

As we jogged along, I can still in my "mind's eye" see the happy group of that exodus to the races. We betted on various chances, hedged on doubts, whistled, sang and joked. Our ringing laughter scared the bandicoot from his ancestral log, and I have no doubt woke up many a slumbering 'possum dreaming the daylight hours away in his hollow tree.

Ah, me! how decimated that lively, joking, boisterous party has become with the lapse of years.

They are gone, all of them, from my present surroundings, disappeared, far away in the "ewigkeit," as Hans Breitmann expresses it. Gone like the passing sunset. "Where is dat barty now? Vere is the lofely colden gloud that rest on der mountain brow?" Eheu fugaces! But to resume. As we rode along we were caught up or joined from bush tracks by other horsemen, squatters, pioneers from remoter stations even than ours, others from the vicinity, stockmen, jackeroos and "various".

Now and then we passed swagmen and shepherds, all merry and determined to enjoy their brief holiday to the extent of their "bottom dollar".

We finally arrived at the "township". In those days it consisted of a bush hotel, a store, a blacksmith's shop, the police barracks, lock-up, post-office, and the stockyard and public pound. In these days it is probably a large town, with a railway running through it and a Salvation Army burning to be immortalized but *not* to be immortalized by burning.

As we rode through the "outskirts," which consisted of the blacks' "camp" and sundry loafing warrigal dogs, we saw that the big town stockyard was in the course of demolition to make way for one still larger. This betokened prosperity and an increase in travelling stock.

Arrived at the one hotel there was (for Brandyville) a great concourse. Many friends turned up. The native police, Queensland black trackers, were in with their white inspector, also a couple of local white mounted constables. Thus the factor for suppressing rowdyism was there in strength and uniform. But they were not required. There was a good

AN UP-COUNTRY RACE-MEETING

deal of bear-fighting and skylarking, and a vast amount of unlimited liquoring up, but evil-minded rioting was unknown. Most of the men who were there—of the crowd, crowdy—had not tasted the cup which both cheers and inebriates for a year or more. We were there to run our respective horses, and to get as much fun out of the meeting as we could possibly cram into three or four days. We also meant to have our full share of the liquor.

The first day we got over most satisfactorily. Things got a bit mixed after all the horses had run, when several over-excited individuals started a buggy race on the steeplechase course. The jumps were pretty stiff, and there were several spills and barked limbs, also contusions, but every one concerned was thoroughly and vaingloriously satisfied. Bacchus generally protects his devotees.

Then the state dinner in the big dining-room at "Gin or Whisky's" was a great, a marvellous success. "Gin or Whisky" was a Russian Pole or Finn, I believe. The name sounded like it, anyway. We never troubled ourselves, and he supplied us with either on application and payment. The dinner was a speciality, well warmed, well lighted and well served. "Gin or Whisky" overlooked us with perspiring, bald-headed beamings of satisfaction and goggles of joy. In the incipient stages of that dinner the ruby wine sparkled and circulated with great freedom, so also did champagne, and festivity advanced with the courses. Then at length, full fed and well wined, every one became loquacious. Speeches were made. Vandyke was one of the stewards, and had been unanimously elected president of that dinner. He certainly filled the chair most imposingly. "Mr. Vice," a very well-known and very small-sized squatter, faced him at the other end of a very long table. The fun and jollity became intense. Songs were sung even by the President and Vice. Men were known to sing who had never been suspected of knowing a song. Everybody began to love his neighbour. They were all jolly good fellows. An hour later they were all jolly goo'flers, and so time passed. A gentleman rose. He had a speech to make. "Imp't'nt speesh, Mista Plesdel." Then came an alarming pause, instantly filled up by the gentleman who sat next me taking a jam tartlet from a full dish of them and hurling it at the speaker. The would-be speaker had a sharp pointed nose, and that tartlet stuck to it as a jam tart might be expected to do. During the roar of laughter which followed, Vandyke, who had been looking intensely solemn for the last few minutes, uttered the most appalling war-whoop, and pulled the whole gigantic tablecloth clean off the table, spreading ruin and disaster everywhere. Dishes, crockery, viands—chiefly pastry—tumblers, wine, spirits, knives and forks mingled in one terrific chaos. There was a wild scrimmage all round, and the "gompany fighted mit daple lecks," or anything they could get hold of. A jam tartlet is a good thing to smear any one's face with, as I personally found out, and so I wreaked my vengeance on my bitterest enemy. The landlord came in and wailed with despair and horror, but was instantly pelted with his own crockery and anything edible or liquid. He beat a prompt retreat. A few of us escaped; I was of that number.

I remember conversing with some of the actors in that hullabaloo, afterwards when all had somewhat simmered down, and have a sort of dim recollection that I thought they all bore a jammy, sugary, confectionary and liquory sort of appearance—also substance. They were not sober. Nobody was. We were not. Various scenes of that festive time became impressed upon our memory as we wandered about in a sort of utterly irresponsible manner. We were in Utopia, a reckless, unreasoning Utopia, full of practical jokes. We passed into a private room. We met a friend there. He was regaling an outcast, a worn and hungry tramp he had picked up somewhere. The tramp had *had* whisky, also ale, also more whisky. He was now filling up with solids. At least a dozen full bottles of beer were on the table before him. He had a pint measure full of it, also one of stout. He beamed with joy. There was a cold wild turkey, the remains of a beefsteak pie, and etceteras. Some one had placed a pat of butter on the top of the outcast's head, and it melted. We left, and went on with time up till two o'clock in the morning, at which unearthly hour the native police inspector and his sub-lieutenant, blandly smiling, were transporting a somnolent individual in a wheelbarrow to their tent. We wandered on and discovered a policeman fast asleep in the open on his back. Beatitude, intense beatitude, was written on his features, and he snored.

AN UP-COUNTRY RACE-MEETING

There was a bottle of three-star Hennessey, three parts full, firmly wedged in his right armpit. We absorbed it. We then came across a flask of gunpowder, "Pigou and Wilkes". We attempted to blow up the policeman. To prevent the explosion injuring any one *but* the policeman, two of us were deputed to throw matches at the powder-flask, whilst two others were to cover the explosion with the policeman's blanket, which we abstracted. In our deep-thinking minds there was no crime about it. The policeman was a black one, and would "jump-up-white-fellow," so it didn't matter much. Our memory becomes hazy from this point, and whether a thunder-storm came on, with occasional flashes of lightning, or we blew the policeman up did not concern us. We began to get hungry and adjourned, whilst one of our party proceeded to capture the hotel rooster on the roof of the stables. Nothing would satisfy him but "devilled" fowl. To attain his project he first walked upon the abdominal parts of a groom who was sleeping at the locked door where his important charges were. He was annoyed, and vituperated us. When we had caught the ancient and scandalised rooster, who made night hideous until he was silenced, we went to the billiard-room and proceeded to cook him under the billiard-table with legs of sofas and chairs. We had an idea that he would grill well, and a deputation set off to search for a gridiron. We went to bed and woke at our usual hour, being much surprised at the advent of another "we" from under the bed, who apologised and said he did not wish to disturb us, but being out late, had come back to find all the beds full, six or seven people in each being quite a common occurrence, according to his account. On entering my room he carefully counted two people in the bed over and over again to make quite sure, and then rolled under it, quite satisfied that there were four. We dressed and adjourned to the bar, partook of a "John Collins" apiece, and set out with refreshments in search of corpses. We found the inspector, his sub-lieutenant and the somnolent one, fast asleep in one of the big holes at the stockyard where the old posts had been dug out. The heels and soles of their feet were alone visible, as the wheelbarrow was on the top of them. We "corpse-revived" them with a "doctor," a potent remedy composed of battle-axe brandy, one egg, a little sugar, some nutmeg and fresh milk, scientifically shaken and frothed up, and the whole of us went on for other derelicts. We found Vandyke asleep, with a smile of cherubic sweetness on his lips. He had taken the great stockyard gate off its hinges, and placed it judiciously across his feet and knees. After we had removed the obstruction, and Vandyke had swallowed his "doctor," he blandly remarked :—

"My dear f'lers, felt shleepy, cold, walted blalket, got one, put it crosh legs, shlept cumforbl, 'sure you. But—wash thish? (producing bits of a favourite gold mounted meerschaum pipe). Smashed! My dear f'lers, musht have been mosh orfully shcrewed, 'sure you, musht have shmoked it *all to peeshes*— mosh strornary." He then got up and went round with us to resuscitate others.

But when we all assembled to breakfast, no derelicts were visible. They were all clean, bright and happy. I don't wish to advise any young men of the present day to follow in our steps, but in those harum-scarum, reckless, jovial old times we were all provided with cast-iron constitutions and could stand anything. That day's racing passed off well, but perceiving that several important people were absent, we relegated ourselves faithfully to duty, and found four of our horses tied up at a refreshment booth. The two grooms, I regret to say, were not strictly sober. We then tried to ride two horses at once, and lead the other two. They became highly excited, and bolted; at least, two of them did. Several fell down, and the others fell over them. We became comets, and after an awful flight through space, struck Mother Earth again twice with our heads most unpleasantly. We would infinitely have preferred remaining comets. We then became unconscious, but when we came to ourselves another "we" was bathing our head, and we began to examine our face and shoulders to see how much skin we had left. There wasn't any. We followed our own party sadly a week afterwards. At least, we should have done so if our infernal fool of a horse hadn't made things lively enough at the start by jumping off a ten-foot cliff right into forty feet of Gunyahgo river water, and compelling us to swim to the opposite shore by hanging on to his mane and the pommel of our saddle. We were very wet, but by the time we had dried, our brain began to work again, and it was extremely comforting to reflect that in that twenty-five mile lonely ride to Stuart's, though the country was not civilised

"RIGHT INTO FORTY FEET OF GUNYAHGO RIVER WATER."

From the Land of the Wombat.

enough for parish mile-stones, nevertheless—and this was the comforting point—the distance had been accurately marked by our party, at every half-mile, with a bottle of special three-star Hennessey, but only the bottle had been employed. They were all empty. What the consequences would have been if they had all been full we tremble to think of. I heard afterwards that Vandyke had made a most impressive speech to a mob of cattle at the half-way water-hole. He had all his new mail home letters in his pockets. Vandyke had a powerful voice, and he excelled himself on this occasion. The cattle were much edified, but gave way to terror after a bit, probably mistaking him for a "bunyip". They bolted with erected tails and much bellowing. Vandyke's watch never went properly again until it returned from Melbourne after a visit to the watchmakers.

Vandyke, in order to give due solemnity to his speech, had waded into the water-hole up to his neck, and we were not surprised to hear that he could get no news out of his home letters afterwards. He wishes to explain this matter, and also the matter relating to his favourite meerschaum pipe, but no one of any sense will listen to him. But he was not in a revengeful mood, and when I next saw him some kind friend had mended his coat, which was split right up the back— with a tenpenny nail. But of that fact he was not conscious, and, beyond wishing to explain, was quite affable and contented. We arrived home all of us in due course, and began to recuperate for our annual festivity again. One thing we are certain about, and that is, that we all experienced most eminent satisfaction at the Brandyville races, and that the fact is evident is a matter of supreme congratulation amongst ourselves. No doubt we should not have done the same things in these enlightened days of sober wisdom and Mrs. Grundy, but we expected neither wisdom nor Mrs. Grundy at the Brandyville annual race meeting, and we went to Brandyville as simple primitive back-block Christians. I forgot to state that the whole of the black police, including their inspector, who ought to have known better, attempted to arrest Vandyke for wishing to pull the police office down on the night of the great dinner. He "knocked-out" the whole lot of them, and the two white constables had important business up town before their turn came. This was before the "gate-blanket" affair. But I don't consider Vandyke morally responsible for his actions if he gets too much aggravated. He only asks for peace and quietness, and these two things should be granted him. But to make Vandyke physically atone for a mere whim of his own is a practical impossibility—and well I know it.

WADDYGĀLO

> Robed, crowned and throned, he wove his spell
>   Where heart-blood beat, or hearth-smoke curled,
> With unconsidered miracle,
>   Hedged in a backward gazing world;
> Then taught his chosen bard to say:
> "Our king was with us yesterday!"
>
> —*Kipling.*

A HOT, bright, cloudless day in the far interior of Queensland, about 800 miles from the city of Brisbane. A blacks' camp—blacks in their pristine savagery and nudity. The camp was about 200 strong, and was situated on a large creek, a mile above its junction with the main river, which ran about north and south, whilst the creek ran north-west and south-east. The time of day was nearly noon. A number of young girls and children of both sexes were bathing, swimming, diving and playing about the banks. Grass was very long and plentiful. Sheep and cattle belonging to the white man had not yet arrived in this country. "Woolibut" or "yapunyah" trees grew all along the lower flat ground on the east of the big creek, for it was as big or bigger than the river the farther one travelled against its stream. A rocky hill, densely wooded, with a number of caves about its base, shot a sloping green sward down to the west bank of this creek, immediately behind the blacks' camp.

This was "Yalli". Yalli, the favourite place of this particular tribe—Yalli, the old camping ground. There was a view from the top of Mount Borré (thunder) close by, all over the country, far and near. You could see much of the winding of the hollow white gum trees which marked the course of the river; over the tree tops again to Meander, that crooked twisting billabong, with a box-tree forest along its banks;

over Meander; over the million mulga tops, forming an almost unbroken surface of greyish silver-green foliage, right away to the distant big blue ranges between the Tarcoo and the Gunyahgo. Yalli, the well watered; Yalli, the wild game and fish-producing.

Two young men, aboriginals, are making a fish trap about a quarter of a mile away from the camp down-stream. The eldest of these two is about twenty years old—a fine, strong-set, active-looking fellow, with expressive eyes, wavy hair, strong, even, white teeth, and a wonderfully quick, piercing look, a true "waddygālo" (wild forest or scrub black fellow). His skin is the colour of gleaming copper. His companion's skin is lamp black, "waddygālo" too, but of a different tribe. A copper-coloured girl, about sixteen years old, sits on the green sward of the bank above, watching the two young men, who are up to their middles in the rushing water.

She sits squatting near a small fire, formed by the ends of three small dry saplings alight, and she pulls these burning sticks forward towards herself from time to time, reaching well over to the dry wood, as they burn a little way from the position, where the glow warms her feet and body. She is beautiful to look at, this girl, with her luxuriant glossy black hair, faultless white even teeth, laughing eyes, and supple rounded body. She is full of grace when she rises sometimes and peers over the bank at her male companions, who have forced six forked poles, sharpened at the single ends with their tomahawks, well down into the mud bottom of the creek. When satisfied that these poles are firm the two come out, and cut a long strong sapling, which is to lie on the forks from bank to bank across the stream.

The posts, with the forks, have been driven in a straight line at right angles to the water, and are to form the commencement of the fish fence and trap.

They pause after fastening the cross-piece sapling at the top into the forks, tying it tight at the junctures with twisted grass fibre and bark string. So far so good. They come up the bank and stand by Eeiya at her fire.

A flight of "budgerigars" come whistling through the hard rough stems of the yapunyahs, and wheel upwards and outwards on to their higher and barer red branches. The copper-coloured youth skims the surface of a branch thirty yards away with a flat waterworn pebble with such wonderful skill that six of the small, beautifully-mottled emerald-green parrots fall off dead and dying.

"A good shot, Eeīya," said he in his native tongue. Eeīya laughs merrily, and looks down.

They have about an inch of stem and bowl of a short black clay pipe, at least—Douràval, the copper-coloured, has. He takes a firestick from Eeīya's small blaze, puffs strongly, and hands it to Eumbon, the lamp-black, who gives it back after a puff or two on the "dottel". But these wild blacks, the pure waddygālos, have got that tobacco and pipe somehow from a far distant town—Fort Bourke itself—and every puff is very precious. Eeīya holds out her hands to Douràval, who puffs until there is a strong glow in the bowl, and gives it to her.

"Douràval," she says, when she has finished, "old man Jimmy had the 'prophet dream' last night. He talks at the 'corrobborree' fire to us to-night when it is all over. 'Ua' told me."

Eumbon opened his eyes, staring steadfastly. He was of a different tribe from old man Jimmy, who was of the "Combo," or ruling tribe, and Eumbon believed in him as the seer of the whole race.

Douràval only whispered in his sweetheart's ear, and she, laughing, gave him a push.

Then the whole three ran off lightly to the back of the densely-wooded Mount Borré. It didn't matter to these children of nature, scantily clad with only skin waistbands, that they had to swim the main river owing to the course they took. They slipped feet first into a long and deep water-hole, disappeared, and came up on the opposite side without a sound or a splash. That is to say, Eumbon and Eeīya did. Not so Douràval.

Eeīya laughed. "He hides, are you quick enough to find him, Eumbon?"

Eumbon glanced around, his fierce black eyes scintillating and vigilant.

He pointed silently with his right fore-finger. "There!" There was the slightest ripple forty yards off, by a clump of water lilies, where the large flat circular leaves, with their edges turned up above the water surface for an inch and a half, formed a lurking place.

Then the whole of Dourâval's dripping head came up. He had thrown himself back under water, bending his head backwards and holding on by the strong stems beneath, with only the holes of his nostrils above the water level. But Eumbon's wonderful sight, and knowledge of the trick, had detected him. "I laugh," said Dourâval as he came across lazily, "I laugh, and nearly choke myself. Did *you* see me, Eeiya?"

She nodded "Yes."

They then passed between two hills up a natural gully, where a thick grove of thin straight saplings grew, and they went to work upon these, cutting out in order about 300 straight willowy gum sticks, about fourteen feet long each, and an inch and a quarter in their thickest diameter. These they tied in bundles, and began to carry them to the fish trap; but Dourâval was up to the lower forks of a large box tree, and cut out a fat "'possum" for dinner before they left, Eumbon securing a big lace lizard, which he knocked dead, clean off a limb, the first shot, with a short straight green throwing-stick, about three feet long, which he cut when he first saw it.

Chatting and laughing, they passed downwards until their voices died away in the distance. A deadly brown snake slipped over the rocks and drew a trail of his sinuous body over the sand, his forked tongue flickering out uneasily, but his stony, expressionless eyes, like death itself, never moving.

Then a buck "paddy melon" came hopping along slowly, as if paralysed, with a huge lace lizard between five and six feet long after him. The paddy melon began to jump backwards and forwards over a fallen tree, but the big lizard went under a slight upward curve of it, only to force the paddy melon to jump back again. He was fascinated, and couldn't go far, paralysed by the reptile gaze of the big lizard.

Then came another forest denizen, with a quick, silent, loping trot, and his vigilant eyes everywhere, his ears cocked to catch the slightest sound of danger, when he would be off like a yellow streak! A wild dog! He snapped up the paddy melon and made two quick, lithe, lengthy bounds to a thicket with it, whilst the lizard scrambled hastily up the nearest yapunyah, his claws rattling against the bark as he did so. The shadow of a passing eagle touched one of the sunlight patches in this forest glade, and some far-off shouts are heard from the direction of the creek plains, where the hills jutted in, as success in some hunting occurred, or noise was necessary to turn emu or kangaroo, whilst down at the fish weir the young men and the girl were going on with their work, laughing and talking merrily as they did so.

Old Jimmy, who had once been among the whites, but had become "waddygālo" again, sat glowering over a fire by his bark "gunyah"—one of fifty or sixty scattered about on the same green flat under the yapunyahs—whilst "Ua," his comely wife, and two copper-coloured "piccaninnies" sat near him. Then the children began to play about, and imitate the manner of their forebears, which they best liked. The two were only four and five respectively, a boy and girl; yet the boy speared a small rolling disc of bark his sister cast for him, with a small hard-wood child's spear, every time it passed him from a distance of about ten yards.

Old Jimmy muttered and glowered, whilst "Ua" sang a waddygālo song, the refrain of a "corrobborree," as she glanced at him from time to time. She was sewing 'possum skins, neatly tanned and figured, together, to make a warm rug for the winter nights. A coolamon full of fresh silver bream roes was beside her. Her "billy" was full of fresh water and her dilli-bag contained a very little tea and one coagulated lump of brown ration sugar tied in a piece of cloth which had once been a part of a white man's coat. In that same dilli-bag too, also wrapped and tied up in an old matchbox, was a piece of a white boy's kidney fat. The white boy was murdered on a far-away river, about twelve months ago, by hostile blacks, having been decoyed thereto, out horse-hunting for his father, by a reputed "gundygālo" or tame black fellow who worked on the station.

This piece of human fat possessed many magic qualities, and, among other benefits, imparted the strength and spirit of the white race to the black fellow who anointed himself with it. Thus it was considered to be a very potent charm.

Douràval, Eeīya, and Eumbon, having broiled their 'possum and lace lizard upon the red embers of their fire, were having another pull at the family pipe, to which a little tobacco, the rest of the inside scrapings and some aromatic bark had been added since we last saw it. This had been done for economy's sake, for Dourâval did not possess more than an inch of the half-stick of Barrett's twist which had made such a proud man of him a fortnight ago.

After their smoke, they brought back enough straight saplings to make a close fence across the creek, with the exception of three feet in the middle which was left open. When they had tied all the sticks firmly on the cross-piece, after pressing their sharp ends down in the mud of the creek bed, the erection looked something like the side of a common stake-fence sheepyard, and pretty substantial, only that it was a water fence and not a land fence. There was just enough room between the sticks for a quarter pound fish to pass through, but the bigger ones would all be stopped.

Eumbon and Dourâval then cut a sheet of box bark four feet broad and about the same length. Then they pressed it flat on the earth, with the smooth, sappy side downwards, and then put small logs and big round stones upon it to keep it flat.

They then cut two more stout forked poles, which they fixed upright in the bed of the river, down-stream from the opening previously left in the fence. Each one of these poles was placed flush with one side of the opening in the middle of the water fence. The poles were twenty feet down-stream. Then they worked hard getting a cross-piece for the forks in these two poles, and two longer ones to go on each side of the opening to the cross-piece, only the up-stream end of each went to the bottom of the last stick on each side of the opening, as before, well forced into the mud. This was the beginning of the framework of a platform to abut on the opening, and rising out of the water at the down-stream end. Then several lighter poles were placed on a level with these two last between them both. Then the workers got long river grass and river rushes and flags and bound them tightly at the root ends, to which anchor stones were attached. When the long waving flags were bundles anchored a little up-stream across the river bottom of the opening in the fish fence, they flowed through it down-stream, but rose upwards at the un-weighted ends. They rose to about the same angle that the catching platform did and flowed upwards along it, thus forming a moving and impervious barrier to any fish coming through the hole. But the sides of the platform from the bottom were

WADDYGÂLO

also staked to a little above the level of the water line. Now all was secure except the trap; the platform was covered with springy grass cut in a particular way. Then the big sheet of bark was brought and forced down half-way across the opening up-stream, securely fastened across, with a clear stream under it along the fence of water flags and river grass, the force of the water bubbling over the top, and also underneath, in a way to boil up anything living on to the grass platform. Every fish beyond the quarter of a pound size came through the opening, stayed perchance a second or so in the backwash behind the sheet of bark, and were cast clear on to the platform. Boiled over on to it, literally. Flap they ever so wisely or determinedly, there was no escape for them. Not one of them could move themselves from the grassy bed they came down on at first, just clear of the rushing water, so cunningly had the yielding grass been arranged.

Douràval now stood near the low end of the platform up to his chest in water, and Eumbon half-way up the bank. Every minute added to the glittering heap of fish in a spot of about three feet square. The grass gave to every buckle, side-flap and flurry of the struggling fish, and there they were just waiting until Douràval picked them up and flung them to Eumbon. He passed them on to Eeīya, who gutted and cleaned them. Some of them weighed as much as three pounds. Eeīya had several coolamons, some with water and others empty. She put all the big roes from the best fish into dry coolamons, where they looked shiny and fresh. It was now getting to the gloaming, and, having about sixty fine fish, Douràval dislocated the platform by pulling out the middle sticks of it and throwing them on the bank ready for the next day. As he did so, the cunningly contrived grass of course floated away down stream, leaving an opening for other fish to pass.

He then came out of the water, and they slung their fish, got all their coolamons together, and strolled back to camp. The low western sun shot the yapunyah shadows across the creek flats and over the waters. Wood-duck, teal, whistlers, widgeon and black-duck began to seek the deeper water-holes, wheeling aside with a whirring of wings and loud quacking as they viewed the blacks' fires, which began to flare out as the shadows stalked among the hollows of the hills, and under rocks and trees and banks, settling permanently in many places, until the moon should bring them out in stranger and more fantastic guise to dance with the wind through the eerie realms and changing scenes of an Australian summer night. The sun is gone, and a silver veil of mist begins to rise from the level grassy flats about the waters, and spreads over the plains. The stars twinkle out, few at first, then by dozens, until all heaven's lamps are lit. The various colonies of nankeen cranes begin to bark from their favourite boughs by their particular water-holes. The kangaroos hop about like grey spooks, well clear of the fires; the bats are beetle-hunting, and a warrigal howls in the distance. They will have an eerie chorus by-and-by when all is still. One huge fire pile is beginning to accumulate in the middle of the camp on an open space. Every one except the dancers are bringing piles of brushwood and logs for it. This pile is to be the great "corrobborree" fire, around which the successful hunters of the day will dance in full corrobborree style the gum tree dance, *i.e.*, very little clothing but a waistbelt of gum leaves, thickly stalk-strung, and anklets of the same. Each dancer will carry a branch of the same material, which he will make to "whish" through the air at each jump, and the whistle and rustling of all the leaves on all the bodies is very remarkable as they move their bodies. Outside the dancing circle, round which the able-bodied male blacks will whirl, ochred in the latest fashion, is the ring of women who keep time to the chaunt by beating hardwood sticks together, and striking tightly-folded 'possum skins with hollowed palms.

In an hour or so the "corrobborree" is over, and the moon is rising. A warrigal howls dismally here and there, whilst the natives' own dogs, half-bred warrigals themselves, growl and snarl as they hear them. Old Jimmy advances to the big fire now a heap of glowing embers, and holding his arms above his head speaks in a loud voice, as follows :—

"Men—Combo men, Murrai men—and Eepai men. Guard your wives and children, also yourselves. The white men come, come to Yalli. Yonder they will build a house. Take care of your young girls and your women. The white man has the gun which kills suddenly with the heavy round thing, and the little gun which shoots often and is never loaded like the gun which thunders twice. I saw it all in a dream last night. Old Combo came and told me.

"After the white men, come the black police, those men of our own race, but of other 'tauris,' who also shoot with the gun that thunders; who fight with the sharp boomerang which sticks to their hand and cuts to the bone—and beyond; those who track us so that we can never get away. In three days' time the white men will be here, and there will be many sheep after them by-and-by.

"Then think you of Oolonga, the secret place over the mountain at the head of Yelcomorn, where the people can hide, and send away your young women and young girls and children to-morrow when the sun rises. Leave here only two or three old wrinkled women to look and see and find out from the strangers what they do.

"And the oldest Eepai man and the oldest Murrai and I myself will be here. We will wait. They will not harm us old people, and I will bring you the news, being younger than these two white-headed old men. They will spy on the white strangers and find out when those black warrigal dogs will come. But stay at Oolonga, the women, girls and children. Come not out on to the river. Stay there, and light not many fires for the warrigal dogs to see. Separate, you men, and go many ways, and do not join the women at Oolonga until after the first rain. Go and hunt, and send scouts up and down the big river, to see when the black dogs come. Then travel lightly to Oolonga in the first rains, and while it rains, so as not to leave a track the hunting hounds can see. I have told you truly."

There was an ominous silence, and then a low guttural growl from many male throats and a mournful wail from the women.

"Long years ago," continued old Jimmy, "I was away with the white men on the big river over there," pointing east-south-east. "I was a child when the black dogs sprang out of the ground and shot at us. What for? Because some of the head men had killed a white man or two because they took our women. And still further, some of our men speared cattle. I got away with my mother, and we came on here, and the other blacks did not kill us because we were 'Combos,' and wanted nothing from them. And I got right back here to my own 'tauri'.

And my mother is dead now many years, and I came back to be a 'waddygālo' again. I like not the white men."

Later, whilst all were asleep, the bright soft eyes of Eelya shone in the firelight, where it caught her face above the folds of her 'possum rug as she lay prone in her father's gunyah—she was Jimmy's eldest daughter by another wife—and she lay awake and thought of her father's words.

She had no knowledge of the white men. She was a pure "waddygālo" (forest or scrub black), and had never seen one. Her wild nature had not yet felt the full force of love. Being a "Combo," a daughter of the ruling tribe, she was a princess in her own right, and would probably be a sort of queen if she mated with Dourâval, who was a son of the late chief or king of the united tribes. Dourâval had not long ago passed the "Bora," or rites established by the blacks from time immemorial, and which brought him to the state of manhood. This would now enable him to take a wife, or more than one, according to his strength and prowess amongst the other rising men. Eelya is making a "corrobborree" in her own mind. She is only a maid, just sixteen years old, but she is a woman, now fully developed, and thinks of her copper-coloured lover Dourâval. And her song runs:—

> Who runs like the emu? Dourâval.
> Who swims like the fish? He too.
> Who climbs the tree first? Also he.
> Who smiles when he sees me? Dourâval, Dourâval.
> Who loves me but Dourâval? Dourâval too.

Silence soon brooded over this far-away camp of these "waddygālo" blacks, and even Eelya closed her eyes in slumber, happy in her own thoughts and knowing little.

Far down the same waters, ninety miles away, is another night camp, where three white men are slumbering, wrapped in blue blankets, with their saddles for pillows. A couple of well-bred kangaroo dogs are stretched at full length between the fire and close against the feet of two of the sleepers. The Southern Cross is well down on the horizon, and the faint steely glint in the eastern sky is rapidly flushing. One of the sleepers stirs and sits up. "Hullo, Prince"—to one of the kangaroo dogs, who is instantly on his feet and by his side —"daylight coming, boy." Then, with a shout that might be heard a mile off: "Show a leg, boys; hurry up, and show a leg," shaking the nearest form, "'Nerangi daylight,' Tom. Get the horses, you beggars. Produce the 'yarramen' along a track. Get up, *I'm* cook this morning. What will you have, eh? 'Hashmagandy' or 'pufterloonas'?—'you bays your money and you dakes your shoice'."

"Get out, you noisy devil!" says the man addressed as Tom. "Any one can tell when *you* are cook! 'Hashmagandy' for me." Saying which he drops a hot coal into the dottel of his pipe, previously going through gymnastic feats of balancing it at a number of different spots on the palm of his hand. He presses it down with a stick and puffs joyously. He then slips three bridles over the crook of his right arm, and steps off over the dewy grass, having given a kick and a push to the farthest off sleeper, who seems loath to rise.

"Awful bore," says the latter as he sits up. "Confound that Tom. He woke me up in the middle of *such* a lovely dream. I was walking towards a river with two remarkably pretty girls. Hang it, I wish he had given me time to finish. How the deuce am I to know now what they would have said and done or what I would have said and done? Perhaps I could have got a kiss apiece from 'em, eh?"

"Perhaps you might, old chap. I say, you know, it *is* rather a pity you didn't have time to finish it. Not much chance of *getting* such a chance now you're awake, out here, is there?"

"Hum," grumbled the other, going through exactly the same performance as Tom Burton with *his* pipe and bridles, and striding off to look for the horses. Roland Dumaresq, the cook for the day, takes a metal bucket and a "billy" and strolls off to the nearest water, carolling an old Australian music hall alphabet song:—

> A—is Australia, the land of the wombat,
> B—is Britannia, a rum 'un to combat,
> C—is a Chinaman, fated to fag,
> And D—is a digger ahumping his swag.
> With a tolderol-lol-dol, tolderolol-dol,
> Tolderol-ol-dol, toorali-lay!

He is a very handsome well-built fellow, tall too, over six feet, with keen blue eyes, curly golden hair, well-kept moustache and teeth, straight as an arrow, daring and active-looking, with an appearance of much latent strength. I have heard an enthusiastic friend of Roland's say in relation to him:

"Roland Dumaresq? Why, there's no better fellow on God's earth!"

And he looked indeed a very manly happy young man, as he stood by the fire again with a half smile, and set to work to make a stew of cold wild duck from the remains of some shot yesterday.

His thoughts were running on the future. How he would form the station in the good country Tom Burton had told him of; how Tom Burton and Richards, the man with the dream, were to be his partners; how old Crowsfoot, the overseer, would keep things all right when he came on with the sheep, and poison every blessed wild dog in the country; how the 10,000 mixed sheep old Crowsfoot was bringing on would increase; how they would invent an apparatus for spout washing. Wouldn't it be a good plan to have a small mob of cattle, and also to breed horses—"Walers"—for the Indian market? And he'd take jolly good care to have a grand kitchen garden, with enough vegetables in it to supply all hands. "I must have water to make things grow in this confounded country; then you can grow anything. Would have an arrangement of buckets (old nail cans!), just the very thing for hauling up on a windlass. Irrigate the whole blessed place, by Jove! Send tons of water over it. Some sort of lever"—looking at a tall, straight woolibut—"might do it. Sling casks up full of water, no end!"

These three young men had left their overseer and shepherds behind, being most eager to come on and see the new country they hoped so much from, and to choose a spot to build a house on. A week after this, Eelya, who had left old Jimmy at Yalli, was at Oolonga, the retreat spoken of at the "corrobborree" fire. She was at a beautiful clear water-hole with a few other young girls catching "bougalis" (small fresh-water lobsters). Most of the girls were in the water, but Eelya was on the bank under a big box tree. Suddenly a stranger rode up on a powerful, good-looking grey horse. A white man! The girls screamed and tried to hide themselves in the water, but Eelya waited, for the stranger smiled pleasantly, and held out his hand with a half-stick of Barrett's twist for her. He jumped off his horse, too, and patted her on her soft warm shoulders, looking at her so kindly, she thought. "Pah, he was nothing to be frightened of. And what a handsome young

"A WHITE MAN."

From the Land of the Wombat. *Page 78.*

man!" She called out to the other girls, and they came out of the water dripping and crowded round. The stranger gave them another half-stick amongst them. "Dear me," thought they, "the very good-looking man is alone. He can't eat the lot of us." So they giggled and whispered amongst themselves, whilst Roland was plying Eeīya with every word of "pigeon English" he could think of. But she spoke more with her eyes. And Roland made out more by their language than by his "pigeon English". He gave her an old pipe he chanced to have in his pocket, and rode off smiling, saying "'Waddygālo,' mine think it?" At which there was a chorus of disapproval from all the girls.

And Eeīya? She had never seen such a man, such a beautiful, beautiful man!

"*This* was a white man, then? He was good to her. And she wasn't the least bit afraid of him. *He* wasn't the sort of man to hurt a girl like her.

"What fine eyes and teeth he had. What a noble presence. Oh! she would like to kiss him, if she wasn't just a little ashamed—and before the other girls, too. Well, *they* wouldn't tell. They all had their own love affairs, and she knew all about them. But they would chaff her properly. Wicked hussies, wouldn't they run after this splendid hero if they only got a chance?"

Eeīya knew that there was a chord of sympathy between him and herself; struck at the moment their eyes met. The blood rushed to her face, under the copper colour. There *was* something in common between them. *What* was it?

As Roland Dumaresq rode away, he hardly knew what to think. Here was a girl of great beauty, a "waddygālo"— never saw such a pretty dark-skin. Just a wild black girl, "hardly black, though," thought he. "By Jove!" said the young man out loud, "I've seen many a white girl that couldn't hold a candle to her. My eyes, what a beauty!"

So these two met and parted for the first time.

Eeīya thought much afterwards about the white stranger— the first and only white man she had ever seen.

She had heard about them often enough from old Jimmy, and fancied them terrible beings, but here was one of them. "Why, he only smiled at us girls. *He* wouldn't shoot us with the thunder gun, not he. Old Jimmy must have been mistaken. Perhaps this fine young man had been a famous fighting black fellow long ago and had 'jumped up white man' again. Very likely. Well, he wasn't a horrid, naked black, anyway. I wonder how many skins he has got on?"

The touch of his strong kind hands on her shoulders she could feel yet. The men were all away hunting. Douràval was far to the head of Yalli, where it ran out into the brigalow and dense scrubby ranges. Only the women were now at Oolonga. Should she tell "Ua"? Perhaps she had better not. "No, I won't," she thought. The young girls were safe enough. "No," thought Eeīya, "I'll keep them all with me," and every day we will come a little farther down Yelcomorn for the 'bougali'. I wonder if I shall see him again? Next time I'll do my hair better, and have my best 'bealbah' girdle on, and the yellow reed necklace and other things."

Back at Yalli, upon the big terrace of the river, ten days afterwards, a quarter of a mile from the old blacks' camp, a big tent was pitched. It was evening, and there was a small brush yard with some merino rams in it on the second terrace. A couple of kangaroo dogs ran about freely, and two or three collies. The camp fire of the would-be station-owners blazed brightly. Two ancient "gins" and a very old Eepai man had crawled up and interviewed the strangers, and when asked by signs and "pigeon" "where were the other blacks?" they affirmed that they were all "waddygālo".

"Shan't see anything of these beggars till we're well settled down," opined Richards, commonly known as "Ted". "I know their pleasing little ways. First they send their oldest "gins," and after a bit, when you've given these some tobacco and a feed or two, their oldest men come. Treat them well, and you'll have an increase of about ten cripples. Then some night, just before you've got the rams yarded, down will come a hunting party, with about fifty blacks' dogs, and it's hey, presto, for the rams then! They'll rush anywhere. Up the river, down the river, into the river, across the river and back again, and some will fight. Next day, three or four bitten, three drowned, and the rest in mobs of two or three, so frightened of a dog that they wouldn't even let old 'Clyde' here within half a mile of them, well as they know him and his bark. Then you make up some strychnine baits, and poison the blacks' dogs, and three or four of your own too, and there is not a sign of the blacks except perhaps a poor old devil of a "gin" left in camp so bad with rheumatics that she couldn't move even if Mount Borré was threatening to fall on her poor old tummy. No, no, old chap, these 'waddygālos' are the devil and all. No fear of their young girls coming here, or any of their young men, so that you could get two or three smart fellows for the milkers and horses. You'll have to train the *boys*. *They* generally turn out well. And by-and-by you'll get three or four warrigals, who've been spearing either sheep or a white man or two, for horse blacks. But the 'waddygālos' know better. I'll bet something a *real* 'waddygālo' or two are even now watching us from the top of the mountain."

Roland had said nothing of his discovery. Indeed, he had seen Eeīya thrice since, and they had begun to understand one another. If the others had remarked anything in an absence it was easy to explain it away. "Overshot a creek whilst kangarooing, had to find his back-tracks," etc., etc. Next day he was riding on Yelcomorn, and Eeīya came to him from a clump of bushes, graceful as a fawn and attired in her best. She always wearied for this stolen interview now, and came fearlessly forward, felt his clothes all over, and laughed softly. Dumaresq tried a little pigeon English, and then gave her a kiss. She made him understand that all the men would be back after the first rains, and that it would be difficult to meet him then; that she loved him dearly and would die for him. When he rode away he thought very deeply and, for him, seriously.

. . . .

It is nightfall the next day. Roland is alone at Yalli. He is sitting outside the tent smoking his last pipe, and his face, if one could see it, is very anxious. It is a dark, windy night, and as he heaves a sigh preparatory to going to bed, "Selim," one of his kangaroo dogs, growls. There is a quick patter of feet, and Eeīya stands before him, breathless, terrified, nearly fainting with the speed of her travel. She cannot speak. She only gesticulates. He clasps her tenderly to his breast. "What is it? Something is the matter? What is it, Eeīya, my dear?" "Waddygālo!" she gasps.

He looks over to his Winchester. Too late! The dogs

spring savagely forward; they have been barking furiously for ten seconds. Two heavy jagged spears, driven with furious hate, by the "womera" from close by, with deadly aim, pierce both their bodies, and, with a savage rush of skeleton-painted men, the "waddy" and the tomahawk do the rest. Eelya had come to warn Dumaresq at the risk of her life, but she was too late! Too late!

. . . .

Oolonga at night, three weeks afterwards. The "waddygâlo" blacks are all asleep in their mountain fastness, when, without the least previous sound, before even their half-warrigal dogs can either growl or bark, a crashing volley of carbine shots wake the echoes into life.

Dourâval, who has grown thin, grave and stern-looking, leaps to his feet, full of fight; as do several others. Crack, crack, crack, crack! A shrill yell or two, and a wild rush of dusky forms out into the scrub and the ebon darkness of the night. Several prostrate bodies, all men! Dourâval lies motionless on the ground; Eumbon also. Nothing else to be seen except the still corpses by the flickering firelight! The fires go out towards morning, and the dead bodies are buried by the black trackers, who come back with the sunlight. They place six stalwart bodies in one deep hole, covering over the level earth with heavy logs and stones to keep the wild dogs out.

"I think we pretty well dispersed that lot," says "Mayboy," one of the troopers, to Richards. "Baal 'waddygâlo' again, none of them pfellers (pointing to the finished grave). I'm pretty hot. I got that pfeller, Dourâval, last night myself. Dam 'waddygâlo'."

"I wonder what they rushed Dumaresq for?" said Richards to the sub-lieutenant. "Girl in the case," responded he, "anybody could see that." "*We* never saw her," said both Burton and Richards. "Can't make out why she came to the camp. As I told you, we knew nothing of it, even of their deaths, for a week afterwards. And the crows and hawks told us that as we crossed the river. We were away making sheep stations with old Crowsfoot and the shepherds. Poor Roland!"

"The 'waddygâlos' knew," said the sub-lieutenant. Pity to have to shoot the poor beggars. But there won't be one of you 'outsiders' left alive, some fine morning, if you don't take better care of yourselves. We *have* to punish 'em, for your faults. Anyway, for the first *murder* done they must suffer. Try and get on with 'em better, and don't have any truck with their women, whatever you do. Good-bye; you're well armed, and I'll leave 'Mayboy' with you until we come back from the head of Yalli. There's some grand country there. I think I shall take up a bit on my own account some day. It'll pay better than this government job. But *some one* has got to do it, and, as I say, there would not be a single white man left alive in the district if it were not for our force here. So long, you fellows. I will stop a night at Yalli as I come back, if I haven't to chivy bushrangers. So long!" And the sub-lieutenant and his troop of six mounted and uniformed men clanked off through the scrub.

THE WRAITH OF TOM IMRIE

> Alas for this grey shadow once a man!
> —*Tennyson.*
>
> Yet this way was left,
> And by this way I 'scaped them.
> —*Ibid.*

"AND so you don't believe in ghosts, you fellows?" said McIlwaine, the squatter, one night as we sat around the cheery pine-log fire at Yerilla. "I do, and I will tell you my reasons. It is not the first time in my life that I have seen one, and I've heard that ghost-seeing runs in our family.

"I saw the ghost of a man, a horse and a cattle dog one night as plain as I see each of you now, but the dog turned out to be real afterwards, and I don't believe that *he* saw the ghost; anyway, he didn't act as if he did. He was very serviceable to me, that dog. Twenty-five years ago, before some of you were born (you may well look, Jemmy, but it's true), I was cattle-droving 'store' cattle from up north, and my chum was a man called Tom Imrie.

"We camped one night on the Lower Tarcoo, and Tom and I left our head man and the others with the cattle and rode on to a bush hotel to put in the evening. There were about a dozen fellows there, a rather mixed lot; and some one was playing a concertina awfully well as we rode up. I never got that imitation peal of bells out of my head. 'Oranges and lemons, say the bells of Saint Clement's,' sort of thing. He played the different changes and triple bob majors, crashes and all the other thingumibobs nearly as well as George Cass himself, whoever he was. I did not know the player then, but I had cause to do so afterwards.

"There were two other drovers in a private room at the

hotel, who had a mob of cattle ahead of ours. So we
chummed up and had a game of whist."

"McIlwaine plays whist everywhere, anywhere and where
he can, so beware," remarked Jemmy uproariously.

"You bide awee, ma fren, and I'll knock spots out till ye,"
rejoined McIlwaine.

Jemmy made a pantomimic gesture, expressive of contempt,
and McIlwaine resumed :—

"Well, as I was after saying, if that infant hadn't interrupted
a man of my age, the name of the place was Bylo. The usual
far-back sort of a township, only the hotel and public stockyard.
And the hotel was combined with an all-round store, where
you could get a variation from a suit of clothes to a frying-pan
—haberdashery and hardware mixed. The police had not
yet arrived, though there were any amount of long, loafing
crawlers in the district, the usual sort who stay about a place
of this description, that promises to be a town some day.
They usually get cleared out in time, before decent people
come. And there is generally a death or two before that
happens—innocent and guilty alike. The police were wanted,
I tell you, and not very long after our arrival either. We tied
our horses up to the verandah posts, along with a lot of others,
on first arriving, and it was there I noticed the concertina.
We stayed about an hour playing whist with the drovers, and
taking an occasional glass together.

"You must know that in the big knock-about room, next
to the one we were in, a lot of young fellows were gambling,
and drinking pretty freely also. Some of them I noticed were
jackeroos, 'jaast like ma young fren, Innocence, here,'" laying
a mighty paw upon Master Jemmy's shrinking flesh and
causing an awful hullabaloo, so that we had to wait until
things assumed an aspect of order again.

"Well, these jackeroos that I was telling you about were
mixed and various, 'poddies,' 'cleanskins,' 'two tooth,' some of
them 'four,' and maybe one or two just lambs unshorn, like
Jemmy ; knew just enough to say ' baa '. It was a wild, God-
forsaken sort of district, right out on the back blocks beyond
the New South Wales border, and young fellows learn bad
things quick enough, unless they stick to their work like men.

"One fellow amongst this lot who were gambling looked
pretty 'old in the horn'. I spotted him when I passed the

door, for I went out once to look if the horses were all right. He was the concertina player. Sort of sharp, by his appearance. He might have been anything from a cattle-duffer to a horse-thief, but he looked like a 'spieler'. He was pretty hard bitten.

"All of a sudden, whilst we were going on with our game (I had the ace, four, five and three of hearts, trumps, I mind, in my hand, and it was my turn to play), there was a fearful shindy! Shouting, swearing, stamping, chairs and tables knocked down and a rush. We jumped up and, just as we got to the door, the very man I have been describing tore out like a maniac, took the first horse he came to and galloped off. The rush of the others coming out after him all of a heap frightened the other horses to such an extent that they all pulled back at once and broke every individual bridle in that crowd. My word, that fellow on the horse *did* scratch away past the pine ridge on the up-river road.

"Tom was a pretty hot-tempered fellow. He managed to catch his horse somehow, got a bridle from somewhere, and was away after the fugitive before I could say 'Jack Robinson'. We had seen a still form lying in that other room as we came out, and some of the fellows were shouting 'Murder!'

"At last I got my horse, and a fresh bridle out of the store, and one of the drovers, another young fellow and myself, started in pursuit. Off we went. The tracks kept on the road, and after a hard ride of about six miles we suddenly came upon two dead bodies—the spieler-looking concertina man and poor Tom! The first had a bullet through his head, as near the centre of the forehead as it well could be.

"Tom was a sure shot with a revolver, and always carried one. So did the other man it appeared, for we found the two pistols close by, just a little way off each body.

"But though there was only one barrel of the alleged murderer's pistol discharged, Tom's had two, and the wound Tom had died from was in the right temple. Apparently he had shot himself. I was terribly cut up. The whole affair was so awfully sudden and unexpected that I could scarcely collect my wits together. We had the bodies brought carefully back to the hotel, and despatched a special messenger for the police, 100 miles away. But we had to bury all the bodies next day on account of the heat. I stayed to give my evidence, of course, but I put on two more hands, and could trust my head cattleman to look after the 'mob'.

"It came out that the man who had committed the murderous assault upon the poor young jackeroo was not well known. He was a stranger, but was named, according to his merits, 'Flash Jack,' and was reputed to be up to any blessed thing, from petty larceny to cattle-duffing, according to my informants. The story went that the jackeroo had several one-pound notes knocking about. One of them was a new one. They were all pretty well boozed, and Flash Jack had got hold of this new note somehow. The new chum accused him of stealing it, and threatened to strike him with a hunting crop he carried. The man swore horribly, and in the scuffle which ensued he wrenched the hunting crop from the young fellow, and hit him such an awful crack on the head with the heavy brass handle of it that he just collapsed to the floor and never spoke again. The heavy end of the whip had sunk right into his brain! The police came at last, a sergeant and a constable, and went carefully over every 'in' and 'out' of the case; after which they put all the witnesses who remained, and myself, upon our oaths before Mr. Fielding, the police magistrate, and owner of Yankalilla station. (Good brand that—J. F. conjoined—was in those days.) Gone off colour since the old man died, and left the property to his son. He's too fond of town, and leaves the station too much to others. Never knew *that* game pay, unless the manager is a partner, or the overseer is a real worthy man.

"Well, it was all finished fair and square, and what is left of those three bodies, whirled to their death in a sudden gust of passion, lies there to this day. I don't suppose the bones would come out of the ground, even if their ghosts wanted to walk, and say a few things they hadn't time for on this earth, eh? We buried them on the rise of the big pine ridge. There's a much bigger cemetery there now, for I passed it only last year.

"Tom's cattle dog, 'Joker,' would not leave the grave until I led him away on a chain, but after a day or two I began to get the poor beggar to eat a little, but I had to keep him on the chain, or he would have gone straight back and most likely died there at the grave.

"When I had delivered the cattle all right I found myself down in Sydney for a spell. I of course made my first visit to Miss Imrie, as I was in duty bound to do. She was Tom's sister, and used to keep a home for him all ready when he came down from the bush to town. She lived at the top of Woolloomoolloo, in one of those quiet streets on the left going out to Pott's Point. Nice comfortable little cottage, with a diminutive garden in front. I rang the street-door bell, and was shown into the drawing-room. Miss Imrie appeared. Nice lady-like girl. I had written the sad news to her myself from up country, so that she had had some considerable time to get over it, for I had been two months on the road with cattle since I wrote that letter. She was dressed in deep mourning, and knew me at once, and we commenced to talk over matters. I knew, of course, that her affairs would not be so comfortable for her after the loss of her brother. Sort of unprotected like. But she had many good friends in Sydney, and I knew that they thought a lot of her. She had a small legacy of her own, just enough to live on. I had brought all Tom's money that was owing to him with me, having got it from our employers, and I handed it over to Miss Imrie then and there.

"'And do you think my poor brother, Tom, shot himself?' said she. I told her 'yes,' but that it might have been by accident (I did not think so myself). What *could* I say? But if he had, I couldn't tell the reason, any more than the man in the moon.

"So ran my thoughts. I knew well enough that Tom meant to *take* the man so as to hand him over to justice, fight or no fight. He was a most determined chap. But he would never have shot him unless the other had been so desperate as to fire at him first. And then perhaps he might have had to do so to save his own life. But the other shot, the one which killed him—a shot from his *own* weapon apparently—*that* was inexplicable. Miss Imrie broke in upon me at this point in my reflections.

"'Will you describe the man who was supposed to be shot by my brother, Mr. McIlwaine?' she asked.

"I nodded, and described him exactly. She got paler and paler as I went on, but when I described what was undoubtedly a birth mark, which I had seen on his chest, and which bore an exact similarity to a fallen autumn leaf, she slid off her seat and fainted!

"I rang the bell at once, and the housemaid came, and between us we brought her back to consciousness. The girl, of course, had heard of Tom Imrie's sudden death, though her mistress would naturally enough conceal the real facts. She (the housemaid) would probably think that we had been talking over the matter, and that *that* had been the cause of her mistress' indisposition. She knew me, too, as I had been there on one occasion to tea during Tom's lifetime. I took my hat and my departure, feeling that I could be of very little use, but I gave the girl a tip as I left, requesting her to give Miss Imrie a message, saying that I would call again if she wished, on hearing from her that she felt sufficiently well to receive me. I also asked the maid to express to Miss Imrie my very great sympathy for her in her sorrow, which I shared also.

"I went to my hotel, and two days afterwards received a letter from Miss Imrie, telling me the most awful thing you can think of. I remember the words well enough. They burnt themselves into my brain!

. . . .

"'That man you described was my other brother! We hadn't heard of him for years. Poor Tom! Now I can see the reason for his own rash act. Please don't call again. I can't bear it. And may I ask you, on your honour as a gentleman, never to mention this subject to a living soul, for my sake, and for the sake of those who are gone?'

. . . .

"Of course, I complied with her wishes, but it was as equally plain to me now as it had been to Tom's sister after the dread revelation of the fatal birthmark. The man's shirt was open at the breast when we found the two bodies, and I saw the mark then and afterwards.

"Strange to say, the refrain of an old drinking song came into my head the moment I saw that fallen leafmark, and there it droned away in my head, pathetically, in the presence of the dead:—

> 'Fades as the leaves do fade,
> Fades as the leaves do fade,
> Fades as the leaves do fade,
>   And dies in October.'

"But the result had not been brought on by the 'small beer,' the prelude to this particular part of the chorus. It was strong liquor, and much of it, which had been the prominent cause of the whole thing. And that tune that droned in my head, the man himself, 'Flash Jack,' had played on the concertina in the hotel verandah, the others joining in the chorus, on the previous interlude to the ghastly tragedy.

"And there he lay himself, and another, both cut off *like* the leaf, and —— Alas, poor Tom!

"Tom must have seen this mark in a far worse and more awful light than ever I did. His own brother! He must have opened his shirt to feel if the heart beat, after the first deadly shot in self-defence and in the heat of passion.

"He probably would know nothing at first. His brother would be altered with a long beard on. They had been parted for long. He had, at the time he started after him from the hotel, no knowledge of his whereabouts, or even existence. What 'Flash Jack's' antecedents may have been, of course, I do not know, but it may be taken for granted that no idea of fratricide had ever entered Tom's head. The man's altered looks, after a long lapse of years, his unrecognised appearance, with long hair and bush clothes, his face twitching with evil passions, the wish to shoot Tom probably working in his mind. So the shots had been exchanged, Tom's with sudden and deadly effect. Then can you fancy the awful reaction, the terrible conviction, and the dread confirmation of the appalling horror of the unwitting deed? Then the sudden despair and anguish, amounting to a passion, a fury, a morbid madness, and culminating at the last in a quick self-annihilation? God knows *what* he thought! I knew the poor fellow's character pretty well—good ideas, kind heart, but stubborn and determined, moved too much by sudden impulse. A man who, once having decided his course, would carry it out unflinchingly, never thinking of the consequences. And he took his own life, after all! I thought he would have lasted for many happy and prosperous years.

"I left Sydney and started up country, as I had another cattle-droving job from O'Hooligan's on the Tarcoo. I should have a chance of seeing to poor Tom's grave, and, strange to say, it had been arranged for me to take delivery of O'Hooligan's cattle at Bylo, the very place where the whole unfortunate affair had happened.

"This new duty was much more satisfactory in detail, to my mind. Four hundred prime fat cattle for the Adelaide market. It paid better, but took a long time on the road. But there is not the anxiety, if the season is good, that one experiences with 'stores'. I had two of my best men with me, and would have to purchase an American waggon and a pair of horses.

"The three of us made Belala, on the Gunyahgo, and we were lucky enough to complete our purchase of waggon and horses there.

"I found, on arrival, a letter awaiting me from Harper of Fassifern, asking me as a favour to travel fifty merino rams, very valuable animals out of the Belala stud flock, from thence to his place, Fassifern, on the head waters of the Tarcoo, the next station but one from O'Hooligan's. Luckily, I had plenty of time to spare. It had been a dry season, but all my horses were in good order.

"One of the Fassifern black boys had ridden in with the letter. His name was 'Boro'. I sent the waggon with my head cattleman down the Gunyahgo and across from Brandyville to Bylo, to await O'Hooligan's draft. I had a clear fortnight, and I didn't want to disoblige Harper, as he had drafts of cattle in prospect from Fassifern, and he always gave me a job of droving when he could.

"So I accepted the rams willingly enough, the more especially as, after having delivered them safely at Fassifern, I could go down the Tarcoo to Bylo, see O'Hooligan on the way for final instructions, take over the cattle, and make a fair start from Bylo. Also there was the welcome prospect of putting a few more pounds into my pocket."

"Always there or thereabouts when 'dibs' are served out!" muttered Jemmy from his corner.

"Ma certie, ye heathen, a thocht ye were deid," snapped McIlwaine *en parenthèse*, and went on.

"I took the Fassifern black boy, 'Boro,' with me of course. He might just as well work for his 'tucker' instead of crawling back, and stopping a night or two at the blacks' camp. That was the worst bit of work I did on the trip.

I thought he might be useful tracking in case of mishap, as the rams were worth over £1000. Well, this black boy, 'Boro,' I did not cotton to. He was all a 'waddygâlo,' but a 'waddygâlo' of the worst tribe—Eepai. You can pick out 'Combo,' 'Eepai,' 'Murrai,' and 'Cubbai'. They have the same types of face, that is to say, a 'Combo' resembles a 'Combo,' a 'Murrai' a 'Murrai,' and so on; but a 'Combo' is the best of all for physique and good intentions. If an 'Eepai' learns anything it is roguery or devildom.

"But with regard to this 'Eepai'—'Boro'—I reckoned I would smarten him up a bit before I had done with him.

"He needed it. One boot, one spur, about a yard of torn blanket for his 'swag,' no shirt, a fearful and wonderful hat with no top to it.

"You know the way some of these 'myalls' ride. So did 'Boro'; one big toe on one side of the stirrup iron—the inside—next toe on the other, and the foot and all the other toes outside; the *one* boot thrust well home into the opposite iron. Doesn't look pretty. But then old Harper never *did* have any ideas about black fellows, never kept them neat and tidy, never had them properly clothed. If one doesn't keep some sort of hold on these 'nigs,' and train them properly, they never will be fit to be seen. I'm particular about it, but the untidiness is in them, and therefore, if you don't keep a good look out on a trained 'nig,' he will disgrace your teaching if he gets a chance. Why, one of *my* own boys, 'Tommy,' a Tarcoo black, about fifteen, broke out on one occasion—lapsed into savagery, as I should term it. I got him from his mother. She was old Biddy from the station camp. It was my first trip with him and he's all right now.

"I was in at Brandyville. Tommy was in charge of my horses. Used to run them up to the town stockyard every morning. I had him nice and neat, riding-breeches and boots, cabbage-tree hat, spurs regular, not one-sided, and a very nice little darkie he looked. Hair properly dressed by the barber, too. He got his meals at the hotel and a small glass of ale with his dinner. He preferred to sleep, however, the first night, at the blacks' camp without my leave.

"Next morning up he comes at breakfast time. 'Horses all right, Tommy?' 'Yowi' (yes). He had someone else's hat and shirt on—nothing else. Positively indecent. Dirty too. Hair anyway. Face all over wood-ash,

"'Where are your breeches, Tommy?' 'Mine been break him trous belongin' to mine!' Quite a new state of things. The little brute was entirely demoralised. Never had any morals until I took the trouble to instil them. This wouldn't do. Was I to go about the country with a nigger in this untidy state? Certainly not. 'Whose hat and shirt have you got on now, Tommy?' ''Nother pfeller, black pfeller, "Charlie," cousin belongin' to mine.' 'Where are your *own* clothes?' 'Mine been give 'em alonga 'nother pfeller, black pfeller!'

"Tableau! '*Give* 'em away.' The suit had cost me about three guineas, and the cabbage-tree hat another ten-and-sixpence, to say nothing of the spurs and boots. But you know their horribly irresponsible style, and how it riles one.

"I took him straight down to the blacks' camp by the ear, and demanded instant reparation, under a threat to the old chief that, unless he complied with my wishes immediately, I should 'yabber alonga policeman'. That 'fetched' him!

"He collared half a dozen youngsters, and brought them up, yelling fit to wake the dead. One had had Tommy's hat, another his boots, and another his spurs, at one time or another, but had halved or given away the articles to others, every one of the kids wishing to wear something belonging to my black boy.

"So these young 'nigs' were sent to collar the others, and a furious hullabaloo then took place, mixed, with chivies round the gunyahs, over and through the fires, and in and out of the creek; and it wasn't until we had collared every kid in camp, with the assistance of old Jimmy and his harem, that we found the missing articles—a boot on one, a spur on another, and so on. I don't know whether they thought I should be willing to take Tommy out of the town in a state of nudity or not, or whether I should just get him some more outfits, until I had clothed the lot of them, but my determined move euchred them all together. So I made Master Tommy put on his duds one by one, till he arrived at hat and boots, with a circle of worshippers round him, telling the frightened youngsters that if I caught them again dividing *my* black boy's raiment amongst them I should have them all hung by the policeman on the big windmill at the town stockyard, concluding:

'Then you baal jump up white fellow, hang alonga sky, wokkaratchies (crows) eat 'em up.'

"You never saw such a scare. And old Jimmy, the chief, quite believed it, and yabbered and howled like blazes to all the 'gins' within a quarter of a mile. Then they began to bring in the rest of the missing articles, but two little wretches had torn Tommy's good Crimean shirt in half to make, as they explained after much browbeating and threatening, 'two little pfeller blankit'. And one of the junior members of Jimmy's seraglio appeared with the collar worn as a necklet. That collar was her sole apparel. However, things simmered down after a bit, and I gave old Jimmy half a stick of Barrett's twist, and bought Tommy another shirt. I made him sleep in an outhouse near the stable in the back-yard after this, but one morning early I caught two other urchins 'coiled' with him, the whole lot under his blanket. They were also 'cousins,' and had arranged to work with him in relation to the horses, hoping, I have no doubt, to get stray bits from the breakfast that my lord did not want himself.

"But it ended in these two others having a separate 'mess,' which I paid for. The hot tea with their breakfasts must have comforted their small 'tums,' and I never like to put obstacles in the way of praiseworthy energy. So Tommy slept warmer at night, and I was the richer by two first-class trackers.

"Eventually I took these boys with me, and they turned out well, and were very useful. And my boy, Tommy, never dared to speculate after this with his clothes. Everything depends upon how you bring them up.

"But, as I was saying before my digression, this boy, 'Boro,' of Harper's, was to come with us, and I did not like the look of him one little bit. He was a holy terror of uncleanness and carelessness.

"We left the Gunyahgo with the rams, and I meant to cross the dividing range with them, straight to Fassifern, steering about north-north-east by the sun.

"Mick Brady was my white man, a regular old stodger with cattle, slow, but sure and steady, well up to every wrinkle on the roads.

"He had been with me for years. We made a creek the first night, and 'camped' the rams successfully by a big 'water-hole'. Mick had his old one-eyed cattle dog, 'Bally,' with him, and I had 'Joker,' who had taken to me wonderfully. We had about fifty miles to make from this water-hole to Fassifern, and a long stage next day of fifteen miles. Next day proved to be very hot, and we made slow progress. At noon we let the sheep 'camp' as usual. I made sure of finding good water over the range at a place I knew of, or I never should have taken this route, but it was a straight track of my own from Belala to Fassifern.

"I let the rams have a good rest and feed, intending to take them on to the water during the night if necessary.

"'Boro' had our water on the pack-horse, and I tell you both Mick and I needed a drink badly at mid-day. We had four big water-bags. The horses felt the heat too, and they just got a 'wash out'—a mouthful apiece. We started on again at about four o'clock in the afternoon, ten miles to go to water. We kept on till dark and camped again four miles farther on. It was the middle of summer, and a horrible sort of haze had set in which would obscure the moon. There would not be much of that luminary in any case, only about a third of the night, but I had calculated on it. As we rounded the rams on to a nice dry 'rise' to 'camp' for the night, I missed 'Boro'.

"Just before we had rounded up we had passed a low spur of the range we had to cross. I had seen him there last, but what with being absorbed with my reflections about poor Tom Imrie's case, and upon my own business, I had given little thought to him. Mick, of course, had been actively employed in heading the sheep in the right direction, and had had his eyes on the flock.

"Well, we lit a fire and sat there waiting for the young brute to come up, so that we could get enough water for our tea to boil the 'billy'. Not a sign of him an hour after, and I began to get uneasy.

"From thinking he had been delayed in cutting a ''possum' out, a conviction was formed that he must have met with an accident. Old 'Chockaroo,' the pack-horse, was a demon to kick if anything went wrong with the 'swag' on his back, and, for all I knew, he might have kicked 'Boro's' head off also. So I told my ideas to Mick, got my horse, which was hobbled, and started to where I had last seen him. Not a sign of him! And the sky got so cloudy, that it very soon got too dark to do anything. So I found my way back to camp.

Here we were, in a pretty pickle, no water, and both of us very thirsty.

"Nothing could be done till daylight. The sky was now completely overcast, with a sort of cottony-woolly haze, which looked as if it meant another blazing hot day on the morrow.

"I resolved to hang it out. About six miles more would do it.

"So we two got a small round pebble apiece, rolling them round in our mouths to increase the flow of saliva. And all that blessed night we didn't get a show to move, and it would have been just madness to attempt a start, for you couldn't see the sheep fifteen yards off, and as to where your horse would go to it would be impossible to judge. My eye, it was a weary watch.

"To make matters worse, Mick's horse smashed his hobbles, and, of course, made back straight to the last water. I just managed to catch mine, as I heard the row.

"Mick's horse must have come a cropper by getting his hobbles across the stump of an old burnt mulga tree. I shouldn't have caught 'Black Jack' if I hadn't run full butt *into* him, and he would have been sure to have followed Mick's horse. It was black dark till the moon rose, but that made very little difference.

"I took the precaution to put a halter on 'Black Jack' and tie him to a tree, hobbles and all. I couldn't afford to lose him. However, I got him a big heap of mulga boughs, and made him as comfortable as circumstances would allow, but the poor old chap wanted a drink as much as I did, and didn't bother about eating.

"Morning broke dull and cloudy. I had had plenty of time to think over my plans, and determined not to be beat. I would try and find 'Boro' and the water-bags, and then come back on my tracks and join Mick. I might find 'Boro' and I mightn't. The horses, if loose, would be sure to make back to the last water. If I had had anything to carry water in, I would have gone on to the other side of the range, and brought some water to Mick, but all our belongings were on the pack-horse.

"The young blackguard had evidently bolted. He had probably ridden well clear, and then jumped off and let the 'yarramen' go. I knew he daren't turn up at either

THE WRAITH OF TOM IMRIE

Belala or Fassifern on horseback without us. Well, I came to the place where Mick's track and mine of yesterday were going to camp. A little farther on I got the two others. 'Boro's' horses, ridden, I could see that. If he had been off their backs they would have been apart *more* than the half length of the head-stall rope. Of course I had given instructions to Mick to keep steadily on; he knew the way. 'Boro's' horses' tracks swerved off our direction of yesterday, then towards the range, and then up and over the first hill. He was probably making towards some blacks' camp. When he knew the country he would let them go—having dismounted—and probably by this time they would be back at Belala. Well, if they were, they would be sent on from the station, and some one with them to see what was the matter with us.

"I paused to think. Should I go back to Mick and take the chance of getting to the water with the sheep, and let the horses be?

"'Boro' had gone, also three horses, and all our water-bags. No doubt of that. I was awfully thirsty, but I could not now leave Mick and the rams. I turned and rode slowly back. My thirst was increasing, and my mouth was dry and harsh. Just as I passed a large cotton bush, a minute later, one of those confounded blue-grey Tarcoo snakes made a dash at my horse's legs. You know well enough what those deadly brutes mean—death in about twenty minutes for a man. 'Black Jack' gave a plunge, and fell clean over, throwing me just clear. He was so startled that he fell for the first time in all his life, I believe. The next moment he was up, off and away, as if the devil had kicked him.

"In the scrimmage and flurry, for we were all floundering about in a lump, I felt a sharp puncture on my wrist. I was certain I had been bitten. I examined it carefully. Sure enough, two punctures, with a small drop of blood in each. The death mark! I got my knife, cut the place out pretty deep, sucked it furiously, and tied a ligature just above the wound (the direction nearest to the heart), with a silk cracker I happened to have in my pocket. Oh, the agonies of mind I felt! Death staring me in the face! But I reflected that I had taken all reasonable precautions, *and* at once. The flow of the blood and the sucking *might* have removed the deadly virus. So I staggered on, half-dead with thirst, bruised, sore and very sick and nervous. 'Black Jack' had sprung into a crab hole in his fright and gone clean over nearly on top of me, right on to the rough stony ground. I had made sure that I saw the snake dash at me afterwards, and that I had put my hand on it!

"I began to feel like a man in a dream, and staggered on and on, not knowing in the least what I was going to do, or where I was going.

"So," I thought, "it has come to this at last. Cut off in my prime by a beastly accident; bitten by a snake, and if the poison has taken hold of my blood, I shan't have very long to live. It's destiny, I suppose—my fate! This is the end planned by a higher Power from the very first moment that I was born! I am not the first or the only one in this world who has had to suffer in the same way, and they had to meet their fate, and must have felt very much as I do now. Death, the end of all things! I wonder what poor Tom felt before he pulled the trigger of his revolver? Hundreds of men and women, thousands of them, perish every year by awful accidents—drowning, burning and shipwreck, plague, pestilence and famine.

"Some are annihilated in a moment. Others die fearful deaths. Well, life has been very pleasant to me, in spite of its many ups and downs, and I must meet death like a man.

"I had better write a few lines describing how I came to my end. I began to hastily jot down the details in my pocket-book, and whether it was with the worry at my repeated bad luck, the unavoidable accident, or terror at the approach of grim, unflinching, unalterable Death, I half lost my senses. I was vaguely conscious of staggering on, choking with thirst, and fighting with something or some one, I could not tell what. I had a sort of idea that my name was Robert McIlwaine, and I had to do something, but that it would be no use because I was dead. Then I must completely have lost consciousness, for I remember nothing until I came to myself lying at full length in a thick scrub. I vaguely wondered what it was all about. What was I there for? How did I come there? Who was I? Then I fainted again. Then—but how long a time after I have no idea—a thought came upon me that I was dreadfully oppressed with thirst. Then I became conscious

"TOM IMRIE SITTING ON HIS ROAN HORSE."

From the Land of the Wombat.   *Page 99.*

that there was a weight on my chest, and that 'Joker' was licking my face. I gradually came round, and, after a period during which my mind refused to work at all clearly, I began to understand that it was really 'Joker' who was by me. I must have been asleep somewhere. No, I was dead and 'Joker' was a ghost. He must have died too, then, to be with me? Was *this* heaven, this scrub? No, I was dead, I had had a sharp fall with a horse. I had been bitten by a snake. What was 'Joker' here for? He ought to be with Mick and the rams. He must be a ghost. I feebly felt him. No, it was 'Joker' right enough. I found myself sitting up somehow, and I realised that it was moonlight.

"'Joker' was whining. I managed, I never knew how, to stagger to my feet, and grasp a sapling to keep myself from falling down again. Oh, this dreadful thirst! I had suffered from it once before, when I had started on a very hot day and ridden thirty miles away from the river to where I expected to find water, but it had dried up. That *was* thirst, but I got relief then, for I found the lid of an old tin 'billy' which some idiot had pricked full of holes, but I plugged these with bits of green polygonum and then milked my mare 'Flirt,' for she had a foal at home. But I shan't get relief from this! No water anywhere. *This* thirst! I can't speak, I can't even make a noise! I shall go mad! *Who* am I? *Where* am I? Bitten by a snake and dying, and no water. Oh, God! what *can* I do? I can hardly walk! Two steps and a frantic clutch at another sapling. Dying, oh, my God! I made a feeble step or two forward, poor old 'Joker' whining with delight. I got a firm hold on the next sapling and rested panting. As I looked up again, as I live and am here to tell you all, I saw a little open glade, with the moon bright on it, and Tom Imrie sitting on his roan horse, as I often remember him doing, half-turned round in his saddle towards me. He pointed with a gesture of authority right across me. I looked steadfastly at him. He was only vapour, so was his horse. I could see the trees through *both* of them. But his gesture was very clear, commanding yet kind, and his index finger pointed straight in one direction.

"I remember trying to say weakly, 'Hallo, Tom, old chap,' but no sound came, and I thought: 'Yes, I'm dead. That's Tom. We are together again. This is the other world!' But 'Joker' jumped upon me, almost pushing me down. Tom was still there, he and his horse. I saw what he meant. I was to go where he pointed. *Must* go, to save my life. *Must* go! I made a line slowly in the direction he indicated, and before I had gone six yards I saw a pool of water—a good clay pan!

"I managed to reach it, fall flat down, and drink a little. And I have a dim consciousness of shouting and singing, and then a long period of rest.

"When I came to myself again it was daylight, warm and sunny. And there was 'Joker' with a bandicoot he had caught. My senses were a little better. Where had Tom gone to? I remembered. Tom showed me the water. Came out of his grave to do it!

"Poor old Tom and 'Joker'! Good dog, 'Joker'. I felt ever such a little stronger. Oh, the snake! What time is it? Time must have passed! Moonlight and sunlight. I was too weak to rejoice; I couldn't take it in yet. I was close to the water; I drank some more, then lit a fire, cooked the bandicoot on the hot embers, and ate it ravenously, slaking my thirst with the life-saving water. I was coming round, but the thought of the snake struck through me like white-hot iron every now and then. I have, personally, a nervous horror of snakes. Some fellows don't care a button for them, and will catch them by the neck and handle them, but to me they are a terror. Well, I wasn't dead after all. And slowly my thoughts came back, and I began to want to go back and find Mick. 'Joker' never faltered. I was in a gully, a good bit off the track, or tracks, we had made. I hadn't the slightest idea of my whereabouts, but he took me in a straight line to more water. Caught a 'paddy melon' and we cooked that. I came up with Mick two days afterwards, a little dazed still. He had got the rams to water all right after a very severe and thirsty trip, but had been terribly uneasy about me. So he sent 'Joker' off to find me.

"You can't beat a rough cattle dog with one blue eye and one brown one. Best breed of the lot. And so you see, boys, why I don't like to make a mock at ghosts. Poor Tom Imrie! I saw him as plain as I see you, ghost or no ghost. I am quite open to argument that I was off my head for a bit. I don't deny it. I know I was, but where did the idea come from—the positive conviction that I saw Tom Imrie at a critical point in my lifetime when I should have gone mad and died of thirst unless I *had* seen him? Was not the idea providential in itself, if I had not been guided? Therefore I believe in this sight of Tom Imrie's ghost as the one means of preserving me, and I hold it sacred. But whether I really saw him or my poor excited over-wrought brain brought the fancy that I did, I cannot tell you. I simply narrate the impression and belief left. And 'Joker' was a bit of a ghost too at first. He turned out real. And the vision showed me the water. We finished our journey with the rams all right. I hunted all over the Fassifern Camp for 'Boro,' but never saw him again.

"The horses were all found and sent over, water-bags and all. We went down the Tarcoo afterwards, arranged matters with O'Hooligan, and made a most successful trip to Adelaide with the fat cattle, topping the market.

"Then I went to Sydney, and found that Miss Imrie had gone to England, but I kept true to my trust and never said a word that would prejudice my old friend Tom's case."

"No, I suppose not," said Jemmy, "you've simply been letting the cat out of the bag the whole bally time!"

"What? You think I have given him away all through, do you? Well, none of you fellows know Tom Imrie or his sister either, for they don't exist. I never told you the real names, and the facts of the case are completely forgotten. It happened too long ago to come to light, as only the actors in it can say anything, and there's not one of them near the district now. What do you say to a game of whist?"

A RABBIT STATION

> Though what he whispered, under Heaven
> None else could understand,
> I found him garrulously given—
> A babbler in the land.
>
> —*Tennyson.*

I AM delighted to say that I have come across "Jemmy" again. I met him suddenly and sympathetically in London at the Earl's Court Exhibition, not as "that jackeroo," but as an Anglo-Austral-Briton. He doesn't like to be called Scotch now—but took two to celebrate our meeting.

Many years have passed over our respective heads since we last met in Australia, and I noticed with pain that his was quite bald, for his hat fell off when I attempted to embrace him, and I could not avoid seeing the state of the poll.

"Jemmy" has travelled far and wide since our earlier experiences, and gave me his story, without any reservations, from the moment I parted from him in the hospital up to the present date, but only in regard to two experiences in relation to attempts in money-making. As he seems to be well-to-do, and possessed of cash, he must have found some more lucrative system out than either of the two related. And he has several years to talk about, to fill in the necessary gap.

Here is his report, *verbatim et literatim* :—

. . . .

"After I grew skin enough to cover my scalds I went back to the land of Burns. (By the way, it strikes me that Burns would have been one of the Scalds, if he had lived in an earlier age. But that wasn't his fault.)

"'I went in' for the ink business after I got home. My 'boss' had a new patent double-distilled sort of green-pink-black ink in the market. It was supposed to be far superior to other sorts of inks, but I found the making of it a nasty smeary sort of business, and some of the pink powder, which was in my department, used to give me a reddish tinge about the nose by constant smudging, so that the governor and the mater were much afraid that I had taken to drink.

"After I had served the time agreed upon, the 'boss' wanted to take me into partnership, but I had had a sickener of his powder and didn't rise. I told the governor I had no inclination to 'go in' for ink, and somehow that made him laugh and put him in such a good temper that he forked out the 'dibs' in sufficient quantity to enable me to 'go in' for sheep out in Australia again.

"You know as well as I do how Australia is always calling for you if you have ever been there and have worked for her. She did not call for me long before I obeyed her summons, going out this time by the Orient line, with my mind made up to study all the different places of note I now had the chance of seeing on the voyage, and to carefully jot down my impressions of the manners, customs and morals of the different races of people I came across.

"I didn't do either one or the other. I talked 'sheep' all the way out with McParritch. You remember him—one of our old passengers? The chap who started a faro bank in his cabin, with 'coppers' as the payable coin, and lost every cent he possessed."

I remembered him perfectly, and said so, remarking at the same time that I never accused him of having any "gumption," whatsoever other remarkable moral qualities he might possess. This roused "Jemmy," who declared that McParritch had plenty of brains if he only possessed the sense to use them! On my complete acquiescence on this important point, he resumed :—

"Well, I stuffed McParritch with sheep—horns, wool, carcass, skin, tallow and trotters—so that he wouldn't look at a mutton chop all that voyage; and though I knew precious little about the whole thing except what I had picked up in books, and learned in my jackerooing days, before I was blown up and boiled, I persuaded him to become my partner, and as he also had lately succeeded in squeezing the family sponge, he was not averse to my proposition, thinking very favourably of my Yerilla experience, and our former acquaintance.

"He himself had been several things to all men during *his* colonial experience, and had at last risen to be a billiard marker at an hotel, but had got his discharge through taking too much 'Scotch,' and talking too much 'Scotch' also, as his clients, being purely Australian, couldn't understand the game when he marked in 'ta Gaelic'.

"One can never tell what one will rise to in the colonies. I remember when shoe-blacking was the height of my ambition as a lucrative business. And I am sure even now that I could have made it so after I had once got a proper start.

"We settled preliminaries before we got to Albany. We would 'go in' for sheep between us. After buying the station in Sydney we packed up our traps, and started to 'go in' for sheep. The coach stopped at a township on the Warren River called Esmeralda. We found that our sheep station was on the Warren River. At present there were no sheep on it. It seemed as if we were a good deal 'on the Warren' when we had to walk five miles, as there was no one to meet us. We noticed a good lot of rabbits *en route*, here, there and everywhere. We shied stones at them, and tramped on.

"Bunivil we found to be a pretty place, close to the banks of the river, and 'embowered in trees'—I think that is the phrase.

"There was rather a respectable-looking house with a fine roomy verandah all round it, a kitchen, store, stockyard, paddocks, etc., and a boat! We instantly made arrangements for picnics, combined with duck-shooting, and McParritch suggested that we might pick up some rabbits also by the way as we 'spurrted' up and down the river. It looked a nice boat, and I resolved to 'go in' for training as well as sheep. So did McParritch.

"I felt elated. I was now, from the moment I got inside our boundary fence, the McNab of Bunivil, Warren River, New South Wales, Australia.

"We had a heated argument about the form in which our firm should be gazetted. I wanted it McNab & McParritch; he wanted it the other way.

"By this time we had arrived at the verandah of our new house, and during the arguments which each of us advanced to place our subject in the proper light, a red-haired, red-whiskered man appeared, who said, 'Tay's riddy, sorr'.

"He stated further that his name was Mick O'Shea. There was stewed rabbit on the table when he had ushered us into our dining-room.

"When we had finished, O'Shea came in with a white napkin on his arm and joined in the conversation."

"I know the man," I exclaimed. "He's an old friend of mine. Wasn't there a Mrs. O'Shea also?"

"Oh, yes," replied "Jemmy"; "she was to cook, wash, make the 'bids' and do the ironing. She was a 'Frinch Ironer,' as Mr. Mick O'Shea proudly informed us. O'Shea asked to be 'kipt on'. 'Sure oim as handy a min as ye'll git, and me missus will be forelore if ye won't kip us on. She's a good ould cook, and oi'll be "rouseabout".'

"So there we were, you see, already provided with a head cook and bottle-washer, and—a 'rouseabout'. We had paid cash down for the station, and were now fixed as landed proprietors.

"O'Shea said that we could buy 'shape' at the township, dhroves of 'em. *That* was all right—'ship-"shape" and Bristol fashion'. We found the seven horses and buggy that had been 'given in' with Bunivil. They were all a bit the worse for wear, but McParritch said they would do. O'Shea yarded the horses. Next morning, after breakfast on curried rabbit with onions, we got two of them harnessed, and drove off to Esmeralda to bring our luggage back and to purchase some stores. Also we resolved to buy some sheep, to make a start with.

"As McParritch said: 'What was the good of having a sheep station without any sheep on it?'

"McParritch bought the sheep on his own responsibility, and I wrote out the cheque for them in favour of the farmer he bought them from, 'a diveesion of labour,' McParritch affirmed. The man sold them cheap, and we were delighted with our bargain. He (the man) said he was 'blanky glad to get rid of them, as there were so many lurid rabbits about the crimson river now. And that he was going to start a canning factory on the proceeds. We had drinks, and parted with enthusiasm.

"McParritch agreed with me that the farmer, broken-down

squatter, free selector, or whatever he was, appeared to be a noble-hearted fellow, and was undoubtedly a brother. He turned over 500 young ewes, with prospective lambs, and 150 'mixed crawlers' for 'killing sheep,' and was so generous that after another whisky or two he said he would bring the blanky lot over the very next day. We 'shouted' another whisky for him immediately, and he departed—wobbling.

"We got back to Bunivil with a goodly supply of stores, including two cases of whisky, and after we had given O'Shea and Mrs. O'Shea a glass each, we asked O'Shea how it was that the former owners had parted with such a beautiful place as Bunivil. 'Sure, sorr,' said he, 'some shtriped lewnattic of a min turned out four rabbits (two bucks and two does), about eighteen months ago, and the anymils is inchrasin' tremenjis.'

"Here was a turn of luck. If sheep didn't pay, we could make the rabbits pay. Canning, felt manufacture, hats, roofs, tents, patent tarpaulins, asphalt, etc. It was a gorgeous idea! Our tea consisted of four different kinds of cooked rabbits, and was voted excellent.

"Why, there was a gold mine in it! McParritch got me to write at once to Melbourne and buy a lot of books for information about rabbits. He was a poor scribe. It was very hard to get him to write a cheque even, at any time, let alone a letter.

"'By Jove,' said I, 'when we have got up our information we can export rabbits wholesale, freeze 'em in barrels for the old country'—and then I felt miserable again. I had just paid for the sheep. Our beneficent farmer came in next day with the 'jumbucks,' and an eye to whisky, and departed satisfied. McNab and McParritch, sheep farmers and sheep squatters to her Maj—— No, that won't do. McNab and McParritch, sheep squatters, Bunivil, Warren River, New South Wales. That's how McParritch headed his first letter home. So did I, and, I believe, the governor showed it to the laird and the meenister of his native town, and the latter averred that it was a great responsibeelitee to be a 'cheepsquatter,' and 'hopit' that there was an Established Kirrk in the neeborhood.

"We put the killing sheep in the home paddock, O'Shea fulfilling his part of 'rouseabout' with an old wall-eyed dog named 'Pat'. The 500 young ewes with prospective lambs we turned loose, generally, all over Bunivil, which was securely fenced with sheep-proof and cattle-proof wire fencing. We had a five-mile block, five miles on the river by five miles back, fifteen miles of fencing. The river frontage was over five miles, as there were a lot of bends and twists and turns in the Warren. The river, of course, acted as its own fence, but I believe the rabbits have now learned to swim.

"The next day McParritch and I took a ride round to survey our country, and note its capabilities. O'Shea had killed one of our killing sheep the night before as soon as they arrived, for he said he was tired of 'atin' rarebits'. So we had mutton chops for breakfast before we started to explore our 'run,' just to get used to the general feelings and ideas of real 'squatters' in possession of real sheep, and even McParritch admitted during the meal that the more 'muttony' flavour we got the more likely we were to understand sheep.

"There is a good deal of knowledge in a mutton chop, and more in two or three, with baked potatoes; but when McParritch said that we ought to get up the 'anattommy of ta cheeps,' I told him to shut up.

"We rode all round the home paddock, our horses exhibiting various symptoms of dyspepsia at starting and afterwards, caused, I have no doubt, by the rabbit-flavoured grass upon which they habitually fed. Mine shied and landed me on the bare ground when we came upon the killing sheep, which were inspecting rabbit holes, but he didn't take the slightest notice of the droves of rabbits he met. Mere habit!

"The rabbits were very numerous indeed, and I saw more *black* rabbits that morning and afternoon than I ever saw in my life before. I must have seen over 5000, and I could only remember about twelve during my home experience. This sight inflamed McParritch to such an extent that he carted O'Shea off to Esmeralda in the buggy that evening to buy three cheap guns, one for each of us. O'Shea was instructed to 'rouseabout' the rabbits with his.

"McParritch's argument in favour of going at once to the township was 'that a new " veesta " of usefulness lay before us'. We could combine sport with the thinning of rabbits, and it would be 'pleasurable' to have recreation whilst we were waiting for our sheep to increase in numbers. Another argument he adduced was that rabbits, combined with mutton, would be a change in our diet. I didn't see the force of his argument, but he didn't care.

"On proper and joint representation by Messrs. McParritch (he *would* have it his way) and McNab of Bunivil, etc., to Mrs. O'Shea, we might induce her to stew, boil, roast, curry, hash, fry, fritter, bake, mince, devil, jug, cutlet and 'shouffly' the rabbits. He added that he had once tasted rabbit 'shouffly' in Edinbro' and it was 'unco guid '.

"And there was the soup. You could make soup in sixteen different ways out of rabbits. The beggar had got rabbit on the brain and no mistake.

"Things went on very well for some weeks, but the more we thinned the rabbits the more they seemed to increase. It was 'too thin' for us. If our sheep gave birth to lambs, the rabbits would give birth to droves ; and by the beginning of the fourth month we were forced to fence. A rabbit-proof fence this time.

"McParritch's idea was to fence them in and destroy them ' vee ate armies,' he said. . At least, that's what it sounded like, and if we ate armies of rabbits, they had far more armies left. We were to poison, dog, shoot, annihilate them. I said it would be better to do that than quote such Hebrew as he had done.

"But his plan certainly looked feasible. In the meantime, I don't know how many tons of rabbit wire fencing had been dumped down along the Bunivil fence; but if you were to judge by the cart and dray tracks all over the place, there must have been a good weight carried. McParritch was always shooting, he did little else. But I soon got tired of it, because if I either hit or missed my rabbit, all the others within ' coo-ee ' bolted into their holes and wouldn't come out again for a good bit, and I hadn't the patience to fool about until they did, but McParritch would wait an hour for a shot! O'Shea used to go with him at first, but stopped because McParritch hit him in the legs with No. 5 shot, and he said ' he wasn't going to be kilt like a blanky rarebit!'

"McParritch and I consulted as to our method of fencing with the rabbit-proof wire, and he affirmed that he 'kent thae rarbits brawly ; ye must jaast pit oop yer fents all round, and then we'll muster the hail o' thae deevils inside. Ye'll ken they'll nae gang ootside, nor come ben.' Well, we fenced, that is to say, we put up the first line of rabbit-proof wire uprightly along the three sides of our cattle and sheep-proof fence, and pegged the bottom down firmly along the ground all the way round. McParritch was delighted. There were all the disturbers of our peace of mind, securely fenced in. Nothing simpler now than to kill the lot. This was the first stage. They had increased mightily everywhere, since we first became the proud proprietors of Bunivil. They romped in solid phalanxes. They scooted in tens of thousands. They burrowed and ate any grass they could discover by the hundred thousand. The young ones of many hundreds of families were grown up, and yearning for family ties themselves, but now the outside ones could not come in for consultation, and the inside ones could not get out for more grass.

"'Ye'll obsairrve," said McParritch, 'they'll aall dee o' starrvaation the noo, but we must jaast thin them off a wee.'

"So he engaged four men with a bullock team for a week to build a huge brushyard to 'yard' the rabbits in. We asked every living soul with a gun, and every living individual dog within a radius of six miles, to come out and help us.

"Nearly the whole township of Esmeralda came, including our publican and the storekeeper, and every one brought a gun and several dogs. There was a huge pack of dogs, and they ate all the rabbit-skins we had carefully stretched and dried as soon as they arrived. Also they hunted O'Shea's dog all over the place, until he sought refuge under Mrs. O'Shea's bed. Then she came out with a broom handle and order was restored.

"We tried hard to 'yard' our pestilent rabbits in McParritch's 'fakement,' but it was no go. We couldn't persuade them to go within half a mile of it. They knew perfectly well that we wanted to rush them into it, and they declined to be 'had' in that way.

"The hundreds of dogs caught and devoured about one apiece. Rabbits were free gifts in the Esmeralda district, and the dogs lived on them habitually. So we couldn't say anything. They ate them skin and all. The townspeople and neighbouring free selectors shot about a hundred more, but what was that out of about five hundred thousand.

"Anyway we chased up fifty thousand that day, and I am sure another fifty thousand were down their holes laughing at us.

"Then the shooting party and all the dogs invaded Bunivil, and nearly drove the O'Sheas mad. We had to kill three sheep to support them. The dogs got all the bones and insides, and finished our fresh rabbit skins. So that the margin of profit was not excessive.

"McParritch expected to clear one hundred pounds after paying for his brushyard. He got out his note-book to jot down casual deaths when the first dog caught and ate the first bunny, but in an hour's time he got tired of it. The real totals did not add up to his liking. And the quantity of whisky our rabbit battue folks mopped up was awful! If I had not at once 'planted' two bottles, with Mrs. O'Shea's connivance, under her 'bid,' there would not have been one left. They finished the remainder. When they were all 'full up' they departed, thanking us for a very jolly day, and expressing their willingness to come to several more 'battues'. That brute of a storekeeper said he hoped we were going to make an instiooshun of it, as he liked a bit o' rabbitin'. Used to have several days off and on in the old country, etc., etc., at Lord Smythe's place, dontcherknow.'

"I suspect him of being a local poacher, and he fell in our estimation from that day. Unfortunately there was no opposition store in Esmeralda, or we would have transferred our affections and our cheques thereto. So we went on dealing with the poacher. He made a good income out of us.

"After it was all over, I told McParritch that we should have taken up about a length of our rabbit-proof fence, and chivied all our above-ground rabbits *out*. But the idiot wouldn't listen, and said that while we were all at the far end the 'ootseeders' would have come in. Did you ever hear tell of such an ass? As if our army would not have made them scoot double quick also amongst the 50,000 we would have brought up. One of the festive crowd who came over told me that we ought to poison our rabbits. He said it was simple enough. 'First,' he remarked, 'get a big boiler, big enough to boil three sheep at once in. Then light a big fire under it, and put a lot of phosphorus in it.' (The fool never said anything about water.) So I jotted down his directions from his own lips to make sure. Then we were to put a bag of oats in the boiler, on top of the phosphorus. 'Then dry the oats and dump 'em down in spoonfuls all over the shop, wherever the rabbits are most numerous.' That seemed simple enough, but as I had not seen any oats growing in the district I wrote a note to the store-keeping poacher chap, and told him to send about a dozen bags out. I reckoned a grain to a rabbit. McParritch and O'Shea started for Esmeralda at once to buy the boiler, and I had a 'nobbler' of my well thought of hidden whisky, and entreated Mrs. O'Shea to have a glass also. She did, three of them, 'wishin' yer all koinds of luck, and a swate young liddy to share the annerrs of Bunivil shape station wid entoirely'.

"She was quite helpless at tea-time, for she had secreted two other bottles on her own account, as I afterwards found out.

"It took McParritch and O'Shea a week to buy that boiler and bring it out on a bullock dray. Then it was found to be too long. It had belonged to an old river steamer, and it had cost a lot of money, as I knew when I paid the cheque for it. McParritch put on another team of men to dig a great hole, and put up an iron framework and a brick fire-place to heat the phosphorus with and I don't know what all. I just gasped!

"We were spending money like water, at least McParritch was, and we had hardly even begun to 'go in' for sheep. And that looney, McParritch, even rejoiced because it was 'self-eevident' that the rabbits would be 'star-rved oot,' and those that refused to be starved would be 'piesonit,' and he added that it 'didna chust maatterr the spennin' a wheen bawbees for the pleesure o' seein' thae deevils dee.' Naethin' could get through 'oor fents,' and, if we got 'thae deevils' off quick enough, there would be plenty of grass next year. Then we could fill our enclosed block with 'ta cheeps'.

I took the brute out with me next day for a look at his boasted fence. I had inspected it 'on the quiet' previously. Not only had all our enclosed bunnies been out to see their aunts and uncles under the wire, but the aunts and uncles had been in to see them. McParritch got out his note-book and began to count 'holes out' and 'holes in' under his twopenny-halfpenny wire fence; but he gave it up before he had gone 100 yards. The total totted up too quickly this time. 'Eh, mon, it's jaast deevilitch.' That's what he said. 'A niver thocht o' the burryin' poor o' thae deevils. We maun gang brisk to tha piesonin', ma certy.' And that is also what he said. Ma certy! indeed. It made me feel *shirty*. They had brought the phosphorus out in packets, being duly warned by the poacher that it was awfully dangerous stuff to play the fool with.

"They put six packets of this stuff in the boiler, dumped two bags of oats on top of it, and then lit the fire. We all, except McParritch, stood round. He attended to the stoking.

"Mrs. O'Shea was of opinion that it would be a great success, and that the boiler would do to boil clothes in afterwards. The success came on the scene as soon as the beautiful boiler got red hot. There was a fearful explosion, flaming oats and oaths shot up in the air in all directions, and that ass McParritch roared out: 'Oh, heell, ave clean for-rgot thae waaterr!'

"I didn't say anything. I was too disgusted to think that a man *could* be such an arrant jackanapes. We all fled except McParritch, who was burning. O'Shea invoked 'Howly Moses,' and Mrs. O'Shea bellowed for the police.

"McParritch lost his whiskers, and was pretty well spotted with burning phosphorus, which pitted him so that people asked him when he had had the small-pox. I didn't either ask or pity, for when I took him to task for his awful silliness in not putting water in to put the phosphorus out, he retaliated by saying that he had acted on the directions taken down from me.

"Then he wanted me to pay for *his* burns. It was no use arguing with such a brute, so I left him severely alone. Next time they boiled the phosphorus, and stewed four bags of oats in it.

"I don't know how they managed it, but they got a lot ready somehow, and then McParritch, O'Shea, and I went about, each armed with a large basket of oats (phosphorised) and a huge metal spoon with a handle three feet long. We walked about ten miles apiece placing the poison down in neat little heaps for the rabbits to eat. And next morning we went out on a corpse hunt.

"We were eminently successful. McParritch had poisoned the home paddock. There were fifty-three of our killing 'cheeps' sleeping their last sleep, every one of them wearing the most agonised expression I ever saw on a sheep's countenance. The rest of them were contortionising round the paddock, doing back-springs, lightning-changes and summersaults previous to giving up the ghost; and one of them butted me in the stomach as if I had been the cause of it all!

"With regard to the rabbits, McParritch was of the opinion that the feelings of heat and general uncomfortableness in their 'eepigaastric reejins' would naturally make them seek the shelter of their holes, or consult a doctor, which accounted for us not seeing so many dead ones on the surface of the paddock as we expected. We only saw about three hundred altogether. McParritch remarked: 'Bit ye see thae pieson's jaast vara eefeective, jaast luik at thae cheeps'.

"Nevertheless, the rabbits were frisking about the 'lignum' in thousands. When we arrived home again, the fair O'Shea was in a state of revolt. She remarked sternly: 'That she hadn't engaged to come to a place where her bidroom would be made a slaughter-house! And she wasn't going to stand it, at all, at all.'

"She had six rabbits in a row in our verandah, which she had found 'clane did, undherr me bid'; and she wrapped her apron round her 'hid' and sobbed. She had taken three more corpses from the parlour floor. After I had quietened her down with a 'nobbler' of her own particular, I asked her what she had done with the last three corpses. Oh, she had just 'chucked' them into the river.

"As we had seen some surprising revelations of phosphorus as a poison already, I wasn't quite sure how it would act diluted with Warren water at Esmeralda. But I held my peace.

"Our killing sheep were dropping now in batches of twos and threes, and would probably be all dead to-morrow; and, as I had poisoned the other part of the run, I deemed it prudent not to make any remarks until we had investigated that part. We had for dinner some stewed rabbit, with rabbit sauce, brains and tongues and hearts and things, mixed with flour and water and onions. These rabbits had been shot by McParritch a day or two before. I said I hoped he had shot them before our boiler exploded and scattered the poison all over the place. He turned ghastly white! So I told him that I already felt a pain in my tummy, and he left the room in jerks, took a strong emetic, and was very ill afterwards. I hoped he would get worse.

"I went out with O'Shea to the part we had poisoned, and he said we should now have to skin all the sheep to save the wool. We certainly couldn't save their lives, for we found them all dead or dying, the whole lot of them. Not one of those 500 young ewes ever had a lamb to utter the word 'baa'. It was a mournful afternoon. We found them squirming in every direction. We skinned as many as we could of those which had done squirming, and rode dolefully home.

"McParritch was better, and swore that he would never eat rabbit again. We told him the news, and I exhorted him to be a man, and sally forth with us the 'morn's morn' with a hone and a butcher's knife, to aid us in skinning the rest of our flock.

"He said his prayers, and after that became contumelious, and accused me of poisoning more sheep than he had. Then he went and polished off half a tumbler of whisky to drown his care. When this took effect he remarked, 'Chimmy, ma fren, never min ta cheeps; we'll jaast gae in for ta rraabeets; we'll stairr-t a cannin' fact'ry!'

"We sent O'Shea buggy-wise to Esmeralda to bring in a lot of tinned meats, and some more whisky; for I did not consider it safe to be eating rabbits any more or drinking Warren water either. O'Shea said that he counted over a million rabbits when he was after the horses, but I didn't believe it, and told him so before he went.

"McParritch and I passed the remainder of the day skinning our defunct sheep. O'Shea returned from Esmeralda rather drunk, about midnight, with all the stores we had ordered, and eighteen cats in eighteen bags, except one who had been put up in a paper bag, and had meandered back. This was a private order of McParritch's, who had read in our rabbit books that cats would kill rabbits. McParritch, hearing the noise of the buggy, as well as O'Shea's vituperations whilst handling the cats, came out in pyjamas, and said that he

"I GAVE HER THE USUAL 'NIP' NECESSARY ON THESE OCCASIONS."

From the Land of the Wombat.

had heard that 'cats were gey fine beesties for ta rraabeets'. Why, or wherefore, or how, I did not inquire. I was past all feeling or curiosity. So I let out the cats, and one of them went and had kittens in McParritch's bed immediately. An hour later Mrs. O'Shea came over, in combinations and an ulster, and said that there had been a similar case in her best box of clothes, and that she wasn't 'goin' to be flummoxed up by them goin's on'.

"I gave her the usual 'nip' necessary on these occasions, and she simmered down and went back to 'bid'. I sat up with a broom and O'Shea's dog to prevent the rest of the cats coming down the chimney.

"What with all these worries and regret at our fast diminishing stock of cash, my hair began to come out by handfuls. I had written nearly all the cheques hitherto. McParritch took dashed good care that *he* didn't, and I knew I was nearly stumped.

"The cats refused to leave the vicinity of the houses, and used to go to roost on the roofs and beams and rafters, causing the O'Sheas to kick up an awful row, and give a month's warning.

"O'Shea, who had got a bottle or two 'planted' somewhere, shouted out from over the way that 'St. Patthrick had kicked arl the shnakes out of Ould Oireland, and that he hadn't emigrated to Orsthrylia to be smothered aloive with bastes of cats, the varmints!'

"McParritch and I loaded up with No. 4, sallied out and shot the whole bally lot of them; the cats, I mean, not the O'Sheas, but I was getting looney enough to do anything. Then McParritch took more whisky than was good for him and wanted to fight me.

"I had been thinking very seriously over matters lately, and resolved to punch his head (verbally) when he was suffering a recovery and felt very low and miserable and, I hope, repentant. I have always noticed that when you have a grudge on a fellow *that* is the proper time to rub it in hard.

"I also meant him to write a cheque for more rabbit wire, and to get seven more hands for an improvement in the fencing which I had carefully thought out and invented. I had noticed that the rabbits burrowed with impunity under our upright wire fencing and I resolved to put a stop to it—to solve the whole difficulty and impress McParritch with my vastly superior attainments. So I went into Esmeralda myself and ordered my seven men and a few more tons of rabbit-proof wire.

"McParritch had been too much 'on the booze' to be fit for anything when I came back, so I started my work alone. He went with O'Shea to the township next day and both of them were much the worse from drink when they returned. They both solemnly declared that the rabbits were playing lawn tennis all along the fence on the Esmeralda side. I tried to bluff that idea of lawn tennis out of McParritch, as I thought he was in for a dose of the 'jim-jams'.

"So I asked him what sort of bats they used. He replied, 'Skeetle aalley bats, of course, jaast theirr honds, mon. Sure as am born'. And O'Shea declared that they used young 'rarebits' just three days old for balls—and took Saint Pather's name in vain over it!

"So I went off to my work next day, taking no further notice of the loonies. But my hair came out in double handfuls. I made my men take the top soil off inside our fence for a little more than the breadth of a coil of wire and go down six inches all round the boundary. This took several days. I then made them lay the coils all along this broad shallow trench and cover it all up again. I had had all the burrowed holes previously excavated by the rabbits filled in with stones and earth by my men. And they told me they didn't mind the trouble, and were willing to work on for months at the present rate of wages. They said if they got tired they imagined themselves on the diggings. I know that I wished devoutly that all the stones and pebbles which they stuffed into rabbit holes had been 'nuggets'. I would have loaded up the buggy and left McParritch to his own devices.

"At last I got my two loonies tolerably sober and repentant by 'planting' all the whisky I could find. I gave Mrs. O'Shea a little in a bottle to pick them up with when the 'jim-jams' became menacing, and they both took their solemn oaths to become Good Templars, and founded a lodge of two with much ceremony. Neither Mrs. O'Shea nor I would join, though they implored us to, for the good of our souls, as O'Shea said. McParritch was Worthy Chief Templar and O'Shea was Worthy Inner 'Gyard'.

"But they had a row at the first meeting and swore 'off' again. If they didn't get their 'nip' to the minute they were afflicted with green and pink rabbits, and McParritch ran right round the house one night with a green rabbit as big as a dog after him! At least, he said it was after him, but when I had loaded the gun I couldn't find it. So I fired the gun off, and the explosion brought on the 'jim-jams' for both of them. They declared we were 'stuck up' by bushrangers!

"I wasn't going to be fool enough to have loaded guns about the place, so I locked them and all the knives, razors and forks up in the store—and had to eat my meals with my fingers. I slept on the key also, and it caused abrasions of the cuticle about my hips.

"After about a month, when they were better, they came out with me to see *my* work.

"I intended to surprise them. There were no more holes, only hundreds and thousands of scratchings six inches down to the hard coil of buried wire. They were very much impressed, but that feeling wore off, because while we were standing there we counted 673 rabbits of all sizes and colours quietly and without hurry climbing our first fence and dropping over on the opposite side. They climbed it both ways, and seemed to think it quite an ordinary thing to do.

"Why the deuce hadn't they done so to our first fence, *before* the underground wire was laid down? I got tired of seeing the 'outsides' coming in, and the 'insides' going out, and went home to think. When I looked in my bedroom glass I found I was bald in patches.

"If McParritch was troubled with rabbits in his brain, they were in my hair! And no wonder. Rabbits soon learn things. They never play their trumps at first. They keep them on purpose to vex you, just at the time when you think you have completely circumvented them.

"I learned a lot of things from rabbits *myself* before I had finished with them. But this new trick of climbing must be stopped at all risks and costs. So I sent McParritch and O'Shea in to order more wire for a top inward horizontal flange, the same breadth as the other two. That would stop their climbing tricks, and we could claim that we had put an end to their burrowing. The underground wire did that.

They would have to learn to fly now in order to get over our treble idea.

"Neither McParritch nor O'Shea turned up for a week, and Mrs. O'Shea remarked that it was not the O.K. idea for a 'forlore woman' to be aftherr stoppin' on the station wid a bachelure jintlemin. What would the folks say? She didn't seem to care a rap what O'Shea thought. Perhaps she knew by experience that he was beyond thinking, as he was where grog was.

"So she decided to ride in herself and bring O'Shea out by the ear. None of them returned. But the wire came, and my seven men and I got the inward flange all ready for fixing on uprights and cross-pieces at right-angles from the main fence itself. Surely that would stop them. They couldn't climb, they wouldn't burrow, and it was beyond them to jump it.

"But I had not yet learned my rabbit lesson. When it was all completed, I surveyed my work with inward satisfaction. One of my men came in to cook, as since the general exodus I had to do that part of the station work myself, besides fretting my brains into pulp with the rabbits. My new cook's opinion was 'that you never knowed when you was upsides with "they robbids,"' and that the whole lot of his mates had better stay until we were aware of the next move. There wasn't enough room for them in the kitchen, so they took all the American axes and other tools, cut down a lot of trees, and built a very nice 'men's hut'.

"That was something anyway to the good out of the general waste and shipwreck. I was so pleased with the completed fence and the hut that my hair stopped coming out for an entire day.

"I fed my men on tinned meat, and as there was plenty of it they did not repine. 'Sam' was a first-rate cook, and I began to put plenty of flesh on. We went out in a body to the fence in three days' time. I was firmly convinced that it would be a great and unparalleled success. But, alas, 'Sam' and the 'robbids' knew better! There were 4580 holes in half a mile, in and out under the whole structure!

"They had burrowed down to the underground wire first. That wouldn't do. So they scratched and found out how far back it extended, and, having got the range, burrowed in earnest, and shot under the whole lot, coming up on the other side laughing fit to break their necks. One hundred thousand on both sides must have started operations to see who would be through first!

"What was to be done with such knowing brutes. We should have to undermine the whole run to do it, and wire the bottom to keep them in. As for the outside brutes, there was simply nothing to prevent them walking up the wire as a convenient step-ladder, halting on the top to enjoy the view, and then hopping over inwards. You can't fence rabbits out or in in Australia or New Zealand either. I felt that we hadn't even begun to cope with the brutes. And as to keeping sheep for wool and carcass, there is nothing left for them to eat where rabbits abound. When we commenced the war in grim earnest, the Lord knows what trump cards the brutes would have to play. Here was fifteen miles of an expensive and troublesome fence completely thrown away. I started my men to fill in the holes again with big stones, but the rabbits liked that, for it gave them a motive in working now, which they did not neglect, and they simply made three fresh holes during the night for every one we had stopped in the daytime. Who could beat that sort of diplomacy?

"Several wise buck rabbits now began to watch the 'possums, took climbing lessons, and educated the youth of their generation to climb trees. After I had seen and counted 300 of them climbing saplings or trees near the fence to the height of six, eight or ten feet, and then throw back or forward summersaults over the whole concern either way, I felt I was not in it, and I went home a sadder and a wiser man.

"I started to cook my own dinner and burnt my hand badly through the lard in the frying-pan catching fire. As soon as I got it out, a policeman arrived in charge of McParritch, O'Shea, and Mrs. O'Shea. He said they were all suffering from the 'diddleums,' and the magistrate considered they would be safer at home, as excursions or alarms caused by 'jimjams' and green rabbits were not conducive to the peace and comfort of Her Majesty's people at Esmeralda. He thought they would quieten down in a few days.

"They looked awful. I liquored up the policeman, gave him half a sovereign, and wished him good-day.

"McParritch took me aside and told me most confidentially that he had seen 311 blue rabbits with orange spots, and was going to write to the *Town and Country Journal* at Sydney about it, as he considered it rather unusual, especially as each of these animals rode a magenta rabbit in a grand national steeplechase, and he was much troubled because he couldn't spot the winner!

"I persuaded him to go to bed, and got him a cup of gruel with a strong dash of 'three-star' in it to steady him, for he was ready to weep, and I feared complications. Mrs. O'Shea came over in the dead of night, after I was asleep, and declared that her 'flure was shakin',' and that O'Shea had killed eleven carpet snakes which came down the chimney.

"So I got up, dressed, and escorted *her* gently, but firmly, with half a bottle of the same remedy to share with her husband, who was far beyond all sense of shame. I took great care to extinguish their light, and departed—shedding my hair all the way.

"Beyond declaring that the butter and jam swarmed with antagonistic and bellicose beetles for the next week, together with several new snake stories and cockroach yarns, the three dissipated and dilapidated wretches got on their legs again in a fortnight, but I had to get the doctor to McParritch, who held conversation with lurid red-hot rabbits, located either on the roof, or under his bed, or in his pockets or boots. One got inside his watch and wouldn't come out. He frightened me out of my wits.

"The doctor said that McParritch had got 'rabbits' sure enough, and that I ought to be jolly thankful it wasn't 'rats'! When I related my own trouble about the rabbits, the doctor said, 'Simplest thing in the whole world, my dear sir. Inoculate 'em; I will supply the lymph and a hypodermic syringe. You will have some fun after you have inoculated say 100 or so in watching them exterminate each other. I have recommended my system to the Government, but they object to anything contagious. However, I can let you have several different kinds of lymph, and will send you over some samples by the mailman.'

"When the invalids got thoroughly well, McParritch and his crony, O'Shea, used to sit about in corners and tell each other stories of the sights they saw during recovery.

"They made some more phosphorised oats and put it up trees, and down the holes, and anywhere else they thought it would be effectual. I was daily in terror lest some of it should get into my food. Thousands more rabbits were poisoned, but tens of thousands took their places from all parts of the country, and the existing live ones romped about in daily increasing quantities. Our fence was no earthly good. It wasn't rabbit-proof any more than McParritch himself was, and we gave up all idea of being able to keep them either out or in.

"There was no grass anywhere, but it didn't matter, as we had no sheep, and we had to stable-feed our horses. The rabbits 'ringed' every tree in our enclosed space, which would produce a great deal of dry firewood in eighteen months. It turned out lucky for our successor, who had plenty of wood for fuel.

"As none of us could bear to even look at a cooked rabbit, much less eat it, we lived entirely on tinned meat, which became monotonous.

"We inoculated several rabbits with the doctor's mixtures, and turned them out according to the prescriptions, and O'Shea declared that the greater number of the home paddock rabbits were suffering from erysipelas and whooping-cough. 'Sure, I harrd 'em barrkin' all over the paddock, and I thought it was the "jim-jams" again,' said he.

"McParritch was sure that the station rabbits had measles and chicken-pox. 'A coontit sax, and a think it's jaast scarrleteena; a kent it fine when a was a bair-r-n.' He was also afraid that one had small-pox, because it was 'doin' a va-a-st o' scraatchin''. He developed personally all the combined symptoms within a week, and set off to hustle up the doctor on his own account. When he returned, he remarked that the rabbits had formed ambulance corps with bits of bark for stretchers, and were taking all the bad cases to the hospitals in different rabbit warrens. He said the nurses wore caps and white collars, and the doctors were all bright blue. Also that one lot afflicted with St. Vitus' dance had met him in deputation on the road, and had nearly scared the life out of him. He apologised for bringing three empty bottles of 'three-star' back with him, but said that he should never have got through the rabbits if he had not kept himself up to the mark.

"It appears that one rabbit must have been inoculated with hydrophobia virus, which the worthy doctor must have imported from England, as no sane Australian dog ever goes mad, and this afflicted rabbit had chased O'Shea home, foaming at the mouth. As I hinted, O'Shea had never quite got over his first 'jim-jam' attack, and used to make me nervous daily with some fresh phenomenon.

"To make a long story short, McParritch got so bad that he was taken off to the lunatic asylum. The rabbits had affected his brain to such an extent that he used to see them going up in balloons, riding bicycles, and driving steam and electric motor cars; whilst he was constantly being chivied round the house by myriads of blue, pink, red and green rabbits. After he had told the doctor all this as a profound secret, it was all up with him, and he was carted off.

"I am told that he is quite happy, but his case is perfectly hopeless. His one idea is that he is a variegated buck rabbit, and he always makes a dash for the cabbages when he is taken out for an airing anywhere near the kitchen garden.

"An American speculator bought the place from me, and I got my share back, clearing all expenses. As McParritch's case was hopeless, I collared his share also, as he owed me a good deal of money. So that I considered myself quite justified in doing so. As he had turned into a buck rabbit, it was no good asking him for it, and I didn't mean to supply him with cabbages to the value of it. Another thing, I don't mean to hold myself responsible to the New South Wales Government for his keep. Let the colonists pay for him. It was their bally rabbits which turned his brain, and shed every hair on *my* head. Let *them* keep him. All he wants now is food, bedding and clothing—with an occasional cabbage.

"I turned the O'Sheas over to the speculator, and I have since heard that they get very good wages in the large 'Canning and Felt Manufactory' he has established at Bunivil on the banks of the Warren River, New South Wales. The manufactory turns out about 500 different sorts of rabbits, boiled, baked, roasted, stewed, stuffed, etc., besides felt hats, felt roofing, felt gasometers, and a lot of other things, all made out of the hides, bones, teeth, fur, and insides of Bunivil rabbits."

, , , , , , , , ,

A RABBIT STATION

"Jemmy" and I dined, after his most interesting story, at Pimms. We had a magnum of Moet and Chandon. It was almost better than old times. "Jemmy" is more serious than he used to be, but his bald and shining head makes him inexpressibly comic, no matter whether the inside of it is serious or not. He has promised to tell me some more of his adventures, especially one in connection with gum digging in New Zealand, at a fitting opportunity.

THE CHASE OF THE WHITE KANGAROO

> The saddle was our childhood's home,
> Our heritage—the steed.
> —*Rolf Boldrewood.*

AUBURN again! In the old days, and myself—after a hard day's work—all alone (save for Tom Barnett and his wife), smoking a pipe of satisfaction and contentment in the verandah during the cool of the evening. It was an hour from sundown. Hoof strokes, and two well-known arrivals—George Guyon and Herbert Mayfair. The first name denotes one of the partners of the firm of Guyon & Barton, owners of the neighbouring station on Seechal Creek, where we experienced the big flood in all its animosity.

"How are you, old chap? Can we stop here to-night?" they ask with broad grins all over their faces. "We're down on business, cattle business; also to show you how to work out that chess problem you failed in, after riding twenty miles to show *us* how to do it. Secondly, to let you know that we are going to take away all those 'cleanskin' scrubbers running out back from your conical hill plain near the ranges."

"The very thing I could have wished for," I joyfully replied. "How are you going to manage it? You won't have a rag on you when you have chivied them through the 'mulga'."

"Oh, we have arranged for all that," cheerily answered George. "By the way, there's an awful old terror of a roan bull on the stramash, a regular 'rager'. He turned me and Herbert out of the buggy, coming over from the Gunyahgo, when we got to within about six miles from Seechal. I know he belongs to those scrub cattle on your run, but he was out of his latitude, looking for a mob of cows. He charged us, upset the buggy and caused Columbine and Harlequin to kick themselves clear and bolt off home. We cleared out also up a gidyah tree, until 'Old Scotty' came up on 'Poteen,' with a couple of cattle dogs and a stock-whip, and caused *him* to clear in his turn. He ought to be shot."

"We will do it," said I. "We'll take the Terry rifle with us, and we'll take the Auburn buggy too, or the American waggon, taking a gun apiece besides. Then some of us can shoot ducks along the river on our way to Baines's, camp there for the night, and go on to the big plain in the morning. We'll take all our cattle dogs, and a brace of kangaroo dogs, blankets, pots and kettles, plenty of 'tucker,' and camp in royal style. It will be quite a picnic, and Tommy and Eacharn can bring out a couple of stock-horses apiece for us all. I'll ride 'Charlie'; he's good all round. But don't tell my brother when he comes back, will you? He hates any one, even me, to ride Charlie."

"Charlie would kick and bite a kangaroo if he attempted to stick your brother up, wouldn't he?" asked Herbert.

"Rather," I answered. "He'll not only kick them, but he'll knock them clean over. Never knew a better horse for kangaroos. It's not a very easy thing for a horse to knock a kangaroo over, both going full speed, without getting a cropper, but Charlie will do it every time. You see he always gallops into the kangaroo full butt, and chests him when the marsupial is *off* the ground. I believe if my brother told him he would bring a kangaroo in by himself and yard him. He is the nicest and best-mannered hack I ever rode."

"But who cometh o'er the hill?"—as a chorus of growls and barks announced the advent of a stranger or strangers.

Looking down to the crossing-place, we noticed the approach of a regular cavalcade. Two men, one driving a buggy with a pair of mules in it; the other riding a mule and driving eight more in front of him. They all had a drink in the shallow rushing water at the ford; and afterwards approached the house leisurely.

All hands were out of doors looking at them—Tom Barnett and his wife, all the blacks and ourselves—for mules had never been seen at Auburn before.

A handsome bearded man about forty years of age was driving. The other was his servant. The principal stranger's name turned out to be Stuart. I introduced him to my friends, and we strolled off to the bathing-place, preparatory to dinner. I informed Stuart that we had never seen mules before in our part of the world, and asked his reasons for employing them instead of horses.

"Well, you see, I'm 'overlanding,' said he. "Waiting for anything I can pick up on the road. A bit of good country if I come across it, cattle or sheep-droving, gold digging, anything else pleasant and profitable. And being thus employed, I find that mules, though new to most people in Australia, are the best animals for my purpose. Out and out useful creatures. They brought me from Adelaide safely and well, and show very little signs of fatigue at present. Turn 'em out at the base of a barren range, amongst loose rocks and boulders, and they'll have a bellyful before morning. They will eat shrubs, scrub, river weeds, anything. They go long distances without water, and are hardier than horses, though not so fast."

We went back to a substantial dinner, with tea as a beverage, and during its discussion elicited the fact that Stuart, our new friend, and owner of the mules, had been through the whole Garibaldian campaign, of which adventure he gave us some most lively and graphic details.

Afterwards we discussed our plans for getting the wild scrub cattle off the ranges abutting on to the Boobara plains.

George was the first spokesman, as he and Herbert had carefully matured their ideas beforehand, being incited thereto in the first instance by the totally unprovoked attack of the wild solitary bull upon them.

Therefore he laid his purpose out before us in this manner:—

"Being sure that you would lend us a hand, I have sent Scotty, 'Jim,' my rough rider, and two black boys out to Boobara plains to camp in the vicinity until we join them. They have about 150 'ragers' (pretty wild station cattle) with them. These cattle will be kept in hand out on the plain to help us, if we succeed in rushing the scrubbers out. If we can only do this the wild cattle will make for our station 'ragers,' and then we can keep 'ringing' them out on the big plain until we reduce the whole lot to order. Then I think if we make a start—it won't do to wait—right away

THE CHASE OF THE WHITE KANGAROO

to your big stake-fence yard at Coolpitta, we could yard them safely. The yard would hold our 150 head with the addition of 100 more. That will steady them down, and next day we can make Auburn stockyard; leaving you a good killing beast out of the 'cleanskins,' which will be a change from your eternal mutton."

I signified my assent, and sent for Tom Barnett, telling him to get the American waggon stored with all necessaries, including a roomy tent, and to hold himself in readiness to accompany us with it on the morrow. After the usual rubber of whist, we retired to bed and dreamland.

Next morning, after a bath and breakfast, we started.

Tom Barnett, as arranged, drove the station waggon, carefully packed with everything we required, including guns and the Terry rifle. We all carried revolvers.

George, booted and breeched, rode his favourite "Narry". Herbert "Poteen," Stuart rode "Doctor," one of our horses, and, as the blacks had failed to run "Charlie" in that morning, much to my disappointment, I mounted "Lucy," a thoroughbred mare of George's, to give her a little schooling in kangaroo running.

Stuart's man was left behind to look after his master's mules, and to be some sort of protection to Mrs. Barnett. I felt relieved at this arrangement, as on one occasion, narrated elsewhere, Tom Barnett and I had left the station on an affair of lost sheep, only to find her "bailed up" by blacks when we returned.

Tommy and Eacharn were of course enlisted and rode their own particular nags. As the cavalcade jingled off, I enlightened Stuart as to a few things he had not before seen, though I was glad to find him both a capable rider, a firstrate conversationalist, and a keen sportsman, with a great love for natural history and botany.

The smooth white trunks of the Auburn watershed river gums kept receding from us on the right. To the left the "yapunyahs" of the Seechal, at its junction with the river, showed for a little way in marked contrast, red shiny upper limbs, with a rugged base, but gum trees also. Then, as we progressed, they were shut out, and overwhelmed in the continuous "mulga" belt on the upper terrace of the Auburn, which we now skirted. Then, over this "mulga" belt, we sighted the tops of the grassy Boolooloo Downs, over which I had had many a successful run with the dogs.

I was forgetting to describe my kangaroo dogs, "Prince" and "Selim," both notable killers. "Selim" was a very handsome large red dog, with a jet-black muzzle, very fast, and a savage killer. "Prince" was a smaller red brindle, but a perfect demon, also very speedy. They trotted together just clear of my horse's heels, where they would remain until I gave them a warning low whistle, or a quick "S-s-t-t".

We crossed the Yalli creek, and pulled up to show Stuart our new woolshed, drafting yards, woolpress, etc., and then proceeded through far more open country, with grassy downs above us, and open patches of small plains in our immediate vicinity, whereon many small and large mobs of kangaroos were feeding.

Every here and there, as our horses clattered over small stony bits of rocky ground, where the iron-grey looking rock itself projected above the soil, the "squatter" pigeons would dart up with a startling flap, flap, flap of their wings in pairs. They are nearly the size of the common pigeon, whitish-yellow-grey in colour, firm, fat and plump. They are also most excellent for the table, and afford capital sport to the gunner. But it is very hard to make them out, and they will "squat" so close to the ground that a horse or a man will almost tread upon them before they condescend to rise. Also they prefer to take up positions on ground much of their own colour, thus favouring the deception. They lay their eggs on the bare rock in slight depressions, but make no attempt at a nest.

I asked Stuart if he would like a spin after a mob of kangaroo, and he willingly assented. So we turned off the main road and edged away along the inner edge of the open "mulga" country on our left until we came to a small plain where there was a large mob of emu feeding, about eight of them.

Well knowing that a sudden scare often enables the horseman to catch or kill one of these giant birds, I touched "Lucy" with the spur, and Stuart following my example with "Doctor," we were right amongst the mob before they realised what manner of terror we were. We were uttering frantic shouts also, and I shall never forget the confusion and panic terror of those emus! They ran in circles, tried to run off but came back again. Our sudden appearance amongst them from high kangaroo grass and undergrowth fairly rendered them senseless, some of them blundering right against our horses. And it was curious to see their gymnastic feats. I could easily have lassoed a big cock bird round the neck if I had thought of unloosing my stock whip, which was fastened in coils to the right D strap of my saddle. But instead of doing so I nearly fell off my mare with laughing. However, "Selim" and "Prince" were not to be denied, but with two fierce leaps at the neck they pulled down two immediately and the other birds rushed away.

A well-trained kangaroo dog always jumps for an emu's neck, and, when "running" them in orthodox style, it is extremely pretty when going at top speed to watch your two dogs, one lying on each side of the bird, to see first one dog and then the other bound into the air to catch the neck, the only vulnerable point. When one of them gets it over goes the emu, dog and all in a cloud of dust, rotten sticks and stones. The neck of course being broken, all is over at this point. We signalled our black boys, and skinned the two birds, packing them off to the waggon by the boys, and giving them orders to join us again when that was accomplished. Some of the wild station blacks, we well knew, would be along on our tracks shortly, and would appropriate the carcasses, as they always did when we took the kangaroo dogs out. Tommy and Eacharn, of course, lived on white men's "tucker," and, although their eyes glistened and their mouths watered, they did not touch them. On our way to join the others, we had a fine chase after a mob of kangaroos, "Prince," as he always did at the start, singling out the biggest "old man" in the crowd, and "bailing him up" by a large bloodwood tree at the base of the grassy downs near us; whilst "Selim" killed a "flying doe," after a much longer run.

Stuart was much impressed by the way "Prince" killed his big red "old man". We sat on our horses close by and watched him, the kangaroo manifesting a great desire to come and try conclusions with us. "Prince" was squatted on his haunches in front of him ready for a spring at the first movement. The run had not been nearly long enough to "wind" him, so he only panted lazily with his red tongue lolling out. The kangaroo always fights with his fore-arms and hands until he can get a grip of his assailant, and will guard a blow as a man would do from a policeman's baton, the most effective weapon to kill them with, except a revolver, that I know of. Only you must know where to hit. If an "old man" can once encircle a dog with its fore-arms, that dog's day is ended, for the kangaroo will then bring up his powerful hind legs, with the terrible cutting toe at the end of them, and the dog is disembowelled. But "Prince" knew all the tricks for and against in the killing process, and was never known to give a kangaroo half a chance.

He suddenly makes a lightning-like leap, seizes the right fore-arm of the "old man" midway between the elbow and the shoulder in his powerful jaws, gives a savage wrench, and breaks it like a rotten stick. Then a slight pause and another spring, when the other fore-arm is broken, and the "old man" is at his mercy.

Then he goes for the throat, drags the kangaroo, big as he is, prone to the ground, well aware of the kicking hind feet and powerful legs. He never lets go, but keeps on biting at the throat until the kangaroo is dead.

He drops in his old attitude by the body, gets his "wind" back, and trots off to the first deep hole of water he can find, where he immerses himself up to his neck. When he comes out again after a few thirsty laps he is ready for another.

We leave the black boys to bring back the tails, which are the only parts of the bodies we touch; the wild station blacks will have the rest. The other dog, "Selim," has also killed, but out of sight, and the two boys are already on the tracks. So we jog on, and catch up with the rest of our party at the eight-mile crossing-place.

A creek, the Boobara, comes in here. We are to go up it and camp at Baines's hut for the night, seven miles further. Old Scotty joins us, and notifies us that the station cattle are camped all right on the "Pottery" creek, at the Boobara plains, our *rendezvous*, and that the rest of the party were "tailing" them (keeping them safe) until we should join them.

Baines was delighted to see us. We pitched our tent on the banks of the Boobara, and Scotty and Barnett stopped at the old man's hut. Baines said he had seen the cattle two or three times, that there was a big mob of them, and they went

THE CHASE OF THE WHITE KANGAROO

to water sometimes at the water-hole in the middle of the plain.

Also, he had seen the bull, but his dogs had chased it off.

Next day we started again for the Boobara plains, and got there about midday. We had dinner, and leaving the men to pitch the camp by the big water-hole, where we saw many tracks of the wild cattle, George and I rode off to take a look round. We passed into a gully between the ranges, and heard cattle bellow two or three times. And we also saw the old Turk of a roan bull, looking down on us from the top of a precipitous bluff, throwing up dust, and tearing up tufts of grass with his fore feet, like the dangerous beast he was, "ready," as George observed, "for anything, from pitch-and-toss to manslaughter". Which was literally true.

From the bellowing of the cattle and the different directions of the noise, we came to the conclusion that there were over 100 "cleanskins" in the ranges.

Then a dispute arose between us as to the ownership of these unbranded beasts, and we finally agreed to divide the number got out, as the mob was on our ground.

"It's my impression," said George, "that the original founders of the mob came from Seechal, and if the few cows who started it are not dead we shall see my brand. A young mob may have joined them, but I don't think it. Still, they may have strayed this way in the big flood, having worked out here from the bottom of Seechal Creek."

Our work would be cut out for us to-morrow. That was self-evident. There would be some hard desperate riding, and we should have to work, both ourselves and our horses, like niggers to keep up with these wild "scrubbers," and finally force them out on the plain, to be "rung" in with our stationary mob of "ragers".

The camp that night was very picturesque. Our tent in the foreground, just clear of a rugged clump of box trees. The horses hobbled and browsing not far distant on the plain behind it, and our party moving about in front of our big camp fire, or reclining on our blankets in comfortable positions. There were five blacks altogether, including our two boys, and they had built themselves a large roomy 'mimi,' and were chatting, laughing and smoking. Last, not least, the American waggon near the water, with all our provisions, comfort and aggressive weapons in it. After tea we lit our pipes, and the inevitable bush yarns started. The cattle were camped on a "rise," about a quarter of a mile away, but the first watch of two mounted night watchmen had been set.

The station cattle seemed comfortable enough at present, but of course wanted looking to all through the night to prevent stampede. It was in relation to some remark about "tailing" cattle, that George, sitting upon his blanket, and assuming an oracular air, began a story, and I well remember his uplifted right hand coming into plain silhouette against the bright silvery surface of the full moon, now rising over the flat-topped hills which surrounded the Boobara plains.

Thus spoke George :—

"Well, you fellows, we shall probably have some sharp riding to-morrow in more senses than one. Sharp as to pace, and sharp as to mulga stakes for both horse and man, with a motto for the riders to look out precious sharp too. But I like work with cattle far better than with sheep any day, and it might not be inappropriate for me, whilst we are digesting that splendid 'bougali' curry of Stuart's—who seems to have picked up some divine wrinkles in his Garibaldian campaign—it might not be inappropriate, I repeat, my lords and gentlemen, to give you a little experience of my own, as a 'jackeroo,' on my very first lesson of 'tailing weaners' on a cattle station in New South Wales, where I first picked up my 'colonial experience'.

"It was on the Lachlan. Merowie was the name of the station, and Booligal was our nearest township. I worked as a rule in couples with another jackeroo named Kilpatrick, and he and I were detailed to 'tail weaners' at an out station. I didn't mean any pun, I assure you.

"You all know what 'tailing weaners' means, and how to do it, or if you don't you ought all to feel ashamed of yourselves.

"To proceed. Kilpatrick and I had been together as chums for over a year on Merowie, and had become great friends. He came of a good Irish family, was rather eccentric, and most awfully superstitious, but one of the best fellows I ever met, saving the present company, except when there was a ghost about. That paralysed him, and he wasn't worth a cent.

"We had had many a camp out together, many a hunt, and many a bird-nesting expedition, often returning to the station in the nesting season with our hats, shirts, handkerchiefs and pockets stuffed full of ducks' eggs, which we knew where to find in the hollow trees along the water-courses.

"'Tooriganny' was the name of the out station where we had to 'tail' those weaners. There were 300 of them, all as wild as March hares, which was not in the least to be wondered at, inasmuch as they had been imported, or rather, I should say, were descendants of the famous Clarence river breed of cattle, from the celebrated Diamond D. and Shield brands.

There was a good dwelling-house at Tooriganny, with two large rooms and a middle partition and door.

Plenty of wood and water, so that we were, or ought to be, content with our surroundings for an indefinite time.

"I knew that there was a decisive qualm in Kilpatrick's heart, however, to which I shall refer hereafter.

"The American waggon had been sent down from Merowie with blankets, provisions and cooking utensils, so we commenced to make a home of the place, and tidy up generally. The cattle yards were very large and extra strong, having been well and carefully constructed, also quite lately repaired in any weak point, so that, once yarded at night, there was no more anxiety about our mob of 'weaners,' and we could smoke our pipes, yarn and otherwise employ ourselves until further orders.

"Unfortunately for Kilpatrick, as I have before this hinted, there was a very unholy mystery hanging about Tooriganny. It was said to be haunted!

"Numerous tales had been told about it by benighted travellers and swagmen who had passed a night there, all agreeing on the one point, that there was something there that shouldn't be there.

"Some had spoken of curious noises, some of real apparitions, others of hearing something following them, whilst again others said that ghosts actually 'walked'. It was surely haunted. The disembodied spirits of a woman and a child, who were buried within sight of the doorway, were said to revisit the scenes of their former life. The poor woman had been the wife of a man who formerly lived there, and had charge of the place before our time. She died suddenly and her year old baby with her. Consequently, towards nightfall, my friend began to exhibit superstitious symptoms, nervously glancing about him from time to time, and nearly jumping out of his skin every minute. We had, up to now, a very easy time with the cattle, as some extra hands, including the head stockman, had helped us down with them from the station, but we were both pretty well tired, as young cattle take an extra lot of galloping after. They are very restless for some days after being separated for the first time from the common herd or mobs in which they were used to run.

"Our horses had been turned out on some splendid grass in a bend of the creek, and as we prepared our tea by a blazing log fire, from which the delicious ever-to-be-remembered scent of the burning pine arose, we could hear their bells tinkling cheerily and contentedly. When I speak of a bell ringing contentedly I mean it. You know perfectly well the accustomed camp sound, and by the very way the horse rings it you know his mood. If feeding, it has the contented sound; if dozing, it is still; if alarmed, there is a quick ring, then silence or more ringing if still frightened; if worried, a constant clatter, and so on. Many and many a night have I told myself what my horse was thinking of by the sound of his bell, and sometimes only dozed off when the 'contented' rang.

"But to return to Tooriganny. Apart from its ghostly reputation, the very appearance of the place was uncanny, no doubt gaining more local colour by the fact of the graves in front of the house, but we happened to have been impressed with the mournfulness of the situation of the house when we rode up that afternoon. It had been unoccupied for about two years. Long grass and weeds grew about it. The stumps which had been cut for fencing or firewood had sprouted dankly and vigorously again, and the whole place was almost buried with overgrowth. The great smooth, deep, black-looking water-holes in front of the door, the great white gums with their swaying, weeping branches, combined to give another ghostly reflection from the smooth, black surface of those dark depths, in whose unhallowed recesses the bunyip might well lurk; perhaps producing those very sounds the travellers were all afraid of. We both knew that not a living black fellow in the district would go near the place, and, as a consequence, the opossums swarmed in the hollow trees, and rioted and fed on the eucalyptus leaves in the depth of the sombre river forest. Now, in the dark night outside, Tooriganny was anything but cheerful. What with the disturbing sudden and constant 'hoo, hoo' of the nankeen cranes, the occasional melancholy howl of a warrigal dingo (wild dog), and the regular cry of the 'more-pork,' our outside surroundings were 'uncanny'. The cattle were bellowing also, and horning each other, not yet having settled down to their unwonted surroundings.

"But inside it was brighter and pleasanter. The hut was quite cheery with the blaze of the fire and the one candle stuck in a bottle; and, as I had my tea, my mind wandered to all sorts of pleasant times spent in dear old Australia. Kilpatrick looked as solemn as a graven image, although he rallied from time to time as if half-ashamed of himself.

"Well, to condense matters, we retired to our blankets after a comfortable smoke, and in a few moments I had lost all consciousness as far as the outer world was concerned. Some hours afterwards I must have been dreaming and half-awakened by something, but the next moment I was in full possession of my senses, and saw Kilpatrick, by the half-light of the fire in the still glowing embers, stealthily crawling towards me from his corner of the hut, his eyes literally starting out of his head with fear.

"'What is it?' I gasped, rather than exclaimed, for his face was so ghastly, the very personification of abject terror, that he fairly appalled me. 'Do you hear it?' he whispered almost inarticulately. 'Listen!' Sure enough, in the next apartment —remember the door was shut and we had securely fastened the windows—there was a movement of something, and a sort of rustling, scratching noise. We gazed at one another in horror. I thought Kilpatrick must have seen something fearful, and his face became paler every second, adding to my belief, and setting my heart hammering away at my ribs like lightning.

"And the dread intruders? Would they open the partition door and come forth in graveclothes to blast our senses by the awful spectre of death moving again on earth, unreal, unsubstantial, ghostly and horrible? Would they speak, or wail, or cry? The suspense was awful, far too much for a mortal to bear, and still the rustling went on. Leaping to my feet, I gave vent to a most appalling and unearthly bellow, the uncontrollable result of my pent-up feelings, in such volume of tone and vigour that it started our horses off, and set all the cattle in the yard wildly bellowing for the next ten minutes.

"Simultaneously with this explosion there was a violent fumbling and scratching in the next room, and two opossums raced up the rough slabs on to the top of the partition, from whence they proceeded to make tracks for the hole in the bark roof by which they had effected an entrance. Seizing the first thing handy, which proved to be a pannikin, I hurled it savagely after their retreating forms, giving another whoop of the same remarkable character, only with a spice more of exultation in it.

"On turning round, to my dismay Kilpatrick lay senseless on the floor! Whether his high-strung imagination had been altogether capsized by my awful war-cries I do not know, but thought it very probable, as at the time they had scared me myself. Suffice it to say that it was a considerable time before he came round, until at last with the aid of a small pocket-flask of brandy which we happened to have with us, and cheery conversation, I managed to force a smile out of him. And this did not happen until 'nerangi' daylight. But the memory of that night will never be effaced from our minds, for we had both worked ourselves up into a very high state of excitement. Kilpatrick perhaps was more overcome by nervous terror than I was. But I was quite bad enough.

"That very day now dawning, at about noon, after a stiff gallop or two with refractory weaners, and feeling very thirsty, I jumped off my horse, and, tying him to a tree, stretched down at full length upon my stomach to get a drink of water at a large pool. Close to my head was a 'roly poly' bush, of the sort which, during a dry season on the plains, get loosed from the main stem, which breaks, and the bush itself, being but a round ball of twisted elastic wire-like fibre, comes bowling in armies before the wind in a way calculated to alarm the best-mannered horse. Judge of my unfeigned alarm, when I saw out of the corner of my left eye, the flattened angry head of a black snake (*hoplocephalus niger*), the deadliest of the species in all Australia, about to strike! That half-glance was enough. Rapidly springing and rolling sideways, I got

THE CHASE OF THE WHITE KANGAROO

out of reach; the snake retreating again into the interior of the 'roly poly' bush, from which he had at first issued when conscious of my immediate presence! Leaping to my feet, I hastily cut a nice pliant long gum whip-stick, and put a lighted match to the bush, which was large and very dry. It blazed immediately.

"At the very first crackle of the flames, the long stealthy sinuous black body came quickly gliding forth, heading straight for the water, its forked tongue flickering rapidly and uneasily. Had any one got in his way then, he would have struck the death blow! Before he could reach the water however, crack! came down the sapling on his back, and there was an end of his trouble and—mine. We had a good time after that 'tailing' those cattle, and were complimented at headquarters for not losing a single head, but if Kilpatrick realised what deadly fear was during the ghost-'possum episode, I am certain I did so equally with him when I saw that vicious deadly flattened head so close to my face!"

So much for George's yarn; one of many experiences he could relate. And after further chat we rolled up in our blankets, and silence reigned over the camp. I felt restless, and after about an hour got up and took the "Terry" and a few cartridges out of the waggon, going away in the bright moonlight to see if I could get a shot at the cantankerous roan bull, if by any chance he might be tempted to come in to water during the night. I walked up to a water-hole on the edge of the plain, and found plenty of cover amongst the bulky sandal woods. Here I lay for about an hour, watching the trembling brilliant stars and listening intently. A light mist was rising anywhere near water, and enshrouding the hills and distant timber. I heard two or three bulls "routing" in the distance amongst the ranges, but our camp fire had no doubt scared them from the open plain. At last two kangaroos hopped up, affording a splendid shot in the moonlight, but at the very instant I was going to pull the trigger, after taking a careful aim, a mosquito got up my nose, and a small caterpillar was crawling on my neck. I wriggled and gave a violent sneeze, coincident with the bang of the rifle and the hurried departure of the untouched marsupials. They went faster than they had probably ever done for the last six months!

I returned to camp, went to sleep, and the next morning saw

George, Stuart, Herbert, myself and "Scotty," accompanied by Tommy and Eacharn, mounted, breeched, booted, armed and ready for the fray.

We jogged off, making for the gully George and I had explored, meaning to get round to the far side of the hills, split into two parties, and *ride* the cattle out. It would be desperate work, as these wild cattle can go through scrub as only "scrubbers" can, and we knew that the riding needed all *our* courage and activity, added to that of our horses, to cope with them in these fastnesses where they were bred, and where they knew the ground far better than we did. As we rode forward the sun was well up over the range, and we could see large mobs of kangaroos on the plain fringes, where the ground rose slightly, and was dotted with sandalwood bushes. They were hopping lazily about, some of them, and feeding, whilst others were lying and sitting up in shady spots, and watching us also with great curiosity. We had left the dogs in camp, as they would make these wild scrub cattle dangerous and unmanageable, and they were practically of no use until we had open country to work them in. I noticed my boy Tommy eyeing one group of kangaroos very curiously. They were near by, almost ahead of us, on the large stretch of open ground which narrowed into the gully where George and I had been exploring yesterday. The ground was quite white in patches where the triturated "copai," or native lime, had been washed from the higher ground of the hillsides.

"I say, Mitta Willie," excitedly cried Tommy, "mine make a light *flourbag*, big pfeller, old man, *flourbag* kangaroo!" By Jove, he was right! A pure white kangaroo, and a monster "old man" at that. Such a phenomenon had never been seen or heard of! What a "curio" the skin would be. I gave the word to the others, and away went George and I, Stuart lying behind on "Doctor" between us two. We rode as hard as we could go, cut him out, headed him towards the plain, and my fast mare was first close to him. I thought I would initiate "Miss Lucy" to "Charlie's" dodge by driving her full speed into the kangaroo, and knocking him over. I had done it when riding "Charlie" many a time. So I touched her with the spurs and she hit him fair, but at the wrong time, just when he had landed from a leap. Over we all went, such an awful cropper, mare, kangaroo and myself, mixed up in a crumpled

"I STRUGGLED TO GET MY REVOLVER FREE."

From the Land of the Wombat.

chaos of dust, kicks, snorts, native phraseology and kangaroo language. The "old man"—oh, ye saints, what a monster and what a white skin!—picked himself up and came straight at me, where I was gasping for breath on the ground, his eyes, claws and forearms working in the way I knew so well as meaning mischief. I struggled to get my revolver free, but could not undo the button of the leather case, do what I would, until he was almost on top of me. "Lucy" was 100 yards off, galloping as if her life depended upon it. Just as I managed to get the revolver out and fire it, the others were close up. What takes so long to write seemed an age to me, but was merely the matter of a few seconds. The flash and bang of my pistol scared the big fellow, and away he went with the others after him; only two yards off, but in the hurry and excitement I had clean missed him! Tommy brought "Miss Lucy" back again, and I was up and off in a moment, the mare's great speed bringing me up again; George lying level on the other side.

Away now, helter-skelter, right along the side of the plain open ground, except here and there where clumps of sandalwood, or high red white-ant mounds and pillars intervened. Forrard away, "lickety lick". And now followed one of those incidents which you try to explain afterwards and fail ludicrously to do so. Mad with excitement, and on the spur of the moment, my revolver, which had never left my hand, was ready. Bang! I went at the kangaroo. Flash, bang, from George's pistol on the other side of him! He was just in a line with me, and his bullet zipped along the ground just clear of my mare's hind legs as we sped past, and mine must have gone perilously near him. Flash, bang, from Stuart behind. Bang, bang, flash, flash, bang, bang, flash, bang, bang! Some one has hit him and over he goes—the fall of a giant!

We feel as if we had come through a cavalry charge, and it was nearly as dangerous, for George and I had been firing right across each other as hard as ever we possibly could. But "all's well that ends well," and in after discussion we could only be thankful that neither we nor our horses had experienced the checking power of a bullet! The white kangaroo is our own, and that remarkable fact makes amends for everything. We "plant" his body by covering it with brushwood, and thick sandalwood boughs, to keep off the hawks and crows.

Stuart has hit him in the spine, a remarkably good shot for a man going at full gallop. We jog off once more soberly, and get into the gully again. By the time our horses get over the flurry, and we are well on the other side of the hills, we see a few young cattle, which go off like lightning, George, Tommy and I—for we have divided our party—after them as hard as our nags could lay legs to the ground; up the hill into the scrub, and now comes the time when you must more or less let your horses take their own way, unless you want your neck broken, when an injudicious pull will certainly and surely accomplish it.

"Lucy" jumps every obstruction and races for the lead. My heart is in my mouth once or twice for low overhanging boughs. That means death, if you are not up to it! You must keep your eyes wide open, and judge your line ahead as far as you can, feel and work with your own will, legs and body, the swift powerful motion of the animal you are bestriding, helping all you can without checking or embarrassing. Throw yourself clean back, with the back of your head on the mare's rump if necessary, or stoop along her shoulders, low down along her withers, with an awful sensation of a coming crush in your back. To jump through a forked stem is another awkward experience, and if it looks too narrow, *you can feel whether it is or not* by the sensation in your *knees!* throw both legs forward *before* the knee-pads of your saddle, and take your riding grip there, instead of down the saddle. Now on for a furious three minutes, crashing through some obstructions and bounding over others. Thank God, here is a little more open space. There they are, a surging mob of horns, hides, fury and red clouds of dust surging with them. They are well together going hard. Here is George, as a veteran should be, on the opposite flank, well up to them, Tommy right ahead to steady them. Then another awful crashing match, under, over and through thick scrub, going full split, elbows up and arms across your face to protect it from swinging and intrusive branches. Let the mare go. "*Swing* them, George, *swing* them!" I roar, and down the side of the hill they come like an avalanche, with George on their right flank. There goes his stock-whip, as he gets the least elbow-room. The ringing crack, crack, crack, echoes in our very hearts! It is the first intimation to the wild mob that they are being *driven* as *we* wish. They recoil from it, and there is a hoarse bellow of fear and fury, for we have turned these "scrubbers" for the first time, fairly out-ridden and pressed them. "Keep them at it, give it to them," and with hoarse yells and shouts, we press them all we can!

"Now, 'Lucy,' good mare, get forrard, old girl!" and away she goes out on their left flank to give them another determined sweep off the slope of the opposing hill. Here there is a small winding gully where we hustle them between the hills, as hard as they will go, and we keep them at it, and in it, with our stockwhips going like pistol shots. Tommy is well forward. His little horse, "Bandicoot," can go through scrub like his namesake, and the boy rides as if he was nailed to the saddle, and is a great help to us. "By Jove, aren't we lucky? Out!" Here's the plain. Away to the left a little to give George a chance to wheel them. Out they come, going harder than ever. "Where the deuce are the station cattle?" Tommy is shouting and gesticulating far ahead. "There they are! See their dust over that ridge!" With a yell and a ringing volley from our whips, we turn our galloping host in the direction indicated, and in a few minutes the wild cattle are in the trap!

They "box" or mix with mutual roarings, but one has had no time to think. "How many did we get?" "Couldn't see for dust, old man, but I think about seventy good." I just cast a glance at him. What a scare-crow. No shirt, hardly any breeches, hat gone to glory, streaked with blood and scratches, and caked with dust, wildly excited, and looking like a mad savage. "Oh, George, George, and you *were* such a nice man for a small evening party, even to hold skeins of wool! What would *she* say now?"

My appearance is quite as bad, I think, but—

> We've got no time to tarry,
> We've got no time to stay.

And we must not wait to think. So we wheel the "station" and "bush" out on the open surface of the plain and give them such a half-hour's "ringing" in a "circle" that they haven't had since they were born. And oh, glory, here's Stuart and "Scotty" with a lot more, about forty head! I believe we have them nearly all. On they come like a travelling dust storm. In they go amongst the mixed lot, and then they get *their* experience of "ringing". We make a circus of that plain until we have got them pretty well steadied. Then we get a hasty snack, give instructions to Barnett to pack up, and come on with the waggon, leave Tommy to get the body of the white kangaroo, and then our strong body of horsemen take charge of the whole mob, and away to the big yard at Coolpitta. No food do they get that night, and just as much water as they can get on the way, and what they can snatch, as they crash and splash and rattle and stagger over the river ford at Coolpitta. But we yard every hoof of them successfully. We have given word to Barnett to drive round with Tommy and get the skin of the white kangaroo, and when he arrives we find that he has taken it off beautifully, tail and all. He soon has it on a clean sheet of bark, slightly pegged, to take off the bits of flesh and fat, and so prepare it for dressing.

The skin we find is a very light cream colour really, but the lime in the plains where he had been rolling, after perchance a shower or two, had made it look snow white in the sun.

But that skin was "a thing of beauty and a joy for ever," when tanned with yapunyah bark and doing duty on a couch. George left us a fine "cleanskin" heifer for killing. There wasn't a branded one amongst the lot, though they had no doubt originated from some of the Seechal stock. The old bull got out of our way that time, and was not seen again until he stuck George up a month later in the same place, but on this occasion he was laid low by a smooth-bore bullet. I never think of that rattling ride without the scent of the sandalwood bushes seeming to creep into my room, to see again the wild panorama of hill, bush and plain stretched away before me, and to say to myself in my inmost heart, "'twas well worth the living for!" And I sing also in cheery remembrance of work among cattle, and of those old days of friendship, health, hazard, and kindly beneficent fortune.

THE STOCKWHIP SONG.

See, as the dawn breaks rosy-red, the jovial stockman issue
From hardy bed, the "tracks" to tread o'er grass and dewy tissue.
His horse is found: on with a bound. He cries, "Why, soh boy, steady,"
We work together, you and I, for "mustering" we are ready.

CHORUS :—

We're off this morn at early dawn, from idling we must sever,
Give us the pace, the rattling race, and the stockwhip's ring for ever.

Amidst those hosts of "horns and hides" what joy to be a rover,
To ride along as the magpie's song with glee is brimming over;
To mark the "pad" as fresh and glad all Nature seems to quiver,
And freedom sweeps upon one's soul—a full and mighty river.

CHORUS: *We're off this morn, etc.*

And there's the herd! How sleek they look, how wild and wanton showing:
They "ring" and gore and fiercely roar, the man and good steed knowing;
And that whip too, its ringing thew, its lash so long and limber—
See, they're away! off shoots the bay, and heads them by the timber.

CHORUS: *We're off this morn, etc.*

When, hard-won day, the work is o'er, night's blue and argent curtain
Brings solace sweet, whilst visions greet his slumber, be you certain,
On those far plains where joyous trains of stockmen meet the rover,
He sweeps on steed of mettled breed, and all his cares are over.

CHORUS :—

We're off this morn at early dawn, from idling we must sever,
Give us the pace, the rattling race, and the stockwhip's ring for ever.

A FREE SELECTOR

> But each for the joy of the working,
> And each in his separate star,
> Shall draw the thing as he sees it,
> For the God of the things as they are!
> —*Kipling*.

TIM GALLAGHER was on his "selection". He had been there for a month. He was an uncommonly good-looking young fellow, about twenty-five years of age, tall, straight, well-set-up, with a laughing, yet determined, blue eye. He wore a cotton twill pink-and-white striped shirt, black silk neckerchief loosely tied, broad brimmed felt hat, riding breeches and boots, and the sleeves of his twill shirt were rolled up above his elbows, showing a brown and very muscular pair of arms. You could not help thinking as you looked at him, "Here is a man whom I would far sooner own as a friend than as an enemy". His character was denoted by his chin, which was firm, decidedly firm. It was also clean shaven, as was the rest of his face. As aforesaid, he had only lately come to live at Possum Creek, as this particular bit of the great Myall Downs cattle station was called, and he did so under the muttered curse of the Hon. Josiah Barnes, who owned every inch of it, with the exception of this insignificant atom, a few acres in a long triangle of land enclosed on two sides by Possum Creek and the Merowie River.

Myall Downs Station proper, with all the beautiful grounds, house and garden, was situated about seven miles down the river. The Hon. Josiah Barnes hated free selectors, and the idea of a nephew of old Gallagher's, the former owner, coming to live there and carry on the tenancy had been a nightmare to him, and his wife was well used to vituperation in his sleep on this subject, and I am afraid he was known to use on more than one occasion extremely bad language before his said wife and three blooming daughters on his *bête noir*.

But Mrs. Barnes and the three young ladies had a way and a will of their own to manage the Hon. Josiah, and under a present and passive acquiescence, generally contrived to do exactly what they wanted in the end. At present the second daughter had an interest of her own about the tenant at Possum Creek, though no one else was aware of it except her youngest sister, Lyddie, who had been in the secret from its inception.

Old Gallagher had been a riotous old scamp, and was more a nuisance than anything else, but he now had gone elsewhere, and it was generally understood that he had sent his nephew up to take his place. Tim Gallagher, the present tenant, had, like his uncle, no stock on the place except two remarkably powerful, speedy and well-bred horses, for whose accommodation and comfort he had erected a four-stalled stable, with ample loft storage for hay and corn.

He also had added to the appearance of the house by an extensive addition, and a new fence stretched across from the Merowie to the stream some distance up the river, enclosing the whole property. Another fence, with a slip panel, had been erected also from river to stream, about three hundred yards from the dwelling-house. It had been given out by passers by up and down the river that "young Gallagher was going in a 'perisher' for improvements," and these reports made the Hon. Josiah still more splenetic and outrageous. As he affirmed, the Gallaghers, root and branch, evidently intended to act upon the Gallic apothegm of *j'y suis, j'y reste*. People in the district also said that either old Gallagher "had struck it rich," or the young man had "made a pile" somewhere else, likely enough on the diggin's. Whatever the real case was, Tim Gallagher and his "mate," for he possessed even that necessary companionship for a lonely "selection," had put in a lot of work on their bit of a holding, and went steadily forwards day by day, in serene and undisputed possession. The reason that made most people talk of the progressive ideas of Possum Creek selection, was a seven years' knowledge of the fact that old Gallagher, or old "cocky" Gallagher, as he was called, seldom had the price of "drinks round" in his pocket, and if he had, he preferred to spend it to "wet his own whistle with," and *he* was never known to be progressive in this particular matter, or in any other.

He had preferred to "let things sweat," as he termed it himself, and it was this trait of the old man's character that provoked comment amongst the uninitiated of a certain class of free selectors further up and further down the river, and beyond the august confines of Myall Downs "frontage".

Unlike his uncle, the present tenant of Possum Creek enjoyed the reputation of being a jovial sort of person, and of being also a true son of "ould Erin". It was also affirmed that he and his friend, after a very free and easy selection of all the free selectors who had happened to be "having a spree" in Lignumville, seduced them all into helping their own selves to paint that town a particularly vivid vermilion before they departed for Possum Creek. This was on the occasion of their first visit to that infantile city, and the incident was remembered afterwards by those who awoke with "sair heeds" the next morning, and by many others also. That crowd declared that the two, Gallagher and his mate, "was out and out the liveliest cockies" (cockatoo farmers) they ever "seed," and the whole fraternity who lived on the river banks and sold "cords" of cut firewood to the river steamers when they were running, generally backed up this opinion, for they were always sure of a night's rest and unlimited hospitality at Possum Creek, whether they passed in boats or on horseback.

But old Barnes fumed, raged, and wished in his inmost soul that he could find some excuse which would justify him in ousting or buying out this free selection, the only one on his celebrated "run," and had expended much thought upon the way of doing so.

He had ridden there once, had been received with great hospitality, and presented with the most undeniable "nip" of pure Irish whisky, and had thought to himself, "Good as my own. Wonder where the fellow gets it? Good mind to ask him." And he did, and received full information, but was assured by Tim Gallagher himself, in a rich and racy Irish brogue, that the "ould min would not be afther givin' up the place widin' his loifetoime," and as improvements which were required by law were going on, the big "squatter" rode off slightly mollified, but completely upset with regard to his purpose of removing the little "cocky".

But he said after dinner in his beautiful drawing-room at Myall Downs, "How do I know that the Irish brute won't start a sly grog-shop there?"

And Lyddie, his youngest daughter, a sweet merry girl of sixteen, said roguishly and mischievously, " I am sure he will not, papa, dear. Tim Gallagher and his mate Bob caught 'Cossack' for me the other day when he broke his bridle after I had got off and tied him up, and they put me in the saddle again, at least 'Bob,' the 'mate,' did, quite nicely. And they mended my bridle too. That was Gallagher's work. And they both lifted their hats as I rode off. If Mr. Gallagher hadn't got that Irish brogue I am sure he would be quite a gentleman."

"That's your opinion, is it, Miss Puss?" remarked her father, visibly relenting. " But I know all the people in the district will do anything for *my* daughters. And the Hon. Josiah felt more important than usual with the recollection. And he also glanced with a parent's pride at his three girls.

They were all pretty girls. Boronia, the second daughter, was a dark beauty, a little stately in manner. Alice, the eldest, possessed brown hair and grey-blue eyes, and Lyddie has been already described. The Hon. Josiah might well be proud of them. I will leave their mother's description till later.

"Well," said the Hon. Josiah, "if Mr. Tim Gallagher does *not* start a sly grog shanty, so that all my grass will be eaten by loafing bullock and horse teams for miles around, and if my own store teams are not delayed by the illicit vending of liquor at Possum Creek, I will not interfere with the man, but if his awful old uncle comes back and begins to worry me again, I'll poison him. D—— free selectors!"

"S-h, papa," interposed Lyddie, "how can you say those horrid swear words? But you're not a bad old daddy, after all (giving him a hearty kiss). Now, I'll find your pipe and mix your grog for being good. Boronia will play and I will sing 'Tom Bowling' for you." And Lyddie, in turning, actually winked at her mother and sisters.

The Hon. Josiah Barnes was a sort of king of the district.

He was immensely rich, still in a vigorous prime, owned the vast extent of Myall Downs, with its many cattle and horses, possessed a charming house and grounds at Double Bay, Sydney, and was a member of the Upper House of Parliament in New South Wales.

Myall Downs, on the Merowie, was a favourite holiday resort for the family, as all the girls had been brought up on the station, and were fond of riding, Lyddie being the most level-headed and fearless of the trio.

Tim Gallagher is getting his tea ready in his house at Possum Creek, and it is noticeable that he is setting the table for two.

His preparations don't take him very long, for the "billy" is boiling, and the chops on a clean plate, peppered and salted, are ready for the gridiron, when there is a sound of horse's hoofs, and he opens the door to descry his mate, "Bob," on horseback outside. He puts his horse up in the stable and returns. Bob is another tall young man, but much darker in complexion and hair than Tim himself.

"Well, old man," Gallagher says, "did you get a letter from Dick?"

"Aye, and the money's invested all right," replied Bob, "£200 for you and £100 for me, in Broken Hill shares—'Wallaroo United'. Here are the papers"—throwing an *Argus* and an *Australasian* on the table. "Went to the tree post-office, coming by, but no letters to-day."

He hangs his felt Queensland hat on a peg near the door, and sits down on a bench by the table.

The place is plainly but very *strongly* furnished, after the usual manner of bush home-made furniture. There are two partitioned bedrooms off the main large room, and in these bedrooms these bachelors repose.

"Yes, our money is invested all right," resumed the new comer, "but I expect it to distinguish itself by following the other with the same persistent and singular fatality."

"All right, Bob; if it does, I suppose I shall have to carry off the girl, or set up as a bushranger and rob a bank or a gold escort to obtain the necessary cash, without which I am a villain and an impostor.

"But"—as the chops now frizzle cheerfully—" we had better have our tea. This sort of food is more healthy than club or hotel dinners, and we shall probably sleep sounder afterwards. The only thing which worries me is that it may be possible that I shall be found out, also that the finder out may be old Barnes himself. Then my cherished idea will vanish—like the marsupial which gives its name to this infernal creek—up a tree!"

"It's not a very aristocratic title," replied Bob; "why don't you re-christen it 'Honeymoon Flow' or 'Wait for the Wedding Streamlet,' or something else equally *apropos*. In any case, I'm here to aid and abet you, according to the arrangement we made together on board the *Australiana*. I don't think, even if I had not been cognisant of your plans, I should recognise you as I knew you then, if I met you suddenly and we had been parted for a week. Shaving off the moustache certainly does alter one's appearance. I'm open to bet that the Hon. Josiah couldn't recognise you anywhere. He hasn't done so yet, and, besides, he only got a glimpse of you with your moustache *on* at a ball in Sydney, didn't he?"

"That's all," replied Tim, and a 'cockie' in shirt sleeves, minus his hirsute appendage—isn't that it?—is very different to a mustachioed lar-di-da."

"Well, they none of them know me at all," said Bob, "though I have also sacrificed my manly beauty to help you. Still we *must* be as careful as possible."

"As you have been away at Graybank, Bob, for the last week, attending to that little bit of business, I felt rather lonely, but that blessed girl, Lyddie, managed to get down with a letter from Boronia to me. Lyddie has always been a true friend to me. There is a lot *in* that girl. She will make some one a good wife, if she marries a man after her own heart."

"Well, you haven't yet introduced me formally, and you have been deuced reticent, which I can hardly consider quite friendly on your part," replied Bob. "Suppose you let me see a few of the 'ins' and 'outs' of the case as it relates to yourself, old man, will you? Of course, I know that it is Boronia you want, but do be a little more explicit. You met me some two months ago in Sydney, told me your very existence depended upon me sacrificing myself on your behalf, and so, for the sake of our ancient friendship, I not only sacrificed myself according to your desires, but utterly obliterated all traces of my being on your behalf, with the sole exception of Dick, who is pledged to secrecy."

"Well, old fellow, I had my reasons," said Gallagher, " and we have been so busy helping the men to make improvements on this place that I have had no time to do so, and my plans were hardly matured enough to anticipate. But, now it is all over and we have spent nearly all our ready cash, I will tell you the whole circumstances of the case. My present name is Tim Gallagher and yours is Bob : as we agreed when we first came here.

"It is four months ago since I first saw Boronia. My affairs then were going to the dickens, or to the deuce, where they are at present. I was walking in the Domain close to the main entrance of the Botanical Gardens in Sydney one day. In front of me were two young ladies, Boronia and Lyddie. Just as they were entering a drunken lout was coming out. He said something to them, and planted himself in the gateway. You know I am not the sort of fellow to stand idly by when beauty and innocence are distressed, and as I quickly stepped forward I heard what he said the second time, and it made *me* blush. So I gave him something to keep for himself—two lovely black eyes, a broken nose, and a knock out, and escorted the ladies through, down into the gardens and along the waters of Farm Cove.

"I was knocked all of a heap myself, with Boronia, who was quite my style, and lost my head and heart at the same time. They told me where they lived, and I saw them home, but excused myself entering, which was reprehensible, and met them afterwards in the gardens several times, which was worse. Boronia and I became engaged entirely on our own hook. But before our first meeting of all, like the unmitigated ass I was, I had managed to lose the nest egg of £5000 I had to start in life with in a bally mining speculation. Besides this, I only had about £500 of my own—£200 of which has now gone as a forlorn hope.

"I was so mad with myself that I determined to see her once again in a proper way in society, and tell her that our engagement must end, also giving her the information that I had lost all.

"I could have shot myself, and the worst of it is that she

only knows me as Charles Wood. I can't well account for the deception, but, having started my incognito, I kept it up. How to break it to her now I hardly know, and after having made the silly mess I did, I cannot ask my brother to help me again, and I can't part with Boronia. There's an awful inducement to ignorant fools like me, fresh arrivals in the colony, to hazard a stake in gold mining with money which, if prudently managed, ought to set them up in life. It was the knowledge of this loss that made me lie to Boronia on the day I first met her. I found out that she was going to a ball at Pott's Point, and I managed to cadge an introduction through old Harding, who was awfully surprised, as I had never been society inclined before. I also got him to say nothing about my real name, and I went as Mr. Charles Wood.

"I danced three dances with her, and found that her affections were unalterably fixed, and that, ruined or not, it made not the slightest difference as far as she was concerned. So we agreed upon this plan of my coming up to Possum Creek, and I managed to square old Gallagher without much difficulty, pensioned him off in fact for an indefinite time. He is to come back to my improvements, and his beloved Possum Creek, when I send for him. And, of course, he knows nothing whatever of the other arrangements. I had to use a great deal of diplomacy to get to the old beggar to allow me to pass as his nephew. He said he hadn't 'got no blanky nephews, and didn't want no blanky nephews,' but I overpersuaded him. What's to come of it all I can't for the life of me see at present. The only thing which stands out clearly to me, is that I have made a bally ass of myself, in deceiving my dear girl.

"But that fatal first mistake and my pride would not let me confess. There doesn't seem to be any chance of picking up gold in this 'one-horse' sort of a place. Write home I won't, but when I get a chance I must tell Boronia my name."

"Well, old man, there's no mistake it was awfully foolish of you to go and risk that money, when you had it safe in coin of the realm. But even then, when all was confessed—about your name, I mean—old Barnes might have given you a share in a station for Miss Boronia's sake. He can well afford it."

"But, you see, unfortunately some confounded fool has gone and told him all sorts of things, not flattering to me, even as

Mr. Charles Wood. 'Fast,' and all that, and that alone would settle me."

"There is no one in Sydney who really knows me except old Harding of the bank. He won't tell, but he thinks me a fool all the same. When old Barnes saw and knew I had danced three times with Boronia, he cut up awfully rough, and told the poor girl never to see me or speak to me again. Gad, wouldn't the old boy be mad if he knew that we had corresponded ever since. Dear Lyddie does it all. S—s—h, what's that?"

Saying this, Tim Gallagher, *alias* Mr. Charles Wood, went to the slab door of the hut, and was accosted by two travellers.

"Good evening, boss," said the first comer. "D'ye mind us two chaps stayin' here to-night? We're strangers in this here part of the country, and we've been trampin' an' campin' out a good way."

"Come in, wid yez," replied Tim. Being only a free selector, and having no "men's hut" for wanderers, he was prepared to do the amiable for the sake of his good name, and ushered the man and his mate in.

They were ordinary specimens enough of the *genus* "sundowner". Each carried the orthodox rolled up "bluey," or blanket, on his back, and each had a "billy" in his right hand. They certainly looked tired.

Gallagher prepared to get them some tea, whilst his "mate," Bob, told them to sit down. After a steady look at the two men, it was noticeable that one of them, a thick-set bearded man, had an uncommonly quick, penetrating eye, and his companion seemed vivacious. They had a bottle of whisky with them, unopened, and, in return for the hospitality shown, produced it, drew the cork, and served out a "nip" all round. Then they had a hearty tea, lit their pipes, and became talkative.

"No work *your* way, I suppose, 'cocky'?" said the fair man. "You free selector coves is pretty well bore down and trampled on by them squatter coves. Any sort of a lay down at the station?"

"Sorra a one of me knows," replied Tim, as he pressed his foot upon Bob's to indicate strategy. "I'm new misilf to these par-rts."

"Come from ould Oireland likely?" said the second man.

"COME IN, WID YEZ."

From the Land of the Wombat. Page 152.

"Well, we're thinkin' o' tryin' the place to-morrow, to see if we can get a job fencin', or suthin' like it. Me and my mate's tired o' trampin' on these here roads. See you've got a bit of a stable here 'cocky'. I suppose you ain't 'ad any time to get stock inside that there fence o' yourn yet? But have another 'nip' mate; times ain't so bad as we can't afford a dram to our friends like." And so they had another glass.

The two hosts could not well refuse, but after a short time they both became so unaccountably sleepy that they turned in, telling the men to make themselves comfortable and sleep by the fire.

When Gallagher and Bob woke again it was noon on the following day, and they felt strangely oppressed.

The men were gone, and so were Gallagher's two famous valuable horses, "Assegai" and "Zulu".

"Bushrangers, by heavens!" exclaimed Gallagher. "Bob, those two devils will 'stick up' Myall Downs, and something may happen to the girls. What shall we do? It's lucky our boxes were locked, and the keys in a safe place. Pistols, my boy, and the boat! We can do it yet; I haven't pulled stroke oar for nothing. Get the oars and something to eat and in you get. Bob and he dashed into the hut, got what they wanted, and returned, when Gallagher resumed:—

"I've got an idea, old man. *We'll go as bushrangers too.* I don't want the old man to know me, even as Tim Gallagher, at first, and we may scare the real ones."

There was a very good strong boat, one of the few possessions belonging to Possum Creek really worth having when they first came there. She had been "planted" a little up the river, in a small inlet, and as "lignum" bushes grew thick about her she had probably escaped the bushrangers' observation. She was furnished with a good pair of long serviceable oars, and also a pair of sculls.

"These blackguards won't come into the river again until quite opposite Myall Downs," continued Gallagher, "for the road cuts out on the plains bisecting the ten-mile bend. We'll land at the lignum in the cattle paddock, and get up to the house under cover. I don't fancy these beggars will 'stick up' the station until pretty well dark, and then they'll have masks on to escape detection. *And so will we!*"

Bob started. "Well, Ha—I mean, Tim, you always were a devil of a chap for surprises. What *do* you mean to do?"

"I'm not going to have Boronia frightened out of her darling wits, that's all," rejoined Gallagher. She'll know my voice, and so will Lyddie, when I speak. You leave it all to me. First and foremost, no one will recognise us at the start, until I speak. Those that know *then* won't tell. If we are successful, we can unmask after our work is done. Those villains drugged us to get the horses. They knew jolly well that they wouldn't have got them without a fight any other way. Picked up some news about them as they came up the river, no doubt. I always have regretted that I rode 'Zulu' in that hurry-scurry down the river at Graybank.

"Horse thieves get to know too much. But anyway, the horses are far too good for bushrangers to have. Nice thing, indeed, to have our two good nags knocking about all over the country under a pair of robbers; and perhaps get a bullet somewhere to ruin them when the police run those brutes down. Now, I think these two will lay up in the two-mile scrub, and bail up the house at sundown. Well, we shall be there, close by, long before them. I wonder what they took us for?"

"Two new chums, of course," Bob answered. "Those two were 'old in the horn,' you can bet your bottom dollar."

"Well," resumed Gallagher, "I have an idea that if we succeed in circumventing them, it will be the making of us in old Barnes' opinion. I should like to gain his goodwill, and perhaps he will forgive me all my delinquencies. But I want to surprise him also, and do it my own way. The old beggar deserves a scare too, for listening to the aspersions on Charles Wood's character. Here's the post-office. Let us see if there are any letters."

The two young men ran the boat's nose into a grassy bend, got out, and, after hauling the craft up a bit, went inland a little way, and on examining an old hollow limb of a river box tree, sure enough there was a letter addressed to Gallagher. He perused it, and handed it to his friend with a grave face. Bob read as follows:—

"MY DEAREST TIM,

"I suppose I must not call you by your real name (Gallagher swore softly). You can't think how brave it makes me feel to have you so near me. Papa heard yesterday that there had been a bad case of 'sticking up' at Pallingerang. The bank was 'stuck up' a week ago at about four o'clock in the afternoon, but the men who successfully accomplished this got clear away. They were both mounted, and when the police neared them they found the two horses, utterly exhausted, but could not find the men, and they say there is no trace of them.

"I don't suppose they will come this way. Have you yet thought of what you are going to do?

"Your loving girl,
"BORONIA."

"H'm, pleasant," quoth Tim. "The worst of it is that the poor darling thinks I have got money, enough to marry on, anyway, and I believe would consent to an elopement and brave papa's wrath for poor, worthless me! Those are *our* men right enough. Boronia's letter accounts for their wanting my horses. They have changed their clothes to masquerade as 'swaggers'. Bushrangers never want for bush-telegraphs.[1] My girl is dreadfully nervous on the subject. Told me that was the main reason for not liking these visits to Myall Downs. She lives in terror of being 'stuck up'. Now we needn't hurry. Let's have a snack."

"Here you are," said Bob. "Here are some cold 'Johnnie cakes,' and a bit of salt mutton I collared in a hurry, whilst there"—pointing dramatically to the river—"flows the shining beverage! We shall find it more wholesome than the last whisky we drank. I haven't got the taste of *that* stuff out of my mouth yet. Eat, drink and be merry!"

After a hasty meal, and feeling much refreshed thereby, the two friends pulled on down the river with long, slow, silent strokes, taking care to keep well under the steep bank on the side the horsemen were, reaching at length the spot they had agreed to land at above the station. It was about half a mile from the big house.

They drew the boat right into some thick lignum in a small creek, where she would be invisible. Then they hid themselves.

---

[1] People, mostly swagmen, who keep them informed of police movements.

"We'd better wait till dark, and then go up and see how we can out-manœuvre these fellows," said Gallagher. "If we go up and alarm them now we shall frighten the girls, and when the 'gentlemen of the road' come and find us prepared there will be some shooting, and some one may get hit. Now, I want to prevent any shooting, if possible, and I believe in waiting for a good chance to get the upper hand of them. But we won't neglect anything on *our* side. We are free to shoot or not, as we wish, if they really 'stick up' the place. So let us carefully examine our pop-guns, and I will make the masks out of a big black silk handkerchief I have with me."

From where they were the two could see the way to the house, and from some distance in front of the door mounted men would have to travel on open ground where they would be distinctly visible.

"They will be certain to have had information that the overseer, storekeeper and stockmen are away," mused Gallagher. "That leaves only old Barnes, Mrs. Barnes, the three girls, and Mrs. Ayles, the cook. The bushrangers will never let such a chance go by; and if there is any money or weapons in the house they will have them. Of course, they had revolvers in their swags. The scoundrels may want to stay all night, and make themselves comfortable. "I'll prevent that."

They waited patiently till dark. Just before that they made out two mounted men ride up to the verandah, call out, and 'bail up' the Hon. Josiah, presenting two pistols at his head. Then they dismounted, tied up their horses, and entered the house.

"On with your mask, Bob, and let us get ahead!" exclaimed Gallagher hastily. "I'm quite stiff and cold with waiting."

A scream from the house broke in upon them when they got nearer.

"By heavens, come along," almost shouted Gallagher, crimson with passion. "I'll shoot any one dead who lays a hand on Boronia! Come on!"

"Easy all, old man; we mustn't give ourselves away," coolly replied Bob. "I'm with you, death or glory; and if any one touches Lyddie, I'm there too, but let us be cautious at first."

During their stay in the "lignum" they had made two very serviceable masks out of a large silk handkerchief of

Gallagher's, cutting eyelet holes and a small slit for the mouth. These when tied at the back of the head and reaching to the chin, gave a very business-like appearance, and completely concealed their indentity.

It was now quite dark, so they stole rapidly to the house, and made out the existing state of affairs. The bushrangers' horses (Gallagher's) were tied up to the verandah horse-pole. Apparently there was gaiety in the drawing-room at the end of the house. The lamps were lit, and there was music. A glance through the window at the back revealed the Hon. Josiah Barnes, safely and securely tied up in his own arm-chair; Mrs. Barnes cowering in a corner. One bushranger was sitting drunkenly at a table, with several spirit decanters and a half-emptied glass in front of him. A frightened girl, Boronia, was playing the piano; the other two, with pale faces, were sitting near her. The other bushranger, the fair one, was tipsily pretending to turn Boronia's music for her, *and both revolvers were on the table."*

"Go round like a cat and collar our horses, mount, and guard the front door, Bob. I'll do the rest," whispered Gallagher. "Make a bit of a noise when you are safely mounted." The window was wide open.

"Sing us another song, lovey," said the fair man. "You play nice, but I want another song now, and perhaps when that's done you'll give us a kiss. I likes a kiss from a gal, and likes it better if she is good-lookin'. The old bloke won't mind, and if he does, why, he can't get out of that there cheer."

Boronia flashed an indignant glance at the speaker, and just then there was the sound of horses' hoofs at the front of the house.

"Damme, Bill, mind them horses, quick," said the fair man, and the other lurched outside; but where he expected to find the horses he was met by a cool, determined, mounted man, completely masked, who levelled a pistol at his head, and whispered sternly: "Bail up, hands over your head at once or I'll drill you! If you move a step or sing out you're a dead man!"

This was at the end of the verandah, and bushranger No. 2 was so sobered by the unexpected, that he put his hands up at once, saying to himself: "Another blanky bushranger, by gum!" Inside, a masked and armed form has entered noiselessly by the window, and taken possession of the revolvers on the table, covering the man at the piano with his own weapon.

"Hands up!" shouted Gallagher in a voice of thunder. The man turned round and did so, with a look of astonishment and alarm, saying huskily: "And who the h—l be you?"

"Thunderbolt," replied Gallagher calmly. "I'm in this game. Go yez over to that corner and stay there," pointing with the hand gripping the robbers' revolvers.

The man went at once. Still keeping him covered, Gallagher went over to the Hon. Josiah, who was purple with rage and indignation, dropped the two revolvers into his lap, and cut his bonds with his sheath knife.

The Hon. Josiah, the very picture of amazement, then removed his own gag himself.

"Tie that min up," said Gallagher to the Hon. Josiah, pointing to the bushranger. "If yez resist," said he sternly to the latter, walking close up to him, "Oi'll shoot yez loike a dog!" Gallagher had a pistol in each hand now, and he motioned to the girls to secure the other. Boronia did so.

Lyddie rushed forward to help her father re-tie the rope which had bound him so short a time before. It had plenty of length however. The Hon. Josiah was a pretty burly specimen of manhood, and thoroughly enjoyed the feat of tying the bushranger securely, hands behind his back, and feet and legs firmly together. He evidently remembered his own treatment. When Gallagher and he had both satisfied themselves that their captive was perfectly secure, the Hon. Josiah appropriated the revolver Boronia was holding, and the two men went out into the verandah, and bound No. 2, Bob keeping *him* covered during the process. Then Bob put the horses in the stable, and that done, the three of them went and carried No. 1 out, and placed him with No. 2 in a small skillion room at the end of the verandah, locking the door, and agreeing to watch one at a time, at the window, where they could see every movement. Then a signal whistle was given to the blacks' camp, and two of them coming up at once, one was stationed by the window to give an alarm of any movement on the part of the two prisoners. And the other was mounted, and sent off for the police.

Then our heroes took off their masks, and made known their identity as "free selectors". Old Barnes drank a glass of whisky with them, and accompanied them over to the kitchen, where Mrs. Ayles put a right royal spread before them. Old Barnes was loud in his eulogies of the daring and discrimination displayed, and the girls peeped in wonderingly from time to time; but every one preserved grave countenances. Barnes had departed with a revolver to watch the desperadoes, and the "language of the eye" had time to speak a hurried message between Boronia and Gallagher.

At daylight, after the captors had carefully watched the bushrangers through the long hours of the night, the police, Sergeant Hiley and Constable Devine, arrived hot foot and carried them off, after they had partaken of refreshment, to the durance vile of the lock-up at Lignumville. The two pseudo bushrangers were warmly complimented upon their tact and skill by the police, Sergeant Hiley telling them that it was a pity they were not both "in the for-rce," and adding, "if the likes of you two 'cockies' were everywhere about, it's little throuble the mounted police would have entoirely. Gallagher, you and your mate are a credit to ould Oireland."

The worthy sergeant knew all about the "vermilion painting," and had his suspicions, emphasised by a knowing wink. Very little escaped the sergeant, but like a wise man he "kipt" his own counsel.

Certain police preliminaries had to be gone through concerning the prisoners, and these were concluded at a full muster of all present before the Hon. Josiah Barnes in his capacity of magistrate. When all depositions had been taken, and a warning given to those principally interested in the capture that their presence would be required for the county assizes at Lignumville, the police left with their prisoners.

Mrs. Barnes expressed her thanks cordially and gratefully to the two young men, and Barnes said oratorically to his family in the dining-room, whilst our heroes were getting their breakfast modestly in the kitchen: "Never thought a blanky free selector would have such pluck. I've half a mind to make that young Gallagher a present of Possum Creek for the rest of his natural life. And everybody, especially Boronia and Lyddie, acquiesced cordially. Lyddie had somehow got hold of a note which had found its way into *her* hand from Gallagher's. This was what was written in it, when the two girls read it in their own bedroom :—

"MY OWN DEAREST LOVE,

"I think we have scored by *this* little adventure. Couldn't you manage to send another letter in a day or so? I could willingly have shot that brute when he was so impertinent to you, but I thought judgment was better than rashness. 'Bob' is a friend of mine, and a very nice fellow he is. We came out together from the old country in the *Australiana*.

"Yours for ever and ever,
"CHARLIE."

Gallagher and Bob rode back to Possum Creek, and put "Assegai" and "Zulu" back in the stable again, where they did not want for a good feed after their bushranging experiences.

Tim Gallagher was always very particular about his horses' comfort, and used to get supplies of hay and corn for them brought from anywhere he could manage. The next day the two of them walked down to where they had left their boat, and brought her back up stream, calling at their bush post-office, where Gallagher found another letter from Boronia.

"MY DEAREST CHARLIE,

"I *will* put that in now. (Gallagher swore a second time.) "I can't find words to express my admiration for your courage and address.

"I think you managed the whole affair beautifully. Lyddie is going to slip down and see you one of these evenings.

"The wife of one of the boundary riders has not been very well lately, and she is going to take her a few little comforts.

"Your own BORONIA."

"P.S.—Mr. 'Bob' is, we all think, very nice-looking. He certainly has proved himself very cool and determined. Of course, we girls see through his disguise. We can see that he is a gentleman. What *would* papa say if he only knew?"

Tim Gallagher looked rather grave as they rowed back.

"What a devil of a thing this money is," he said out loud. "Here is as nice a girl waiting for me as a man could well hope for. Here am I, having introduced myself to her under a false name—a crime in itself—and using another under disguise to prevent her father finding out the false one, crime No. 2, only more pardonable under the circumstances. I'm blest if I can see my way out of this business, Bob. It's the want of cash, and the lack of respectability that capsizes me, and I see nothing for it but to make a clean breast of my sins to Boronia."

"Oh, she'll make that all right, old chap. You haven't done that much to grieve over, only told a few crams and used some one else's name. *Heaps* of 'so-called' respectable people do that every day."

"I meant to have told her at first, and would have done so, but that confounded loss, and my equally confounded self-estimation came in. I had made certain too of getting something out of that confounded mine, and lost every halfpenny, and that upset me. I'll tell her everything the very next chance I get."

Lyddie Barnes came down one evening riding "Cossack," one of her many favourite horses. She blushed when she saw Bob, but very soon placed herself on a perfect equality with him. She was a fresh, pretty, bouncing girl of sixteen, a regular romp, fond of fun, and very good-natured. In fact, she was a healthy, hearty Australian girl, and in saying that I have said all I possibly can in her favour.

"Oh, Charlie—I forgot—Tim Gallagher, Mr. Tim Gallagher, if my father catches me talking to his pet *bête noir* I don't know what he will do. Pack me off to Miss Crutchison's again in Sydney, I have no doubt. But, Charlie, dear, Boronia wants to see you so much. I think we might manage to arrange to meet, if you come down in the boat as far as the end of the river home paddock. My horrid parent is going away on business somewhere up the river to-morrow."

"Well, dear," said Gallagher, "we will come to the spot indicated on Tuesday, say by ten o'clock in the morning, without fail. Give Boronia my best love, and give me a kiss my dear, good fairy. I don't know what I should have done without you, Lyddie. But I am afraid I shall have bad news for you. Now be off. We mustn't risk anything. Bob's at the boat, you had better say good-bye to him. I rather fancy he thinks a lot of you."

"Oh, you bad brother, putting such ideas into my head. But there, I'm off. Oh, I forgot to tell you that there's a friend of ours—no, Alice's—coming to stay at Myall Downs, who will arrive before papa goes. A Mr. Meakin. He is dreadfully inquisitive. Oh, good-bye, Mr.—Bob. I don't suppose for a moment that that is your *real* name, but it must do for the present."

After Mr.—Bob had very adroitly placed her in her saddle, and raised his hat to her, she cantered gaily off, kissing her hand to them from the turn of the road by the pine bridge.

"By Jove, Tim, the young one *is* a beauty! I'm half gone with her already. She's sweetly pretty, and I'm blest if I don't think she's far away the best of the three."

"Every man to his own taste, Bob. But Lyddie *is* a darling, and as plucky as she is good. A real downright honest girl!"

During the interval of two days to the fateful Tuesday a mounted trooper called with an official letter containing a subpœna each for the coming trial. After his departure the mailman rode up with several home letters and papers, including one from Bob's mining agent in Melbourne, which hinted favourable things. Bob had also invested £200 in "Wallaroo United," as he said he meant to back Gallagher's luck.

"And, Ha—Tim, I mean. I shall be letting the cat out of the bag some of these days. Hang it, man, why can't you stick to your own name as I knew it in the old country. What does your brother say?"

"Says he thinks he has done well for me and expects me to do well for myself. I knew that already, but feel the worse now for his hints. He has, of course, claims of his own, and it's a deuced expensive regiment. He's spent a lot of money too since he came to the ti—— But *I'm* forgetting too. He has acted like a brick to me. Paid what money I owed, not much, thank God, but he gave me a clear five thou. for a start. And then I go and chuck it away. I ought to be shot!"

"Not you, old man, or you might have been the other night, only we held too good a hand of trumps for *that* to happen. But to-morrow will bring to pass our eventful meeting, perhaps parting. I only hope that I shall get a sight of the fair Lyddie."

The expected day came, and they rowed the boat to the place appointed, and had not long to wait, for Boronia and Lyddie joined them almost to the minute. Gallagher took Boronia out of earshot to a piece of rising ground covered with bushes in the bend of the river, where they sat down on a fallen tree to converse, whilst Lyddie chatted with Mr.— Bob.

Boronia was *brunette* to Lyddie's *blonde*. She was beautiful to look at, with dark blue eyes, and all other attributes which make up a maiden's charm. She was distinctive from her other sisters for a certain queenliness of manner, a sort of great lady air, which was entirely devoid of pride or ostentation, being simply natural to herself; and although this particular manner of hers imparted a sort of *noli me tangere* effect to strangers, she could be particularly soft, lovable and winning if she cared for any one, as Gallagher well knew.

"And now, my dear Boronia," he said, breaking the ice at once, "I must plead guilty to practising a deception upon you, innocent enough in intention at first, yet now to me unbearable, for I love you very dearly. I have only to tell you my story and you will easily see for yourself to what extent I have been justified, if indeed I have been justified at all, in your sight for what I have done."

"My dear Charlie, why do you speak so mysteriously? *What* have you done?"

"Well, here is my confession," replied Tim quickly.

"I had arrived from England with my friend, Bob, only about a month or so before I first saw you. I came out here under a false name "—Boronia started—" with the set purpose of making money somehow. I had been living beyond my means in the old country, and, like many another younger son, was of the opinion that I could better my circumstances in the new world and achieve an independence.

"My eldest brother paid my debts and gave me £5000 to start with. It was a most generous act, but, unfortunately, just before I met you and Lyddie, I had risked every penny of it in a mining speculation and lost it all. It was but a bankrupt concern at its best, I believe, and heavily involved; and I have melancholy reason for knowing that the very man who represented it to me as a splendid investment was a defaulting partner in the mine, for he disappeared with my money. My endeavours to trace him were futile, and I paid bitterly for my fruitless and foolish trust.

"Of course, I was utterly ignorant of these mining matters, only trusting to the prospectus I saw on paper, and was led away by the specious and friendly manner of the man himself. He represented it as a grand form of investment for my money, and likely to treble it in six months.

"I have a little money of my own still, but I shall have to work hard to earn a living. I thought it right that you should know this, and also that my name is not either Charles Wood or Tim Gallagher."

"Oh, Charlie—I suppose I must still call you that—how dreadful. But you know that it is quite as much my fault as yours. In the first place, I never should have consented to meet you in the rather clandestine manner I did without my parents' knowledge, but my heart was yours, Charlie, from the very moment you protected us from that wretched drunken man, and since then you have saved me from another ruffian. Oh, Charlie, dear, my heart will break," and she sobbed drearily.

Just at this moment some one on horseback, a gentleman in clerical garb, appeared close to them. He was apparently greatly discomposed, and astonished beyond measure.

"Dear me, Boronia, what is all this about?" he exclaimed, as they rose hastily to their feet (the blessed friend, I suppose, thought Gallagher), "has this—er—young man been making you cry?"

"Mr. Meakin," said Boronia angrily, "will you have the goodness to mind your own business for once in a way? I did not think you would come prying down here at all, being sure that you would be much more in place with mother and Alice."

"Dear me, Boronia, if that is your opinion I will take myself off, but is your respected mamma aware of your meetings with this—ah—gentleman?"

"You had better take yourself off at once, sir," said Gallagher fiercely; "I also brook no interference."

"Very well," replied the Reverend Topaz Meakin severely, "I will. Good-day," and raising his hat he rode off.

"Oh, this is dreadful," exclaimed Boronia with much concern. She had completely recovered herself now, and became a heroine at once.

"Topaz is a dreadfully prying man," said she. "He must have noticed us coming down this way, and then set off to find us out. What *shall* we do?"

"There is nothing to be done now, my dear," said Gallagher calmly, "except for me to make your mother acquainted with the whole gist of the matter and abide by her verdict. No chance of the Hon. Josiah dropping in casually is there?"

"No, indeed," replied Boronia, "he won't be back for a few days. He said he couldn't bear to leave us before the Reverend Topaz came up, but he has most important business to attend to. And he was also comforted by the thought that the overseer, storekeeper and stockman are expected back to-morrow without fail. We shall be all right when Mr. Beresford returns. Poor mother, what will she say to us?"

"I'll 'coo-ee' for the others," said Gallagher, and having done so Lyddie and Bob joined them.

"Oh," said Lyddie, "what are we to do now?"

"I am going to your mother at once, dear," replied Gallagher. "You had better come too, and Mr. Bob will wait with the boat."

And the trio departed on their way to an interview with an indignant and exasperated mother at the big house. They entered. Boronia showed Gallagher into the drawing-room and left him there. Presently Mrs. Barnes came in, and Gallagher was face to face with a crisis. Mrs. Barnes was a portly dame, with a good-looking and good-natured face, but she was, by her manner, evidently in ignorance of the whole affair. Indeed, she thought it was quite natural that the girls should have come up with Gallagher. Had he not saved them from the bushrangers but a short time ago, and were they not all under the greatest obligations to him? The Reverend Topaz was too much of a gentleman to say anything until he was quite aware of Boronia's wishes; and, pending those, reserved any disclosures. If not satisfied on this head, however, he would deem it his duty to acquaint her father.

On Mrs. Barnes' entry Gallagher stood up, hat in hand, waiting for her to speak.

"How do you do, Gallagher?" said she. "Do you wish to see me particularly? I hear you are the nephew of the man who lives on our run. My daughter told me that you wished to see me. Can I do anything for you? I know that

Mr. Barnes is going to express his thanks and gratitude for the timely and brave manner you and your friend, Mr.—eh? —'Bob,' helped us against those dreadful bushrangers. I freely express my thanks now—warmly shaking Gallagher's hand—and the thanks and gratitude of my daughters. Mr. Barnes is away at present."

"Madam," said Gallagher colouring, "I had better come to the point at once. I love your daughter, Boronia." (Mrs. Barnes' start of incredulity and amazement was splendid.) "I know your daughter loves me." (Another worse start, and Mrs. Barnes walked determinedly to the bell-rope.) "Madam, hear me, I implore you," exclaimed Gallagher interposing. "I met your daughter not long ago in the paddock by the river below the house by appointment." (Another reach for the bell-rope.) "But, madam," continued Gallagher, "pray restrain yourself and your very natural feelings against me until I have finished my explanation."

"He certainly is very good-looking, quite *distingué*," thought Mrs. Barnes.

"One day I was walking in the Domain towards the Sydney Botanical Gardens when I saw two young ladies, your daughters, just about to pass through the entrance gates. They were unceremoniously treated by a person who, unfortunately for himself, had taken too much to drink. I interfered, offering my services to escort the young ladies further down the gardens where they would be unmolested. I was much impressed with your daughter Boronia's beauty, and gave her on the impulse of the moment the name I had borne on the steamer I came out in, which was not my real name. I have been very sorry for it since, especially as I have got to love her better than my own life, but I was in a peculiar position at the time, which I will further explain. I had lost all the money I had safely put by to start in the country with. I drew it out of the bank and lost it in a mining venture, and I was too proud, or too thoughtless, to tell your daughter the real truth. But before our interview ended, I found that she was the girl I had often dreamed of. Her wit, her education, her great beauty, completed my subjugation, and I was in love with her, for herself alone, before we parted. The next time we met accidentally, and I found myself more hopelessly entangled and more in love with her than ever. I knew that I should have called, even in my assumed name of Charles Wood, but I had no means, and no visible present way of making a living. And somehow, now, I *could* not give my real name, as I was entirely dependent upon my brother, and felt that I had treated him very badly. I pined for a sight of your daughter, and I persuaded her to meet me again and again. Then I got an invitation to a ball I knew she was going to, and Mr. Barnes saw me dancing with her and made inquiries. Some false friend circulated injurious reports about me, and Mr. Barnes cautioned his daughter and forbade her to speak to me."

"Oh, then, you are Mr. Charles Wood, that hopeless young man, and you are merely masquerading in the *rôle* of old Gallagher's nephew? What does it all mean?" cried the bewildered matron. "I can forgive you a great deal for your noble conduct the other night, but under the circumstances I must request you to give me your *real* name, as you have stated to me that you have assumed one. You must be aware that that sort of conduct is very serious."

"And that, dear madam, is the very reason that makes it so hard to give you my real name. To assume one, and get it talked about disadvantageously was bad enough, but it made me ashamed to own the truth, because I should not like my brother to know about my loss, and he doesn't know me as Charles Wood. It was a mere whim of mine at first, and after deceiving your daughter it was very hard to think of it even. Of course, you could not expect me to ask for your daughter's hand if I could not support her in the way suitable for her rank in society. I am only, owing to my own culpable folly, a man who will have to work for his daily bread. I have been compelled to come here to-day to tell you the circumstances and to free your daughter from all blame, for I respect her equally with yourself, and would lay down my life for her cheerfully if I thought it would do her any good. It was our meeting with Mr. Meakin that brought me up here at once."

Mrs. Barnes, who was a very worthy lady, relaxed a little at the lover-like idea of Gallagher's laying his life down, and interposed with a slight smile:—

"I should rather say, Mr. Woo— Gallagher—oh, dear me—that it would be better for you to think of *living*. Have you no friends?"

"Only 'Bob,'" said Gallagher despondently, heaving a deep sigh.

"But in England, I mean?" reiterated Mrs. Barnes.

"Yes, a few," responded Tim.

"Well, I should advise you to write to them. Of course, I cannot permit you to see my daughter any more, and what I am to do with that tiresome Mr. Meakin now, I am sure I do not know. He will be certain to speak to Mr. Barnes, and we shall have a stormy time. But whether Mr. Meakin saw you or not has nothing to do with my duty, Mr. Gall—Wood—and I must forbid all communication from this day forward."

"Madam," exclaimed Tim excitedly, "don't blame your daughter in any case; you can easily see that it was entirely my fault."

"I don't blame her," said the poor lady to herself. "I should have done exactly the same when I was a young girl if I had been rescued by such a handsome young man." But she only said aloud, "Oh dear, oh dear, what *will* it all come to?"

"But, madam," said Gallagher uneasily, "you have been so good to me, so lenient in spite of all the trouble and grief I have caused you, that I will tell you my name, if it will only satisfy you that my intentions were honourable. Only don't mention it to any one. Think of me as an honourable gentleman at least, and one who loves your daughter most dearly. Until I can claim your daughter in a more orthodox and reasonable way than in my present circumstances could ever be granted by you, I will abide by your decision. I had a mother very dear to me a few years ago, but she is dead, and, pardon me, madam, but your voice, manner, and even your face, remind me of her. Here is my card." And he handed it to Mrs. Barnes. Mrs. Barnes adjusted her gold-rimmed *pince-nez* and scanned it. It bore his London address, and was the last he had.

"Dear me," said Mrs. Barnes, reading the card, "I have a sister in England who knows that family, and she has written of you to me. You will be the Hon. Ha—Gallagher, I mean."

"Quite so, my dear madam. Your sister spoke well of me?" (anxiously).

"Indeed, she did. Mr. Ha—dear me, how you do confuse me with your three names. Then, if anything untoward should happen to your brother you would be Lor—Woo—Gallagher, I mean. I will write at once to my sister. She has met your brother often, and knows all about your family. She has, in fact, told me that you have been extravagant."

"Far too extravagant for my means, madam," replied Gallagher.

"Well," said Mrs. Barnes, "I will not tell a soul; but how you will get on with Mr. Barnes after this I don't know. You must remain as Tim Gallagher for the present, anyhow. Mr. Barnes will probably send you some money, or make you a present of Possum Creek, in that character." And Mrs. Barnes laughed.

"Madam," said Gallagher, "I have, of course, told your daughter to-day all the story. The one thing which stands between us is money, and that I must earn myself, or I can never ask her parents' permission as to marriage. And now may I take my leave? I think I can promise to save you from any annoyance through Mr. Meakin, by speaking to him privately."

Mrs. Barnes left the room, and sent Boronia in, all smiles and tears. There was a hurried embrace, a parting word of "Cheer up" from both of them, and then, as Mrs. Barnes re-entered, Gallagher actually shook hands with her. Nay, he did more, for he deliberately and solemnly kissed her. Then he kissed Lyddie and Alice, and departed, waving his hand.

He then went down to the boat, joined Bob, and the two pulled laboriously back to Possum Creek. The river was high, three-quarters full, which told of rain at the higher sources, and the weather had been threatening for the last few days. As they sat down in their small house to their frugal meal of "Johnnie cakes," chops, tea, and bread and butter, the latter imported from Lignumville, through the kind offices of the mailman, Bob said, "I never saw any one like you for getting out of scrapes, Gallagher. I say, I have proposed to Lyddie; and now what on earth are we both to do?"

"Like your cheek," said Gallagher smiling. "And what did Lyddie say?"

"Took it like a lamb," answered Bob. "But hark to that."

There was a roll of distant thunder. The forenoon had been

very hot, and dark clouds had been banking up to the south all day.

"H'm," quoth Gallagher, "we had better finish our tea, and see to the horses and the boat. I expect there will be a general break-up of the dry season now, and as this selection lies rather low, we must take all precautions in case of flood. I am more uneasy about the horses than anything else. Should much rain fall, they must be taken away to a place of safety. Have another chop?"

"Thanks, we're both getting to be rather good cooks now, I fancy. What a bother that fellow Meakin turning up is. He'll split to old Barnes for a certainty."

"I'll stop him if I catch him," said Gallagher.

It was now raining in torrents, and having by this time finished their meal, they went out and secured the boat, hauling her right up and fastening her securely.

Then they attended to the horses, fed them, watered them, and littered them down for the night. They were just going into the house after the conclusion of these necessary duties, and Gallagher was in the act of closing the door, when he exclaimed hurriedly : "Look out, here comes that chap Meakin! He's just putting up the slip rails. He has been caught in the rain and is no doubt seeking shelter here. Look sharp, on with our masks and get the pistols! Hurry up!"

This was done in double-quick time, and Gallagher having shut the door, sat very near it. The Reverend Topaz came up gingerly. He was very wet, and the rain was increasing. Seeing a stable, he thought he would ask permission to put his horse up. As he had never been in the Myall Downs country before, he knew nothing of Gallagher's location. He meant to ask permission to remain until the storm had ceased, so he knocked at the door after fastening his horse to the horizontal pine bar outside. "Come in, wid yez," said Tim with his back to him. "It's wet ye'll be?" Bob was leaning out of the opposite window, with a slouch hat well down on the back of his neck. "Sit down on the binch by the table," continued Tim. The Reverend Topaz Meakin did so, pulling off his black gloves, and was immediately confronted with two masked men with a revolver a-piece pointed straight at his august and reverend head.

His surprise and alarm were self-evident.

"And pfwhat might yez want wid de loikes of huz?" said Gallagher pointedly. "Is it to rob and plundher a church?"

"Oh, good gentlemen, kind gentlemen," shrieked the unhappy Topaz, "spare me. I did but call and ask for shelter for myself and my quadruped. Spare our lives, we never meant you any harm."

"We're not clane sure of that same," remarked Gallagher sternly. "There's a frind o' mine, a sort of first cousin, tells me that ye're interfherin wid a young liddy he was spakin' wid this marrun. I'll blow your brains out of yer hid if ye ivver brathe a wurrud forninst her, or him ayther."

"Oh, spare me, gentlemen," wailed Topaz, now terribly apprehensive.

"Will yez swear ye'll not say a wurrud of spache about it?" questioned Gallagher, advancing and collaring Topaz by the reverend scruff of his neck, and placing the revolver's cold muzzle against his forehead.

"Oh, I'll swear *anything*," said the agonised young man, utterly forgetful of his own Bible teaching, "*anything*, good gentlemen, if you will only spare my life. I'm too young to die yet," sobbed he.

"Bring the Bible, mate," ordered Gallagher.

Bob did so.

"Now, repate these very wurruds afther me :—

"I, the Riverint Topaz Meakin, hareby solemnly swear niver to utther a wurrud to any livin' sowl about Miss Borony Barnes, or anny of her sistherrs. Niver to tell Mr. or Mrs. Barnes or anny one else in the wide wurruld. So hilp me God."

And the Reverend Topaz swore in great fear and tribulation.

"Very well, then," exclaimed Gallagher in a sepulchral tone, "ye have now taken yer Bible oath of that fact. Mate, get some tay riddy for the English praste. Now, Masther Meakin, come over wid me to the shtable, and I'll put yer har-rse up. It's little we'll have to say to yez if you kape yer wurrud loike a gintleman and a praste, but howly saints and angils, if yez don't ye won't live outside of an howerr. We've got thrusted agints all over the counthry."

"Oh, my good sir," said the relieved clergyman, "you can depend upon me. I will never, on my honour, say one word to any person living. Besides, I have sworn on the holy book," added he with great reverence, "and I should be false to my cloth if ever I broke my word."

"Good," replied Gallagher, "only kape to that and we'll thrate yez as a frind, but moind yez don't break your Bible oath or we'll thrate yez worrse than a poisoned dog."

"I assure you, you may absolutely depend upon my silence," murmured the wretched Topaz, much impressed by the reiterated threats.

"Well, come along an' I'll put your baste up." There were four roomy stalls in Gallagher's stables. It was a good building, and well and carefully put up. He had paid a good price for it, for the sake of his much-cared-for horses.

"And now come in and get yer tay loike a Christian, and a warrum by the foire," said Gallagher, when the Reverend Topaz's steed had been duly seen to. "I'm thinkin' yez'll have to stop wid us to-noight, for ut's wor-rse than ut was."

The Reverend Topaz thought so too, with due regard to both circumstances.

Here was a clergyman, a young and shining light in a suburban pulpit, compelled through stress of weather to spend a night with a couple of murderous bushrangers. What would the bishop say if he only knew it? But the reverend gentleman comforted himself with his promise and felt rather less afraid than he had been.

The Reverend Topaz Meakin was an ordinary mild-mannered young man. He possessed too much curiosity, perhaps, but he had "points" also. He wasn't at all a bad fellow at heart, but his position in regard to Miss Alice Barnes had made him disposed to avail himself of anything unusual in the behaviour of her sisters. However, he stifled his feelings, which under the existing circumstances partook of the nature of compulsion, and was indeed very glad of the warm fire and of the hot cup of tea and other good things which the bushrangers pressed upon him.

He took off all his dripping clothing, which was put to dry, whilst Gallagher and Bob rigged him out in some old garments of their own, and provided him with a pair of dry socks and slippers.

A FREE SELECTOR 173

They then lent him a pipe, and told him to make himself quite at home. But they did not remove their masks the whole evening, despite the fact that they produced a very capital bottle of whisky afterwards, and made merry during a more appalling storm of thunder, lightning, and rain than had been experienced in those parts for years. The hot whisky warmed the Reverend Topaz Meakin's heart, and he thought his hosts were both capital fellows, and that it must be rather jolly to be bushrangers—but this latter thought was evoked by his second full tumbler.

As they all sat round the fire, what more appropriate way of whiling away the hours could there be than by singing songs?

Gallagher started and sung "Finnegan's Wake" in a rich and racy Irish brogue. Bob followed with "Sam Hall," which he considered suitable to the occasion, and this impressed the Reverend Topaz very considerably, accompanied as it was with torrential rain, vivid lightning, and deafening crashes of thunder. He paled visibly, and had his glass filled once or twice more before he forgot it, being much impressed with the part.

> The parson he comes too,
> He comes too, he comes too, etc.

He afterwards volunteered a song himself, an innocent and harmless ditty about a maiden, and spring flowers, and frisking lambs, with a general chorus of "Rule Britannia" appended to each verse.

At last they all went to sleep—the Reverend Topaz being accommodated near the fire with a mattress and blankets. He had breakfast next morning with the two masked men ere he departed for Myall Downs, having been also aided thereto by a potent stirrup-cup concocted by Gallagher. The Reverend Topaz hadn't been quite sure when first he awoke whether he had not taken rather too much whisky overnight, and was uneasily suspicious that he might have slightly transgressed the bounds of strict decorum, perhaps, by being a little too jovial. This feeling was hardly allayed by Gallagher whispering in his ear as he mounted, "Remimber yer Bible oath!" And so he departed, inwardly resolving to be as secret as the grave.

When he was well out of sight and hearing, the two friends removed their masks, and burst into a roar of laughter. "I fancy the Reverend Topaz wont peach now," said Bob. "That was a capital dodge of yours, Gallagher. By Jove, we'll have to camp like 'possums to-day! See how it is coming down! But here is the down-river mailman. The Reverend Topaz got away in good time. Hulloa, Tom, what's the news? River going to rise, eh?"

"Looks like it," answered the mailman, who was riding a grand horse, and leading another fine animal with the mailbags.

Good need of good cattle had Tom Hardy. An Australian bred and born was he, a first-class rider, as most of Australia's sons are. Civil and obliging to all was Tom—a good specimen of a good class.

And he needed to the fullest of all his reserve of pluck, hardness and vitality in flood-time. He had had several dangerous swims, at one time or another, over suddenly flooded creeks, with dangerously boggy approaches at various seasons, when the slightest mistake of horse or rider might have been fatal.

But he always looked as cheery and as "jolly as a sandboy". He wondered, and had wondered, at Gallagher and Bob, as he could see they were different to their surroundings, but a judicious tip or so, and a glass of whisky at trying times, made him keep his own thoughts to himself, and he often brought them a small parcel from Lignumville of anything particularly desired.

"All the people up at the township are talking about you and your mate, Gallagher. It was a dashed plucky thing of you to yard those two bushranging fellows up at Myall Downs. I wish I had been in it to help you to tie them up and hobble them. The sergeant tells me you passed yourself off as 'Thunderbolt'."

"Oh, I explained matters wid him," said Gallagher, "those two villains had got my harrses. But have a dhrop o' the cratur, will yez? And it's wet yez are, and wetter ye will be, before ye get to the ind of yer stage."

"Don't mind if I do," said the mailman. "This rain's plaguy cold riding through it. I've got a few letters and a paper or two for you and your mate."

When he had gone, Bob and Gallagher sat down to read their letters. One addressed to—
                    Mr. TIMOTHY GALLAGHER,
                        Free Selector, Possum Creek,
                                                    Myall Downs,
attracted the owner's attention, and he was soon deep in its perusal. He finished it with a shout of laughter.

"Here, read this, Bob," he said, handing it to his friend. "It seems to me that we are beginning to make our fortunes already. Read it out again."

"All right," replied Bob, and did so. The letter referred to was as follows:—

"DEAR MR. GALLAGHER,

"I daresay you are well aware, if you have heard your uncle speak of me, that I have always considered him an ill-conditioned old dog, and a great nuisance to me." ("It seems that I have got a nice relation," murmured Gallagher.) "I've always wanted him off the place, but wouldn't buy him out, as I was sure he would drink himself to death with the money. But towards his nephew I have totally different feelings, and in consideration of your heroic conduct the other night, and your friend's, in rescuing my family and myself from a position of much embarrassment, perhaps worse, I herewith enclose a cheque in your favour for £600—£500 for yourself and £100 for your friend. I wish you to invest this money for a start in life; and, as far as you are concerned, I think I could put you in the way of advancement, but on the gift of this money I strictly enjoin you to have nothing whatever to do with your worthless old uncle. But for your sake, as regards yourself solely, I will withdraw all opposition on my part to his free selection on Possum Creek for the term of his natural life. I hope to see both you and your mate at the station on my return, to speak to you, and learn your qualifications, before I decide in what way I can further help you.

                    "Yours faithfully,
                            "JOSIAH BARNES."

"Oh Lord, oh Lord! Did you ever hear of such a thing?" laughed Gallagher. "Bob, my boy, what do you think of it? For my part, I won't touch a penny of his money. It would make me feel mean. To have proposed to his daughter, being without visible means of support, was bad enough, but to go and take such a generous offer out of the old man's pocket—why, it would be positively shameful."

"Don't you be in a hurry, old man," calmly replied Bob. "I just vote we keep on as usual, put the money to our respective credits at Lignumville and let it accumulate. Then if anything untoward turns up, we can adopt the injured innocence style, and return old Barnes' money with a deprecating wave of our virtuous hands. Of course, I couldn't touch it either in view of my matrimonial prospects. But it would be of no avail to show our hands now. The old man might get to suspect something, and the game would be up. Let us each write him a letter of thanks and deep obligation and wait. I am of opinion that our luck has changed now. Look here," and he pointed to a paragraph in the *Argus*.

"Broken Hill, 'Wallaroo United'. A rich lode has been struck in this mine. Shares rise £2."

"That has doubled our money at all events. No, I say keep on as we are going, and back our luck. How it rains; I think I shall go into Lignumville with Tom Hardy when he comes back, and I shall probably stay there a bit, on the banking business connected with this letter of the Hon. Josiah's and a bit of my own. I will take both the horses. I can raise another £100, and I'll write to our agent to invest it in 'Wallaroos'."

"So be it, old fellow. Let's go out and see if the river is rising."

Ten yards from the door showed them an altered state of things. The river had risen two feet, and great blobs of yellow bubbly foam were sweeping down its broadening bosom.

"I tell you what it is," resumed Bob, "I shan't wait for Tom, but start right in for Lignumville to-day, send this cheque of old Barnes' to the Melbourne branch on deposit, and fix up things generally. If you have a visit from the fair Lyddie during my absence, you can give her my love, but the weather doesn't promise to favour 'visiting'."

Bob was soon "saddled up" and away, leaving Gallagher in a rather lonely mood.

However, he indited a long letter to Boronia, cooked his own food, tidied up the place, and dawdled over his newspapers, varying this employment by keeping a watchful eye on the boat.

By night the river was steadily rising, and the rain was coming down harder than ever. He was much relieved that Bob had gone and taken the horses out of danger. There was a most terrific downpour during the night, and the river began to "talk," murmuring with the ever-increasing current—swollen, vast, irresistible. He got some good logs in and kept a watch all night, but fell asleep towards morning.

Sure enough, when he looked out of the door, he was thoroughly aroused to behold the selection at Possum Creek changed into a veritable island.

But the river was over the banks, in different parts also, and a vast sea was beginning to form on both sides, whilst the rain came at intervals in fierce showers. He began to think his position untenable, and the water being nearly up to the boat, he put things in the house as high as he could, provisioned his boat, got the oars and sculls, also a small tarpaulin, launched out, and shot away down-stream. It was anything but safe, for large undermined trees and big branches were whirling down, rolling over and over in a highly objectionable way, but he kept clear, and at last he found the entrance of the station "billabong".

He went away down this and it proved to be much better going. "Good-bye to Possum Creek," thought he; "the water is coming down brick red. This is going to be the biggest thing known in floods."

He had ample store of provisions, blankets, and a good strong new boat under him, so he felt perfectly secure, and was very glad that Bob was away out of danger with the horses.

No fear of Lignumville being flooded. The town was built on a hill, back from the river, and there were many natural outlets for any flood water for miles around it. He determined to camp for the night. So he made for the still water, tied his boat to a tree, and rigged his tarpaulin stem and stern on a cross pole, with two subverted letter V supports. He had plenty of clothes line, and made himself quite comfortable. He had to do without a fire, but was dry, warm and well sheltered. Next morning, even in the out-water where he had passed the night, he could see by the position of his boat rope, or "painter," that the water had risen another two feet, and he then began to think that affairs would not be very prosperous at Myall Downs. He then heard a faint "coo-ee" on the out-water straight ahead of him, down the direction of the billabong. He skirted along as soon as possible, and found—of all people in the world—the Hon. Josiah Barnes, in the lower branches of a white gum tree on the edge of the billabong. He rescued him easily enough, by keeping inside out of the billabong current, and the Hon. Josiah hung by his hands and dropped into the boat. "Luck keeping by me," thought Gallagher. "Old boy has been making a short cut for Myall Downs, and got into difficulties."

He then earned the Hon. Josiah's eternal gratitude by giving him a stiff pannikin of whisky and water. He had been wet through, and was very stiff with an all-night exposure. He told Gallagher that on the previous evening he had ridden post haste homewards, had been delayed by swollen creeks, and got to the "turn off" too late. In the darkness his horse had floundered into a deep billabong, and thinking he was in the river in earnest, he had flung himself out of the saddle and had been swept into the lower branches of a tree into which he had climbed, had heard his horse land lower down, and had not dared to move from where he was till daylight. He had kept some warmth in him by holding on to a bough, and stamping with his legs and feet on another. Doing a step dance he called it.

"Not the first time," quoth the Hon. Josiah, "not the first time by one or two chalks. Had to camp on the roof of an out-station one night. Water up to the eaves. Stayed there three days. Place got rather shaky, and roof began to go. Short of 'tucker'. Log came by. Swam out and floated down with it. Picked up lower down by some men in a boat prospectin' for corpses. I'm a pretty hard case, Mr. Gallagher" —and the Hon. Josiah swigged off another jorum, which did him good. Then he took an oar to restore circulation.

The Hon. Josiah was of the type so prevalent amongst some of our Australian legislators, both of the past and present. Hardy pioneers of civilisation first—living, working, exploring, settling, stock-raising, civilising—until in their latter days they became moving powers to make laws, to abide by them, to help like true Australians, their grand young country to move ahead on the path of progress, reform, science, culture and resource.

"THE HON. JOSIAH BARNES IN THE LOWER BRANCHES OF A GUM TREE."

From the Land of the Wombat.   Page 178.

May they live for ever in their young land's recollection, and may there always be the right men at the right time to carry forward their life's work, undauntedly, steadfastly and victoriously.

"I don't believe much in the position of Myall Downs house for an extra big flood," resumed the Hon. Josiah. "Billabong all round it. Water rising steadily all night. Had plenty of time to observe it from my tree. By Jove, Gallagher, it was lucky for me you were in the way! Possum Creek selection under water?"

"I expect it is by now," returned Gallagher. "I sent my mate aff wid the har-rses. I must thank you for the chick, sorr; my mate's goin' to bank it, and oill mind yer wurruds."

"Well, we've time enough to talk about it later on," observed the Hon. Josiah, "but now let us get ahead. I'm very uneasy about the station."

Two miles further down along the out-water they got into the station billabong again. The water was out for miles on each side. Heavy freshes from up-stream still continued, as did also the rain, which poured in torrents.

It was a lucky thing that the Possum Creek boat was extra large and roomy, for the house at Myall Downs was submerged to the level of the sofas and chairs, and all hands were busily employed making a large raft to float off on; so the advent of Gallagher with the Hon. Josiah was hailed with hearty acclamations, mixed with astonishment. Then Mrs. Barnes, the three young ladies, and Mrs. Ayles, were taken in the boat at once to the end of the out-water, where a beautiful red sand pine ridge shot up above the flood, and made a temporary home for them, Gallagher's tarpaulin being at once rigged for a brief shelter. Many other journeys were made in the boat backwards and forwards to the station, and all sorts of necessaries brought. Large dray and waggon tarpaulins were taken over at once, and converted into weather-proof and comfortable houses, being stretched over strong, properly-built frameworks, and the big raft did good service that day in saving furniture and sundries. The overseer, stockman, storekeeper, and the Reverend Topaz Meakin worked double tides, and so did old Barnes and Gallagher. At night Providence Camp, as it was elected to call their refuge, looked splendid with the large fires blazing amongst the pine trees.

Gallagher was introduced to the Reverend Topaz by Barnes as the free selector from Possum Creek. The Reverend Topaz had an uneasy suspicion that Gallagher must be the young man referred to by the principal masked bushranger. But he of course held his tongue, never suspecting that he was the man himself. Every one praised Gallagher, and he worked like a hero, he, the overseer, storekeeper and stockman performing prodigies of valour in rescuing valuable articles from the house and store during the rapid rising of the waters. They all remained at Providence Camp for about two months, until the ruthless devastation of the flood was made good, and everything about Myall Downs was placed in proper working order again. Bob turned up in due time with the horses all safe, having come on to Myall Downs, because he heard from the mailman that "old Barnes says Gallagher is the very best fellow he ever came across, and won't part with him on any account. Says he is going to make his fortune. And he has sacked the new storekeeper and given Gallagher his place as he is very good at figures." ("So he ought to be, as a Cambridge man," thought Bob.) But the news paved the road to many a speculation, and opened up vistas of future well-being.

Bob had also most important news to communicate to his friend. Wallaroo shares had gone up enormously. He had sold out and realised £10,000 between them, £5000 each. With this sum safe to their credit in the bank, they found courage to mention their hopes to old Barnes personally.

When the Hon. Josiah found out who they were, he extolled himself to the skies for his great perspicacity in discovering their merits, especially Gallagher's, and gave his consent with the greatest urbanity. They were also greatly aided and abetted, during the interim of the hard work which fell to their lot in renovating Myall Downs after the great flood, by Mrs. Barnes and the three girls.

It eventually turned out, when the whole matter had been explained to everybody's satisfaction, that Tim Gallagher, *alias* Charles Wood, was in reality the Hon. Harold Woodward, the next successor to a peerage as Lord Forrester, and Bob, his "mate," was known in home circles as the Hon. Robert Trevar, also another highly-connected young man. Of course, after all this, every one was quite sure that they had suspected something all along.

A FREE SELECTOR

The last news I heard about them was that they possessed many flocks and herds, and they and their families are in great evidence on certain festal occasions at Government House.

The Reverend Topaz Meakin married our two friends to Boronia and Lyddie respectively, but had to seek the assistance of another clergyman, who also officiated on this important occasion, to marry Alice and himself.

He turned out a much better all-round man since the time he dropped his prying habits, and quailed before the masked and armed bushrangers at Possum Creek.

The trial came off at Lignumville just after the wedding. The real bushrangers got a lengthy term of penal servitude, and "Gallagher," being overjoyed with a handsome present from the Government of a beautiful double-barrelled gun, and a revolver for "Bob," for their "gallant conduct in defence of the laws of the country," gave vent to his emotions by inviting every free selector in the district to a handsome collation at the principal hotel in the town. And the free selectors drank his health with three times three, but on this occasion, as his young bride was with him, he did not "paint the town red".

FATHER'S "FORTUN'"

Where the gully sang of springtime with its bubbling brook and trees,
Where Nature's breast was wooing, where softly kiss'd the breeze,
'Mid scent of burning resin from grass-trees on the range,
And perfume of bush-blossoms with hues of glorious change.
—*Coo-ee.*

YEARS ago, in the heart of the hills situated about forty-five miles from Melbourne, and near to the borders of Gippsland, a boy and a girl were playing on a gully flat near a rough slab cottage or "humpy," as the settlers thereabout called this species of building.

The "humpy" or cottage was situated clear of the wooded hills which rose in every direction around it.

Out on the flat, which extended for a visible half-mile down the creek meandering by about twenty yards from the door, were clumps of wattles here and there, in full bloom, and amongst these the children ran and laughed, making the gully ring with their merriment. The creek itself sang and bubbled on its way amongst, over, under, and around waterworn boulders of all sorts and colours, from white quartz to blue-grey granite, from yellow quartz to red jasper, until the clear reaches showed a bottom of pebbly mosaic composed of smaller fragments of the boulders above. Then the creek ran smoothly past grassy, bulrush-fringed banks, and again out into the sunlight over boulder cascades.

It was a sturdy stream, and at times it would light up and fairly dazzle your eyes from where the sun struck its rolling, dancing ripples into diamond flashes. It would lurk smoothly and darkly under wattle shades, where a soft green-blue of the water, in a deeper, longer, broader pool, would swirl more gently with a sidelong sweep and a back-water, and then off it would go again with a quick leap over a six-feet fall, where it would chatter noisily and joyously as it was stirred into rollicking, leaping, foaming life.

And so winding, darkling, gliding, sparkling, murmuring and rushing, it wended its way between densely-wooded hills, ever and anon joined by other little creeks along its route, until at length the combined waters found one channel, and lost themselves altogether in the greater flow of Wattle River, which shot onward through a pasture land of wealthier farmers, where sleek cows, calves, horses, mares, and foals grazed on greener and lushier grass, and where larger and more artistic homesteads came in sight, with stockyards and post and rail fences about them.

For a good deal of fresh butter, cheese and eggs were sent to Melbourne from this open country beyond the ranges, the watershed of Wattle River. But the sturdy little stream from the hills thought it was going to do all this great work of fertilising the bigger flats itself, until it was absorbed and hurried away towards the sea with the mightier volume of the river. So it passed on, a mere unit in a greater whole, in a rather saddened state, and darkened over deeper pools, where larger trees and bigger wattles grew than it had been accustomed to.

Back in amongst the hills the smaller stream had a name of its own, which gave it dignity. It was generally known there as Taylor's Creek, because it ran through the land where Taylor's cottage stood.

Taylor's Gully and Taylor's Creek were known to the few hill and valley denizens as one of some small holdings scattered about in the many gullies where their owners made a precarious living by keeping a few cows, a work-weary horse or two, a wandering flock of ear-marked goats, and a few pet sheep, which latter had mostly originated from stray wild lambs picked up in the hills, and bottle-fed at home. Their destination when they grew up and got fat was the cooking pot.

But they paid for the trouble taken with them. There was generally spare milk at these little homesteads, and once weaned and able to support themselves, these tame sheep cost nothing. They would eat anything—even damper, tea leaves, old newspapers and shavings—about the house of their adoption. These were delicacies. Grass and herbs were the staple food.

They were shorn at the proper season, and their wool hand-scoured and sold; and their rendered fat was made into candles or slush lamps. Most of the hill settlers had a saw-pit and a team of working bullocks. The bullocks grazed about the alluvial flats, and added a certain picturesqueness and homeliness to the scene. These bullocks were used for hauling logs of red and forest gum, stringy and iron-bark, to the pits, where they would be split, sawn across or length-ways, as occasion and experience directed.

Taylor possessed a team of bullocks. Here they were, on the flat, the oldest leader with a large "bull-frog" bell on. So had the chief milker, "Blossom". And the girl and "Ballie," the collie dog, kept the stock in order. And "Ballie" "rounded them up" and mustered them when told to do so.

Bessie Taylor, the little girl, was ten years old, a bush child, as wild and shy before strangers as a kangaroo rat, or a bandicoot, and as pretty as a cluster of wattle blossom. Her timidity arose from the comparative solitude of her life, also from the simple fact that it was too far for her to go to school, for in those early days there was no school nearer than Dandenong, the township, which was at least eighteen miles from Taylor's Creek. Seven miles of bridle track through and over the hills must needs be traversed by either equestrian or pedestrian before they would reach the Gippsland and Melbourne coach road, which passed the small bush public-house at a point where Wattle River was spanned by a bridge, in the more open country of that vicinity. From thence was a steep hill with a long straight bush road right up to the top, down the hill on the other side, and continuing the same straight line to Dandenong, with a variety of coach and waggon tracks at the sides curving round and past any dangerous muddy places where bullock drays had been stuck up to the very axles in the raw new soil. The extreme breadth of the road, as it had been first made, allowed plenty of room for any latitudinarian driving.

It had been cut in a bee-line, through forest gum, stringy bark, wattle, iron-bark, tea tree, etcetera, wherever its course took it, over a hill or down it. Wherever the country was level, clumps of forest gum, open wattle and river timber was its characteristic. And a patch of half a mile or so in breadth of this particular sort of country obtained about Taylor's cottage back in the ranges. All along the creek flat it was open until narrowed in by opposing hills.

The little girl is more like a civilised being to-day, because she has a companion—and a well-known one—Tom Ritchie, the son of another small landholder from Native Bear Gully, about two miles distant. He has come over the ridges and hills, and through the bush tracks, to find a stray milker of theirs, which used to belong to Taylor; and she, being a young cow, with a liking for old friends, in which idiosyncrasy she partook of Bessie's nature, has come over to her mother, "Blossom," the chief milker of Taylor's "mob," to have an interview, and to pick up all the current stock news about the calves and "Polly" and "Native Rose," the other milkers; perchance also with a keen recollection and appetite for a particularly sweet patch of grass on Taylor's flat, her birthplace.

Tom's mother has taught him to read, write and cipher a little, and his father has taught him to milk, to dig a patch, yoke a team, either of horses or bullocks, use a bullock whip or an axe; to hobble a horse, to split shingles, and take his turn with the pit-saw.

He has also taught Tom various other items of bushcraft, and has even taken him down to Melbourne in the old spring-cart, and he has seen the rapidly growing metropolis, the great swarms of people, the enormous houses, as compared by the Native Bear Gully standard; and Tom has even been to Sandridge Pier to see the ships which have come all the way from England over the great sea.

The girl and boy are now sitting on a giant quartz boulder at the edge of the creek. The boulder is flat on the top, and must have been brought down to its present position by pre-historic flood or upheaval, for it weighs considerably over a ton. It is a capital seat, and is wedged into the bank, and garnished with patches of bright green and yellow moss, at a place where the sturdy little creek has formed one of its miniature still pools of twenty-five yards or so long by ten broad and three or four feet deep.

Tom is a strongly-built, berry-brown boy of twelve years, wearing a blue Crimean shirt, moleskin trousers and an old felt hat. As he sits on the rock his feet are dabbling in the water,

Bessie has a light, newly-washed pink print frock on, and an old straw hat with a ribbon, which might be of any colour except the one it was when new; and her brown face, sunny hair, and wistful blue eyes make a very apt and striking contrast to the all-brown of sturdy Tom Ritchie. What a painting these two children, and their surroundings under a warm Australian sun, would make if done by a skilled artist! The two are sitting on the quartz boulder chatting in undertones, and anon silent as the grave with expectation and excitement, the little girl, with one hand on Tom's shoulder, gazing with strained expectancy at his rough cork float when it bobs, for Tom is fishing. The scene is varied.

The sunlight patches on the grass around. The coigns of light salient on the craggy opposite shore, about ten yards off, where a small, rocky bluff rises sheer up, with a tree fern here and there, flashes of varied colour in clumps along the bottom and sides, and top of it, where pink, and white, and purple, and scarlet, and yellow wild flowers come in amongst the bushes, and under the tea tree. Then here and there a strong, straight, white, forest gum sapling with dashes of blue-grey, and dark red-brown on its smooth bark. Feathery, beautiful wattle trees around and near where the children sit, and all up and down the bright little watercourse. These numerous shady wattles, with their brilliant golden clusters of dancing yellow fluff-balls and their delicious scent, complete the scene, with the addition of the soft warm air and sunshine for everything to live and grow and breathe in.

All around, up and over and down the creek, away on the hillside forests, everywhere as far as the eye can reach, the yellow-crested white cockatoos are flying, screeching, perching, feeding, but never still or noiseless for a single moment. Then there are hosts of "rosellas," "blue mountains," king parrots, pigeons, honeyeaters and other birds, and parroquets are twittering in hundreds on comfortable boughs, where they are resting before they depart on their afternoon forays. It is high noon, and that marvellous, all-pervading, sweet, aromatic, Australian bush perfume, like no other in the wide world, makes the scene what it is—an Australian bush scene. Without that scent you could not realise that it was Australia.

It seems to me to be made up of everything *in* the bush concentrated together. Even the scent of the wild animals are in it; and I think to one who knows it well, this will always seem so. If an Australian is away, say in New Zealand, for a term of years, he will notice it at once when the steamer enters the Sydney heads. It is very faint, but very perceptible, and is always there, off the coast lands. There is one flower that carries it and one only—the "Native Rose". There it is strong, lasting and very aromatic, a scent that would drive a perfumer mad with envy, made up of odorous resin, and hundreds of other delicate tributes from eucalyptus and other scented trees, with the odour of every wild and curious bush blossom and flower consummated in its wondrous whole —the scent of the Australian bush itself. This scent permeates the whole atmosphere where the children sit, very silently now, and lo! of a sudden that living flashing gem, the peacock-blue Australian kingfisher, shoots like a darting emerald and sapphire combined, and alights motionless, a king of colour, on the boy's rude fishing-rod!

As aforesaid, the children have been very still lately. There have been a few bobs of the cork, and the shade, the various bush sounds, and the murmur of the stream have a quieting effect, but there is a real bite, and away goes the cork under water.

Up goes the rod, away darts the kingfisher, and the boy, with a gratified smile, lands a dark-coloured kicking fish, having caught him with a grub worried out from under the rough bark of a tree near by.

"Oh, what a beauty," says little Bessie Taylor. "It's a toe-biter, ain't it? Leastways, that's what *I* call 'em. Bites your toes, they does, when you wade in the creek. If dey's very big, might bite your toe right off. I'se feared o' dey things."

"Toe-biters, you silly! It's a blackfish, same's the other one. They's big ones down at Wattle River. Went with Bob Dargan once. Got seven of 'em, much bigger nor this one. Toe-biters! Only gals calls 'em toe-biters."

"Well, dey *do* bite your toeses. They've bit mine all along the creek, and I've run out."

"That's little crawfishes what bites yer, or leeches. How'd yer like leeches all over yer? Heard Bob Dargan say his father knew a man who got nearly killed with them leeches. Nearly sucked all his blood, they did. But I've never seen none of 'em here, nor on Native Bear Creek neither. There's another one, that's three. S'pose we go and cook 'em for dinner?"

"All right, Tom," said Bessie, springing up with active grace. "Come along in and I'll cook 'em. But you take out the insides and clean 'em; I don't like cleanin' live things. Look how they jump!" she exclaimed with a suppressed shriek, "just like 'goannas'. Oh!"

Tom, however, is not moved by any such qualms, and settles his captives at once by a good hard blow from a short, smooth, throwing-stick he always carries, and with which he can knock a sitting bird, a "'possum," or even a "goanna" itself clean off a bough with positively startling dexterity. He has picked up this accomplishment, a great one to a boy, from an occasional visit of a few blacks who come at certain seasons, and from the young boys especially, who are adepts at it. The main tribe live nearer Dandenong, where they get shillings and tobacco for finding stray horses and cattle, but even in these early days the tribe is but a remnant, and a very small remnant, for they dwindle with great rapidity near any town where they can indulge their fatal love for "budgeree white pfeller nobbler".

Bessie twines one hand and wrist round her playfellow's neck as they go towards the cottage, which is built on a slight eminence on the edge of the flat, with rising hillside behind it, hillside that trends gradually upwards until it reaches the summit of one of the main ridges of this hill and valley country.

She gets out the frying-pan, lays the cloth, and sets the table. She places on it a clean, light, yellow-brown damper of her own baking, which occupies the place of honour. Then she adds a couple of plates, some butter, knives and forks, salt and pepper, a jug of milk and a *terra cotta* coloured earthenware "monkey," filled with water. When the fish, which weigh nearly a quarter of a pound each, are ready they will have a healthy, hearty, happy feast.

Tom expatiates about a mother native bear with a young one which he had seen when coming over the hills.

Bessie knows all about the bush animals, and her eager face and expressive eyes show plainly enough the interest she feels in the narration. She fairly dances with delight, to the imminent danger of the frying-pan, the fish, and herself, as Tom describes how he tried to catch the young native bear when it was low down.

"I could ha' killed un easy, only it was such a teedly little un," said he. "And the old un, she were frightened, and took it right up, up, the old hollow gum, until I couldn't hardly see it, before they both clomb into the top hole. And she rattled that hard on the bark she did, that she frightened a black cockatoo sitting on the top. And he flew away, screechin', screechin'. And *he* frightened a big 'old man' kangaroo. And he come down the hill quick not far off me. If I'd had father's 'Rover,' our kangaroo dog, he'd ha' nailed un sure."

"But," said Bessie, as they fed like little Christians, sitting down side by side, their hats duly hung on pegs, "do tell me more about the great, great, big, big town. Did you see any great ladies, Tom? Was they like Queen Victōry over there yonder?"—where, above a latticed window (Taylor had his "points") our gracious queen's portrait hung, attired in a reception dress of her younger days and a blue riband of her order over her shoulder.

"I saw lots on 'em," replied Tom; "some was in carriages, but most on 'em was a-walkin'. No," added he, "they wasn't like *her*, leastways, I didn't see any. But they was nice enough. There was any amount of 'em. And lots o' little gals."

"Was any of them little girls nicerer than me, Tom?" said Bessie hesitatingly.

"Well, I didn't ask 'em," replied Tom. "You're nice enough, Bess. Oh, mother says I can fetch you over, same's I do when your father goes away to town, next Wensday, 'cause she's got a sister coming who knew your mother very well before she went to Heaven."

"I think dad'll let me," answered Bessie. "Dad's awful good and kind to me, he is. It's *my* little lass, he says. Says I've got to be mother and all to him now. So I takes pains with my cookin', and mother she taught me a good deal. And father's a good cook himself, and he shows me. And my butter's nice, and I keep the place tidy and clean so's dad can see things nice when he comes home from his hard work. And I sews and mends dad's things. And I washes, and milks, and dad he says, 'I'm a wonder, for a ten-year-old'. But he wants to get book larnin' for me, he does. And he's taught me a little to read and write. But I'm not much at figurin' sums. And I never sees no money to figure up for. Poor dad. Seems he feels lonely like, now mother's gone away. If mother knew that, I think she'd ha' stayed a little longer."

"Well," said Tom, "I must loose 'Crab' now. He's got to take that wild thing 'Five-corners' back. She *is* a 'Five-corners' too. Knocks down our slip-panel and lets herself out of the yard, over the fence and away here, every chance she gets. But 'Crab' 'll manage her, and when she knows she has *got* to go back, she'll go straight enough, else old 'Crab' 'll worry her hocks and heels proper. He knows where to 'heel 'em up '."

"Tell your mother, will you, Tom, that I've sent her two nice brown eggs laid by that little white pullet she give me? I've packed 'em so nice in a little box, if you'll be *very* careful with 'em, and not break 'em. You be over 'bout 'leven o'clock Wensday. Good bye, Tom."

"Good-bye, Bess. You tell your dad how I caught them three blackfish, will you? Young Bingalong showed me. He says, 'Little pfeller frog best pfeller,' but I couldn't see none. Good-bye, Bess."

And off went Tom Ritchie, and the gully presently rang with shouts, bellowings and barkings from the astute "Crab" and "Ballie," who, of course, went to help to drive off the intruder. The two dogs quickly hustled young Mrs. "Five-corners" on to the top of the ridge and over it, when "Crab," giving his friend the wink, "Ballie" trotted back.

Bessie washed up, set the entire house in order, made some "Johnnie cakes," and put them in the cold, clean, camp oven ready for father's tea. Then the fire had to be replenished, and wood and water brought. The big iron kettle and the billy had also to be set in readiness.

Then the child washed herself, and took out some sewing and a new straw hat to be trimmed with some ribbon for her visit. Quite a little woman was Bessie, though strange and shy before people she did not know. But the prevailing thought that she had her father to look after, made her remember all her mother's maxims, and she was curiously self-reliant for her age. She had worked hard as long as she could remember, because she always used to be her mother's help before she died, about a year ago.

She sewed away until her milking-time approached, and had mended several articles by the time the sun began to sink towards the western hills. Then she put away her materials in her little bedroom, tried on her hat before the looking-glass, and ran out calling for "Ballie".

He came at once, barking and bounding from the side of the ridge nearest to the house, where he had succeeded in frightening an unusually fidgetty and preternaturally early bandicoot nearly out of its wits, by chasing him frantically through the scrub, and "treeing" him in a hollow log, where the terrified little animal took half an hour to moralise upon the late imminence of sudden death for him, and to get his breath back.

Bessie soon found her three cows, brought them home, and put "Blossom" in the "bail" for milking. She got a bucketful from the three, and then, having placed the contents (strained) into her milk dishes in the tiny dairy, began to look out for her father, who was later than usual, and did not turn up until after sunset. Then she heard him "coo-ee," as he always did on approach, and shortly afterwards he came up.

Ned Taylor was a man of fifty or thereabouts, tall, strong, embrowned by the sun, and with rather longer hair than he would have had if he had lived in the vicinity of a town.

He was a hard, muscular, fair man, with beard and moustache, and a kindly look in his honest blue eyes.

It had been a hot day, though not unusually so, but there had of late been a somewhat lengthy period of dry weather, and the grass on the hillsides was yellow and wispy, and the thick undergrowth dry and harsh.

"Well, my little lass," said Taylor as he entered, catching the child to his arms afterwards when he had sat down on the bench, "I've found that as will make a little lady of my girl yet. Look at that now!"—and he produced from his pocket two or three lumps of broken quartz which, even without a gold glass, showed gold. There's a 'fortun'' there, my lass! But mind you tell no one, for I don't want folks to know. I must go down to town at once, and take out a miner's right, then I must peg out my claim and some more ground for one or two of my neighbours, until we see what we can do with it. But I don't want my little lass to say a word."

"Not me, father. I won't say anythink. Tom's been here to-day, after 'Five-corners,' and he caught three blackfish, and we eat 'em for dinner, we did. And Mrs. Ritchie's got her sister coming up, and she wants me to go over on Wensday."

"Well, my little lass, that'll just fit. I must get to town at once. I'll start to-morrow and leave you at Ritchie's. Then I'll go on."

"Shall I be like Queen Victōry when your fortun''s made me a lady, father? A real grand lady like her with a blue riband?"

"I'm afraid not, my little girl. Queen Victōry's the first lady in the land, and, 'sides, she's a queen."

"But what's a 'fortun',' father? 'Fortun'' same as you say will make a lady of me?"

"Why, money, lots of money, my lass, so's you and me can go and live in a big city like Melbourne."

"Oh," said Bessie, for she often thought that would be the greatest of all earthly treats, and she remembered Tom Ritchie's various descriptions.

Ned Taylor took Bessie over to Ritchie's next morning. She was to go back daily with Tom to milk the cows. Taylor went right on to Melbourne, and afterwards to Heidelberg, where he interviewed the mining registrar at his private house, and took out a mining right for four, including extra ground for two other neighbours besides Ritchie and himself. He came back in three days, but during his absence most of the hills had been swept by a fierce bush fire, and though he had marked trees on the way from the reef towards his home when he first discovered it, in a lonely place some miles away, these trees were completely obliterated, and he was quite unable to find the place again. The hills had been so thickly wooded, there had been so much scrubby undergrowth in patches, that the all-devouring fire had changed the very aspect of the country. The fire had wiped out all the pre-existing land-marks. One ridge looked exactly like another, a mere blackened mass of *débris*, with heaps of charred trunks still smouldering in some places.

In fact, so changed were many old familiar spots amongst the hills, with the utter extermination of tree and scrub growth, that Taylor declared that he might have walked over the spot again and again without in the least knowing it. Even the young trees growing off the ridges were scorched and would die.

There would be no new upspringing forest now for years where the fire had held its ravaging course. It was absolutely easier to find one's way about before the fire than after it, since now there was such a sameness about your surroundings that you could travel for miles without noting one salient point.

After a week's search all over the place with the greatest minuteness, Taylor gave it up. But he showed his quartz specimens to Ritchie and the two other men for whom he had taken out licences, and they scoured the neighbouring country in all directions, but the gold reef had vanished from human ken. Taylor repeatedly described it to those interested as being on the side of a hill near a heap of granitic stones, but whether the heap and reef of which Taylor had discovered the "cap" was covered with a jumble of fallen tree trunks, or whether he had failed to strike back to it in the proper direction, could not be proved. The marked and blazed trees were certainly gone, and thus no clue remained.

Ned Taylor told his troubles to his little daughter, described the heap of stones, and the position of the reef from them, saying that it ran across and through the hill, would probably dip into both valleys in the same linear direction, and extend for miles.

"I've had some experience on the diggin's," added he, "when I first married your poor mother, but I lost all the money I had made, and I haven't enough now to work a reef, nor have any of our neighbours. But we might have sold it to them as has money; and if the yield had proved valuable, I might have got the thousand pounds bounty from the Government for a payable goldfield, and now it's gone past all findin'. When all that bush grows up again, all that cleared ground'll be thicker and greener than ever, and the fallen tree trunks will decay and make more soil, and the rain will come and wash still more down, and that there cap'll be covered two feet deep, and nobody'll know nothing about it. I don't believe I should have found it at all, only I've a quick eye, and I know what quartz is, burnt or not. I'd stopped to light my pipe, and sat down on that there heap o' stones that I told you of, and saw it while I was thinkin'. Some three or four head of cattle, workin' bullocks, had been up there a day or two before, and one of them had slipped, and in scramblin' to get up again, had knocked a long slither o' turf and moss off the top of the 'cap'—and 'twas *then* I saw it! The quartz is all burnt like, yellow-brown with old, old bush fires, but when you crack it with the back of the axe-head like I did, there's the 'colour' right enough. And below it, down in them creeks near by the reef, there's sure to be gold for surface diggin' and on the 'bottom' too."

Thus half-talking, half-musing, Taylor laid bare his thoughts before his little daughter.

And Bessie started thinking, and formed a great plan in her own little mind.

"If father has sharp eyes," she thought, "mine are sharper. I always finds the hens' nests, I do, when they lay away in the bush, and I'll look and look all round. Maybe I'll find father's 'fortun'' yet. It was a tiresome thing that this big bush fire had happened. It hadn't come near the house, but it had gone over the reef and all about it. Poor old daddy, he had found the 'fortun',' and it must be lying in the hills somewhere. It was near a heap of stones, and it was yellow-brown in colour. That would be the colour of a dead leaf, or one of the patches on old 'Blossom'." Bessie's mother had taught her to say her prayers, and she prayed morning and night to find father's 'fortun'.

Taylor recommenced his saw-pit work again with Ritchie's assistance, having several green logs left here and there about his pit, but nearly all the good growing timber in the vicinity was now gone, and he was beginning to have serious thoughts of shifting to some other locality where he might get a contract for a big lot of fencing or bushwork, for like most of his class he was very handy with either axe, saw, adze, mallet and wedges, a master, in fact, of bushcraft, with a great turn for carpentering and building besides. His knowledge ranged from splitting shingles to shearing.

About a week after this, Bessie, being left at home, started out on her own account to look for father's 'fortun',' which had been running ever since, day and night, in her busy but perplexed little brain. After wandering in various directions for about two hours she completely lost herself through the changed condition of the country. When she became sure that she was really lost, a terrible thing in its inception even to a strong man, she became wildly terrified. To add to her alarm and horror and sense of utter isolation, almost amounting to the well known "bush madness," a fearful tornado swept suddenly down an adjacent ridge, as they not infrequently do in Australia, clearing everything before it. The mighty force of the wind cut a road through any standing timber for the exact width of the whirlwind itself. Bessie saw logs and blackened trunks of trees lifted off the ground and hurled yards away. Saw trees, wherever they happened to stand, levelled flat, as if hundreds of axes were at their roots, and ran wildly away out of danger, without in the least knowing where she was going to. She then got quite dazed, and wandered on, talking to herself, and it was not until after dark that she fell exhausted to the ground.

Her father was astounded and terribly alarmed when he returned home, and after taking a turn round, shouting and coo-eeing, went over to Ritchie's, half thinking that she might be there. But no one had seen her, and as the night was dark, nothing much could be done. But Ritchie, Tom and he, left as soon as possible to begin the search with bottle lanterns. Tom was stationed at Taylor's cottage with orders to fire off the gun at intervals to be a guide, perchance, to the lost child. The men were good bushmen and would not need it. But the child?

Before poor Bessie had experienced the dreadful feeling that she was lost she had indulged in many bright hopes of success. How pleased father would be. His "little lass" had found his "fortun'" again after he himself had lost it. But, afterwards, before her mind got too dulled to realise things, and the knowledge of being lost rested with her, she passed through every phase of childish terror, mixed up with her own childish fancies. Regret at losing her little circle of friends, sorrow for her father's sorrow. "Oh, poor daddy, wouldn't he be sorry?" And she had "coo-eed" and screamed until she could do so no longer, and then that merciful want of knowledge, that oblivion of outer events, the "bush madness" came upon her, and she wandered on and on as if in a dream. When Bessie fell exhausted, unconquerable sleep came upon her, and that was a crowning mercy. She might have been scared completely out of her mind had she been obliged to face the long dark hours alone. Providence had dulled her brain, and exhaustion had done the rest.

All through the night Taylor and Ritchie searched far and near, the father with an agony at heart past expressing. "His bright little child—would he find her alive or dead?" And the strong man felt a despair at even living himself in such suspense. Leaving Ritchie to continue the search, he made back by daylight to his "selection," caught a horse, and galloped wildly over the hills to the small coaching public-house at the bridge by Wattle River to see if he could find any blacks about. White men volunteered at once, on horseback, but Taylor was fortunate enough to get "Old man Jimmy," a famous tracker, who wore a polished copper disc of large size on his breast, which had been given him by settlers for finding a previous lost child.

The new party started, "Jimmy" loping along, and keeping up with the walk and jog of the horses, and when Taylor's creek was reached Taylor made a few preparations. Tom was placed under the same orders as before, and Ritchie joined them. "Old man Jimmy" then took up the running. The father's heart lightened a little when he saw the dexterity with which the black fellow made a wide cast, and picked up the child's track. The circumstances were favourable in some parts, even to the white men, but over hard ground, rocks and stones, where would they have been without the born instinct, knowledge and unerring certainty with which the black fellow pursued the object of his quest; halting here, regaining his clue, and on again? At times he ran.

At last he stopped. The horsemen and others had kept well behind so as to give him free play. He held his hand up.

It was the spot where Bessie had seen the tornado desolate the hillside. "Piccaninny white gin, big one pritened," said he oracularly, "yan burraburri, this away, that away. My word, that one debbil debbil alonga cobra, now burraburri, big one priten." And "Jimmy" passed his hand over his shock of hair to indicate the "bush madness".

"SHE HAD FALLEN NEAR A NUMBER OF MOSS-GROWN BOULDERS."

From the Land of the Wombat.   *Page 197.*

From thence they went deviously, "Jimmy" running the tracks like a sleuth hound. He continued to show the others where she had stopped, showed where she had fallen exhausted, and demonstrated the movements of the tracked one with his own body. Then he stated how she had got up in the early morning and wandered away again. He pointed out a shred of her dress, caught by a branch splinter of a fallen tree. He marked the blood that had spotted one place from her wounded left foot, pointing to his own left foot at the time, and after three hours of most anxious zigzagging, suddenly exclaimed with great excitement: "Wokkaratchie sit down" (crows waiting), and, dodging forward suddenly, hurled his throwing stick with such unerring aim that he killed a crow dead not more than ten feet from where poor little Bessie lay pallid, cold, and quite insensible. The others of course flew away, but there had been four of these satiny blue-black fiends, with their steely-blue eyes, hopping nearer and nearer to the unconscious child. Had not that benign Providence, "which shapes man's ends, rough hew them as he may," willed that the rescue party should arrive in this the nick of time, poor Bessie's sufferings would soon have been over. For the crow attacks the eyes of man or beast when helpless. The Australian crow (*corvus vastatrix*) and the dingo are the end of all things in the bush!

Taylor's bushcraft had taught him a thing or two. During the brief stop at his cottage, before "Jimmy" started "on the tracks," he had annexed a flask of brandy and one of milk, and with a horn spoon he administered a little of the joint mixture to poor Bessie. She had fallen near where a number of moss-grown boulder stones had been hurled flat from a heap, and in the exact spot where the child's golden hair swept the ground, as she had fallen, was—Taylor's reef!

Bessie, though all unconscious of it, had indeed found Father's "fortun'"! And Taylor saw the reef again and wondered, but like a wise man held his peace.

When Bessie came to, the horsemen departed to tell Mrs. Ritchie the joyful news that the child had been found.

Taylor told Ritchie the good news when "Jimmy" was cutting out a "'possum," but very guardedly, and with a wink of caution.

The brandy and milk brought poor little Bessie round, and

Ritchie and Taylor carried her home. Mrs. Ritchie came on to nurse her, and, when she was completely established, Taylor and Ritchie went back and pegged out their claims, saying nothing to any one. "Old man Jimmy" was suitably rewarded, and was a constant visitor at Taylor's afterwards to see how the "piccaninny white gin" got along.

Bessie gradually recovered, and in two or three days, under Mrs. Ritchie's skilled nursing, nature and her own good constitution came in to help, so that in a fortnight she was quite recovered, but there was a knowledge in those pretty blue eyes of hers that had not been there before.

In a short time Taylor had his specimen stone assayed, and the "prospect" was so good that an expert from a mining company arrived in a secret manner, and in the disguise of a farmer. He concluded a bargain which completely satisfied Taylor and his friends, and departed unknown. When all this had at length become known, the firm began, and the ball being once set rolling, kept on at it.

People came in hundreds from all parts, and Taylor's Flat became a small town in a month. He sold the whole of his selection at an enormous profit, and when the value of the reef and neighbourhood became known, netted another £1000 from Government as the discoverer of a payable goldfield.

Ritchie sold out too, and made a considerable increase in his income, because a speculator, after paying him cash down for *his* selection, immediately started to build a large hotel at Native Bear Creek, as it was on the direct line for the new road to Melbourne. In a couple of months the little coaching public-house at Wattle River disappeared, and another huge hotel sprang up there, where people used to sojourn as time went on for the express purpose of seeing the great goldfield, which originated from the discovery of the Queen Elizabeth Reef (so called after Bessie). Taylor and Ritchie bought large sections of land on Wattle River alongside one another and settled down on fenced-in property with a fine dairy herd apiece. A town sprang up around the big hotel at Wattle River (I have no doubt but that it is a city now, with a railroad through it), and amongst the substantial buildings, which nevertheless grew like a lot of mushrooms, there was erected a county school, and to this school Bessie Taylor and Tom Ritchie went. Being sharp, clever children, they progressed wonderfully. The years rolled on for Taylor and Ritchie with increasing prosperity, until the two departed for another world, strange to say, within six months of one another.

Then Mrs. Ritchie also departed, and only Tom and Bessie were left. After a decent period of mourning, and being now both grown-up and educated, they joined their lands, and their lives, and amongst their own children often narrate the story of how mother found her father's fortune.

ON THE LEAD

> The hollow orb of moving circumstance
> Roll'd round by one fix'd law.
> —*Tennyson.*

JACK FALCONER and Willie Routledge were "mates". Both of them had been through every phase of colonial experience.

Jack Falconer was the squire's son at home in the old country, and Routledge was the son of a farmer on the estate.

With the levelling experience of the colonies before them, where every man on the field of labour, be he prince or peasant, is accepted according to his merits, they did not, and were not, likely to forget their old friendship, which was cemented when they were boys together. It had but grown stronger and more enduring, because they had gone through hard work together. They had tried nearly everything available where thew, sinew and muscle were required, and had come through with fair credit, before they found themselves partners in the Nil Desperandum Claim, which they had bought for a small sum from a party of broken-down and disappointed diggers; and from the moment that it came into their possession their luck began to turn in royal style, for in a new tunnel they had hit upon a "lead" of surprising richness, and then they began to employ labour.

It was what is called "alluvial digging". A shaft was dug to various depths, say from fifty to a hundred feet, and then, if fortune should so direct that the "lead" was there, it was tunnelled along.

The old diggings had been but very sparsely populated before the new turn was given to it by the discovery of the "lead," which really was the hollow of a prehistoric watercourse, buried by ages of earth-forming years with the aid of attrition by rains, deluges and *débris* of all kinds, geological evolutions, eruptions and changes, extending far beyond the ken of the time when Falconer and Routledge went to bed at night, thinking that the fortune which they had journeyed together to Australia to seek for was within an ace of being realised.

The partners were men of a similar age—about thirty. They were bearded, bronzed, strong, hearty and good-looking. They had not bothered with the shaft sunk by the previous miners, but had tossed up for choice of localities close by, which each one selected according to liking, and the winner—who was Falconer—had the "luck" with him all through the venture, for though they sank a good hundred feet before they got to the "bottom," yet that one sinking proved to be a mine of wealth.

As they tunnelled along it, and took out the coarse and ragged-looking bits of gold from the bottom of the angle made by two strata of rock, they were amazed; for there, by the evidence before their eyes, there must have been a mighty upheaval of underground forces sufficient to throw these strata at an angle of forty-five degrees to each other, thus forming a wedge-shaped cavity into which the valuable metal had been cast by the denudation of the old existing hillsides, and had found its way to the arresting rock by its own specific gravity.

The reason for the sparseness of the digger population about the vicinity of Waratah Gully was because, though gold was known to exist throughout the district, nothing reliable had as yet been found, and therefore the crowd of diggers were merely nomads, hunting and prospecting for the buried gold all through the ranges and gullies far and near.

But when once the worth of a certain claim is even whispered, the very rocks and trees seem to catch the echo, spreading it abroad, and the paucity of the population which obtained when Falconer and Routledge first "located" in the spot alternated to increase and influx by leaps and bounds.

Thus an hotel shot up almost at once. Several stores were erected, and in a few months a town was building by rapid stages.

The partners made £10,000 in four months, and had formed

a strong syndicate with men who were attracted by the richness of the "lead," which syndicate obtained possession immediately of a vast acreage along the "line". And the original prospectors were now drawing a large weekly sum.

The man who "ran" the new hotel, by name Martin, had a daughter, and it was currently reported that she was "setting her cap" at Jack Falconer. And here another element of this story came into play, for a certain young unmarried schoolmaster from the nearest town, about ten miles off, who had been hitherto helped in the management of the girls' part of it by his own sister, threw up a small but steady income, and came to try his luck on the goldfield.

He soon found out, greatly to his chagrin, that he had thrown away his birthright for "a mess of pottage," as far as he was personally concerned, for being totally unskilled and physically unfitted for miner's work, the very preliminary of sinking a shaft was enough for him.

And this dearly-bought experience, coupled with the belief that he had made a fool of himself, and exposed his sister to unnecessary tribulation, had the effect of making him gloomy and misanthropical. But Jennie Holroyd, his sister, was a fine stalwart healthy girl, who had no petty weaknesses of her own, and she had actually supported him by washing all the clothes she could collect from the diggers, who, in admiration of her spirit, came on various days in bodies of three or four, and being expert bushmen, as every Australian miner has to be, very soon erected a most comfortable and substantial log shanty for the brother and sister, and put up a nice laundry for Jennie besides.

Holroyd did not seem to get over the shock he had experienced. He suffered from wounded pride very much indeed, and with some that faculty is most sensitive, when it experiences a sudden and unexpected fall.

And his utter inability to adapt himself to the curious and very varied experience of camp and mining life was never made more apparent to him, and in the presence of his sister too, than on a certain morning when she had been working with him in the first blush of his belief that he was quite fit and experienced enough to make a rapid fortune. On their arrival the night before, he had brought a load of very inferior calico out on his back, and he and his sister had camped for

the night under a "mimi" or rude brush shelter put up by
Swanhill Jack, a digger of great experience, who patronised
them and cooked their breakfast for them next morning.
On this particular morning he had said, when the roll of
calico was produced with ostentation :—
"What's that thing for, mate?"
"That is going to be our tent," said Holroyd proudly.
"That thing?" quoth Swanhill Jack, with infinite scorn.
"'Twouldn't keep water out, let alone the first puff of wind
that came along. Where are you goin' to sink yer shaft?"
"I don't know," said the unfortunate Holroyd.
"Well, as yer a new chum, I'll show you," said Jack.
"You can peg out your claim next to mine. I've shepherded
it for ye, me and one of my mates—for the young leddy's
sake," added he, taking off his hat with a low bow, as he
gazed admiringly at sweet Jennie Holroyd.

And after a morning's work at the selected spot, Holroyd,
his back stiff, his shoulders feeling as if they had been well-
nigh dislocated, and his hands blistered all over, was startled
and not at all comforted by Swanhill Jack's sudden re-appear-
ance with the statement that "if he went on like that with
the pick and shovel, he might expect to get to the bottom by
about Christmas time!"

They were two months this side of it, the season being the
Australian spring. Then came the next pertinent question
from the stalwart digger :—
"And what are you goin' to do with yer shaft when you
get to the bottom?"
"Why, get the gold out, of course," answered Holroyd;
"haul it up in a bucket."
"Not much, you wont," said Swanhill Jack ironically.
"There's a water-drift in this here gully, and your shaft'll
have to be timbered as you go down. Of course, you don't
know nothin' about splittin' slabs, nor cuttin' corner-pieces,
nor puddlin' back, nor nothin'; nice sort of loony you are to
come minin'. Why didn't yer stick to your book larnin'?"

But all the same Jack helped him to timber his shaft with
the greatest good will, but Holroyd became ill, as he was very
different to his robust sister; and some internal trouble
made him daily more melancholy, irritable and miserable. He
only worked by fits and starts, and Jack and one of his mates

actually washed his first "prospect" from the "bottom" gravel and drift themselves. They had sunk his claim and timbered it almost entirely by their own labour, having put two more mates on their own, for as Jack said confidentially to Bill, "That chap's no more use nor a fly. He's sickenin' like, I think, and, by my word, he's no more like that fine hearty young leddy, his sister, nor chalk's like cheese."

It came about that Jack Falconer, whose claim was half a mile away at the upper end of Waratah Gully, chanced one day to be taking a stroll by Holroyd's log hut, which had been erected by sympathising miners, and after exchanging a few words, and leaving a book with the invalid, of whom he had heard, met Miss Jennie a quarter of a mile farther on, carrying a nosegay of bush flowers.

He raised his hat, thinking at the time that he had never seen a prettier face, a more graceful form, or a more ravishing complexion. Jennie Holroyd's attributes of beauty were many.

Her hair was glossy black, and as fine as silk. In style she was a brunette, with eyes of a dark, limpid blue, and dazzlingly white and faultless teeth, but Miss Jennie had a temper of her own, not often displayed however, so that if nothing ruffled her particularly she was sweetness itself. A rich dark crimson flushed her cheeks as she looked upon Falconer for the first time, for he was the handsomest and strongest-looking man she had ever seen. They were a noble pair.

And Falconer said, smiling pleasantly, "I have just called upon your brother, Miss Holroyd. I heard he was in ill-health, and we, you know, that is Routledge and I, happen to be the founders, so to speak, of Waratah, and naturally take a sort of fatherly interest in our co-dwellers and workers. My name is Jack Falconer."

"Yes," replied Jennie, "of course we have often heard of you. In fact, your name mentioned as having 'struck it rich' was the first reference to Waratah that we heard, but my poor brother is not strong, and I often think that I myself could stand the mining part of the work far better than he can."

"Are you botanising, Miss Holroyd?" continued Falconer. "Would you like some waratahs? I can show you plenty if you will permit me to accompany you for half a mile off the track. Will you?" he added eagerly.

"Certainly, Mr. Falconer. How pleased I shall be to get them. It doesn't seem possible to get any about here."

"For the very good reason that they are always picked," said Falconer. "Very few people of the unthinking class care to let these beautiful flowers alone, and either tear them out of the ground, root and all, or ruthlessly break the stem, which practically destroys the plant for at least two seasons. But they never seem to think of cutting them neatly off with a knife and a decent length of stem, which, of course, would do no harm whatever. But that mode of procedure, the act of tearing up or wantonly breaking, is prevalent among all English-speaking races. Look at our Australians with the waratah, native rose, and the beautiful Christmas bush. These three unparalleled flowers are torn up, injured, and purloined wholesale, unless strictly guarded. Then take another phase of destruction in Great Britain. Suppose an unusually atrocious and appalling murder takes place, say near a wood. In that case the whole of 'Birnam Wood will go to Dunsinane,' that is to say, the coppice near the scene of the ghastly tragedy will be taken in bits, splinters and branches to the great Cockney depot for all things—the greatest, the best, the noblest, the most valuable, and also, alas! the worst and the most horrible—London."

In a short time Falconer and Jennie reached the top of a neighbouring gully where the "waratahs" grew.

Here they were, small forests of them, with the beautiful dark scarlet blooms rounding off the ends of the long straight stems, and their green serrated leaves, few, but judiciously placed by nature, that great artist of effect, giving just the contrast that this curious and somewhat rare Australian coast and mountain bush flower requires.

There is always something fresh and startling with Australian flowers. There is the flannel flower, that curious creation of greenish-grey, silky, flannel-looking texture; the lovely epacridæ, those triumphs of beauty; the sarsaparilla creeper, with its amethystine clusters; the large and small bottle brushes; the strange mixed pea-blossom-shaped dark and light yellows; but all being put together, and I have not mentioned one-thousandth part of them, what can compare to the thrilling joy of the practised bush-flower hunter when his sense of smell informs him that the native rose is in his vicinity?

In those small and rare vivid pink petals there lie the odours of the whole Australian bush, epitomized and etherealized into a strong, yet delicate and most delicious odour.

The flower-gatherers soon had a large bunch of the rare and precious "waratahs," and Jennie had as many as she could well carry in both arms, all carefully cut to a good length of stalk with Falconer's sheath knife.

As they walked back towards Holroyd's hut, Falconer asked to be allowed to call occasionally, and Jennie accorded a gracious permission, asking him to come in and see her brother for a moment, which he did.

The invalid appeared querulous and fretful, in spite of Falconer's manner, which was kind enough to obviate any splenetic display.

But kindness failed in this instance, and Falconer very soon took his departure.

Falconer and Routledge now lived in state, but though their increasing affluence gave them comforts which they had not previously known during their somewhat lengthy period of roughing it together, they still worked in the mine.

But they now lived in a substantial weather-board building, and they were attended personally by a celestial valet and cook—who went by the name of Lu Appa.

Lu Appa was a young Chinaman scrupulously neat and clean about his person, and was a valuable factotum.

As a rule, on Australian goldfields, Chinamen generally look after the main chance of getting gold themselves, but Lu Appa had had a fight with a countryman, and had managed to get about three inches of a knife stuck into his thigh, which necessitated a compulsory sojourn in the hospital for two months.

He emerged therefrom quite impenitent, and thirsting for revenge, but his assailant had fled, and he had accepted Falconer's overtures to look after the house and persons of his masters. He bought all the necessaries himself, and managed about as well as a housekeeper of the opposite sex would have done, if she had had a personal interest in the *ménage;* but Lu Appa's cooking was above comparison.

Falconer got this paragon of a celestial to make up a few dainties, and took them over to Holroyd's place to try and get him to eat them, and rouse him out of the apathy into which he had seemed to have fallen of late, but apparently to no avail. And one night he was greatly startled by the advent of Jennie Holroyd herself, who appeared to be in much tribulation, and declared that her brother was getting worse.

"I don't know how it is, Mr. Falconer," she said, "but Edward seems to be getting very strange in his manner to me. He always used to be such a kind brother, but now nothing I can do for him seems to please him, and he says unkind things. He wanders off into the bush too, and stays away for hours. I sometimes think he has some trouble on his mind, but what it can be, unless he broods over the unfortunate circumstance of giving up his school for a life to which he is hardly fitted, I cannot say. I have come over to you to ask your help, for he went out three hours ago and has not come back. I fear he may either have lost himself or met with an accident."

It was now an hour after sunset and quite dark, but Falconer soon lit a lantern and accompanied Miss Jennie back to her dwelling, though, when they got there, they found that Holroyd had returned, and for some reason or other did not seem at all pleased that Falconer and Jennie had come back together.

Falconer went home, sat down and ruminated over his pipe for half an hour. Then he read the *Australasian* until his partner turned up.

Routledge had been over to the Waratah Hotel, where he had played a game or two of pool, and said, in a casual way, that he had met Dora Martin in close confabulation with Holroyd, which seemed to explain a great deal to Falconer, and accounted for Holroyd's absence.

Dora Martin had made overtures to Falconer before this, being much attracted by his handsome face and figure, and also by the fact that he was a prospective millionaire as one of the two first holders of the Nil Desperandum Claim.

A day or two after this Falconer called at Holroyd's location, and interviewed Miss Jennie over her washing tub. Her brother was away; and if Miss Jennie looked attractive in her Sunday best, she seemed in Falconer's eyes infinitely more so when slightly heated by honest labour, and with her beautiful arms bared to the shoulder, as she seemed to assert her own sturdy independence, which refused to be beaten by adverse circumstances.

"That's the girl for me," thought Falconer. And told her so, but in much more flowery language. Jennie seemed to be much moved by her would-be lover's ardour, but said parenthetically :—

"Why, Mr. Falconer, we all thought Dora Martin was the young lady?"

Falconer would not admit this, but hinted that even if he had had a predilection for Miss Martin, which he stoutly denied, it would have been entirely obviated by Jennie herself from the first moment he saw her.

Then the girl, having satisfied herself of the reality of this denial, and being the more convinced by Falconer's earnest eyes and ardent manner, gave in gladly, and was immediately kissed by her lover, albeit she had to hold her pretty arms and hands behind her, because of the soap suds.

Who should come up at this extremely inopportune moment but Holroyd himself, and was at once informed by Falconer that his sister had consented to become his wife !

A curious change came over Holroyd's face. He turned deathly pale, and seemed in such danger of a sudden faint that Falconer and Jennie supported him to his hut, where, after a glass of brandy had been promptly administered, he came to himself, and said brokenly : " Then it was—not Dora —Martin —you were after—at all !"

"Certainly not," replied Falconer. "I never had such an idea. I suppose the report got about through my being pretty constantly up at the Waratah, but beyond talking to the young lady in question now and then, I never said anything to her more than a gentleman would say to a fair casual acquaintance."

Now, Dora Martin had a cousin, a hard-up, reckless scoundrel of a fellow, who was just about at the end of his tether in more ways than one.

This man was commonly known as Dick. He had been born of respectable parents, farmers in the neighbouring district, but had got into bad company, and was only just beyond the clutches of the law for many a stolen horse or effaced cattle brand.

He was a splendid rider, but of late had taken to drink a great deal, and that had begun to tell upon his nerves. Dick had at one time made considerable money by breaking-in

"ALBEIT SHE HAD TO HOLD HER PRETTY ARMS AND HANDS BEHIND HER, BECAUSE OF THE SOAP SUDS."

From the Land of the Wombat. *Page 208.*

highly-bred colts, but latterly he preferred to earn or lose it by dubious card-playing, and had dropped into the Waratah occasionally on the strength of his relationship, which, however, Martin and his daughter kept carefully concealed.

Dora Martin was very vain; more than that, she was bitterly piqued by Falconer's attentions to Jennie Holroyd and utter neglect of herself, and she knew that Jennie Holroyd was much above her in the social scale. She, Dora herself, had spread the report about that Falconer was paying her attentions. As a matter of fact he had never done so. It had been a mere passing flirtation, such as any young fellow might have had with a pretty and attractive young girl.

And Dora undoubtedly was both. She had also been well-educated, and could sing, play, and dance very well indeed. But the main attraction had been on her side, and she had cherished the idea.

Two days before the events related above she had detected Dick in the very act of taking some one-pound notes and some silver out of the till, and had told him that unless he put them back at once, and left the district for good and all, she would inform her father, who, in spite of the shame of such a relationship coming to general knowledge, would, Dick felt sure, consign him to the care of the police, to await his trial for larceny. So Dick slunk off, baffled, but with a bitter rage in his dark heart, now so callous with repeated breaches of the law, that he actually considered himself the injured one.

"Curse her," muttered he, as he stole away through the miners' camp. "I'll be even with her yet, for all her fine ways. If I hadn't been afraid of her making a darned row in the house I'd have taken that money; for I know enough to force her to give me anything I want, and I will too. If I get her alone and off her guard I'll make her suffer for it, see if I don't."

It was Dick who had casually overheard part of Dora's conversation with Holroyd a night or two previously when the couple were met by Routledge. He had heard Dora tell Holroyd that Falconer had paid her the most marked attention before he met his sister, and gathered that her vanity had suffered a great deal.

Next day Dora Martin, who was very fond of horse exercise,

was riding her favourite mare towards Blue Rock, the town through which Cobb and Co.'s coach passed on the way to Melbourne, and where there were several good shops. She was about half-way, and when following a lonely bridle track on the top of a hill, she was suddenly confronted by Dick, also on horseback, and in a very nasty and revengeful humour.

Noticing the desperation and anger on her cousin's face, Dora Martin, though a plucky and determined girl, became alarmed, the more so because Dick had sprung his horse alongside hers and made a prisoner of her by fixing a firm grasp with his right hand on her mare's bridle.

"Now, my lady," said Dick savagely, "you were pretty high up on the stilts with me yesterday; it's my turn now. What were you saying to Ned Holroyd the other night? I may just as well tell you that I was close by and heard every word you said about Falconer."

Dora paled visibly, but she exclaimed with rising anger: "Let go my bridle, sir, or it will be the worse for you!"

"No fear," said Dick coolly. "You were egging Holroyd on to get his sister away from Waratah, because she was in your way. And I know a lot more besides. Now, I shan't let go your bridle until you give me a couple of pounds and swear that you won't say a word about that little matter of the till. You would never have missed it, for the governor and yourself have just been coining money, and every one about here knows that *that* is a solid fact."

"If I do, Dick," said Dora, "will you in your turn give me your solemn assurance that you will not say a word to any one of what I said about Mr. Falconer?"

"It's a bargain," said Dick relenting. "And now for *your* part of it. When I get those two pounds I will let you go."

Dora produced her purse, gave her cousin the sum required, and they parted.

Dora rode on and made her purchases, but Dick disappeared. Dora was perfectly well aware that the ex-schoolmaster was violently in love with her, and she had exercised all her arts to induce him to leave the diggings and take his sister with him. As she had flown at higher game, she did not feel in the least inclined to be coerced into love-making, and did not care a bit for the new object, or his penury either. She was the mistress of a facile tongue, and she had employed it for her own ends, making the unfortunate man believe that it might all end favourably for him.

But things so came to pass that Swanhill Jack, having "bottomed" on Holroyd's claim and found it a "duffer," put in a drive and suddenly "struck it rich" also; and as the trend of the "lead" deviated from the adjacent claims, and went straight for Routledge and Falconer's Nil Desperandum, those two, who had instant news supplied them by trusty agents, in conjunction with the syndicate, took up more ground on the line, but only *after* the astute Swanhill Jack, who shifted his ground, and pegged out for all his mates instantly upon his discovery, to his and their great advantage.

Then the back line of the lead was snapped up by the syndicate, and they also offered Holroyd a good round sum for his new claim, that which was taken up by Swanhill Jack. He accepted the offer, and thus became possessor of a sum of money which he could never have earned, in the teaching profession, even at the very highest salary. Jennie was now an heiress, not a very wealthy one, but still possessed of enough and to spare.

And poor Holroyd renewed his suit to Dora Martin with increased hope. When the payable "lead" was followed away from Holroyd's old claim, Swanhill Jack and his mate had sunk a new prospecting shaft, untimbered, again on the deposit, and Falconer and Routledge found in this quite enough assurance to satisfy them for the recent purchase, and enough to justify them in hopes of a considerable profit, far and away beyond the sum the syndicate had given. There were only two dissatisfied people on the Waratah goldfield. One was Holroyd himself, in despair of the ultimate success of his suit, feeling that Dora did not really care for him, and surmising that Falconer was the favoured one. The other was Dora Martin. She was utterly miserable and a bit revengeful besides. She had hinted to Dick, who had again waylaid her for more money, that she wished she could make it even for Falconer, who had utterly destroyed her happiness.

"Well, look here, my lass," said the scoundrel, "I'll get you your revenge; I think I know a way to work it. You give me twenty pounds, you can easily manage it, and when I've got it I'll clear out of here for good. You just take four or five pounds out of the till every day, till the sum is made up. Your governor will never know, and there's such a crowd of people going to your place all day, and all night too, that a small sum like that spread over a week or two, will never be missed. You leave it to me, I'll fix it up for Falconer somehow, never you mind how, but I'll work it so that no one will ever be a bit the wiser. He deserves something to aggravate him too, my girl, for the way he has treated you. Such a pretty accomplished girl as you are," said the artful Dick, with such seeming earnestness that the unstable Dora instantly collapsed and burst into tears, agreeing that Dick, in his own terms, "should work it somehow".

That day week she handed over the twenty pounds agreed upon to her cousin, and he vanished again. Next morning Falconer and Routledge were about to be lowered into the new shaft by a primitive contrivance of windlass, bucket and rope, one of their working diggers standing by with his hand on the winch of the windlass; when, to their surprise, Holroyd himself came up and asked to be allowed to go down first, as he had "something to show them". He seemed rather excited. Holroyd had of course been down before several times, but his illness and internal pain generally made him disinclined for much exertion, though he told Falconer, who suggested it, that he felt perfectly well, and believed that he was going to get all right again.

Somewhat astonished, Falconer told him to get a foot in the bucket, and himself prepared to lower him. After about six steady unwindings of the windlass, there was a jerk, a total absence of resistance or any weight to Falconer's grasp, and Holroyd had gone!

The rope had been cut so deftly that it was not apparent at once until the windlass revolutions had sent the whole weight of the unfortunate man upon the nearly severed strands eight or nine feet back, with the awful result recorded! And the rope had been cut in a line directly *under* the roller of the windlass and from the inside of the rope!

With blanched faces the party above ground hastily examined the rest of the rope, attached another bucket, and went down to the shaft bottom, where they found Holroyd quite dead! He must have turned downwards somehow for his neck was broken.

Then came a curious time for Falconer and Jennie Holroyd,

for after Jennie had heard the fatal news from her lover and had somewhat got over the shock, amongst her brother's effects she found his diary, which he always kept locked up, and which in fact was locked itself.

In this diary was the following extract:—

"1st July. Went down to the new shaft near my old claim and saw a way. To-night I shall do it, and my enemy will be gone for ever." It was the last entry in the book. On 2nd July, Holroyd had gone to his final account.

Jennie Holroyd was nearly distracted with the horrible thoughts which ran riot in her tortured brain, and almost broke her heart. "Was it really true that her brother intended *murder*? To murder her own sweetheart? True, by his very own action he had himself become the victim of his own dread purpose. He must have gone mad? Was it in the family? Should she go mad too?" She felt very like it. Her brother, by his action, had destroyed his own life and hers too. She could never marry Falconer now. And she did love him so dearly. Such a fine character and disposition he had, and such a noble young fellow. "Oh, what shall I do, Jack?" she sobbed. "I can never marry you now." And she showed him the fatal entry.

Jack Falconer looked very grave, but pooh-poohed her reasoning, saying that even if her brother had really intended to cut him off, it would make no possible difference to his feelings towards her; that no one but themselves need ever know. And he threw the diary into the fire, and burnt every trace of the accusing entry.

But Jennie was perfectly firm, and, despite all her lover's assurances and entreaties, left for Melbourne shortly after her brother's funeral, determining to support herself by setting up a school for girls.

Falconer departed that night to his own house, deeply chagrined and greatly shocked at the deplorable character of his betrothed's brother. "I suppose the beggar did it to get me out of his way," thought he, "and repented, or went mad, at the last minute; coming down so much elevated by his new way of thinking that he no longer felt pain, but only the sublimity of a lofty self-sacrifice, knowing the rope to be cut for a deadly purpose of his own. I had a narrow escape indeed."

And that was the only conclusion he could come to.

Some three months rolled on, and Dora began to pay attention to Falconer again, much to his exasperation; but he noticed that the girl was different, and didn't seem to care for any allusion to the fatal accident.

She once or twice asked him if he knew where Jennie Holroyd was, but he could not tell her, as he did not know himself.

Firm and unflinching as to her resolution, Jennie left Melbourne and went secretly to Sydney, and Falconer who had followed her down in the hopes of persuading her to become his wife without delay, was totally unable to trace her, though he spared no expense, and even employed a couple of smart detectives.

At last one day a mounted trooper rode up to his house at Waratah and said that he must come with him at once to Blue Rock, as there was a man dying there who earnestly wished to see him. It was Dick, who, moved by a guilty conscience and the effects of heavy drinking, desired to unburden himself of a ghastly secret. He, in the presence of a magistrate and the doctor, did so. He had suffered a severe fall from a young unbroken colt, and, though able to speak, had not much time to live.

"Mr. Falconer," said he in gasps, "I tried to set—Holroyd —on to—do—you a bad—turn, but so help me—Bob, I thought you would get off with a—broken leg. Holroyd—said he would do it—but—he never did, for I watched—him—near —to the shaft. There was no—one about. It was not a very deep—hole—and I meant no—murder—I was half—drunk— too. But I saw—Holroyd's—face. He shuddered, and turned —away—and I—*swear*—he did not—do it—as God—made— me—I swear it—for—I did—it—myself!—"

The blood rushed to the wretched man's lips and in a few moments he was a corpse!

"And Holroyd never knew the rope was cut!" thought Falconer.

This confession was duly attested by the authorities.

Falconer felt now that Holroyd, being exonerated, there was no longer any bar to his union with Jennie, so he at once went to Melbourne and gave his detectives such instructions that they finally found Jennie established at Balmain, near

Sydney, and delivered to her keeping a letter from Falconer himself which filled her with joy. He shortly afterwards joined her, and facts were made still clearer by Swanhill Jack informing Falconer, that when he had bottomed the new claim on the rich "lead" he had told Holroyd, and he had been down the shaft to see it. As the particular richness had occurred in some ground dissimilar to anything Swanhill Jack had ever seen before, it was probably this news, Falconer thought, that Holroyd's repentant soul had urged him to give on the morning of the accident.

Falconer and Jennie were married at St. James's, Sydney. Willie Routledge was best man, and Swanwill Jack, who had always been a humble adorer of the bride, was asked also, and appeared in his best clothes and a tall hat, both quite new for the occasion. He also wore the most portentous and wonderful tie ever seen, with an enormous gold nugget as a scarf pin. The colour of the tie was an enthralling blue, which fairly made you wink, and could be seen at least half a mile off down the street.

Swanhill Jack also presented the bridegroom with a massive and valuable nugget ring of the purest gold, and Jennie with a most beautiful waratah and bird's-nest brooch, also of gold. The latter he had had made at Hardy's, in the most approved and newest style, also providing the gold for its manufacture. At the wedding breakfast he said that Jennie had always brought him luck, and he wished the same to her and her husband for all their days.

He then raised a brimming glass of champagne in his strong tanned hand, and concluded: "And here's to Miss Jennie—I mean Mrs. Falconer. For a bright, independent, plucky young ooman, I never seen her ekal, and wherever she goes old Swanhill Jack'll be glad to hear of her happiness, if so be as she will deign to let such an old 'shellback' as me know." And down went the champagne!

Falconer, always prosperous, went home to England with his bride by way of commencing his honeymoon, and the old squire having passed away, leaving everything in a pretty good muddle, he, as successor, began to restore order in the most exciting style for all the tenants, and dependants, in the village. Never in the oldest man's memory had they experienced such wonderful times, for almost everybody was employed at remunerative rates, and Falconer's Court began to feel its ancient glories reviving after the decay of three-quarters of a century. And he kept improving it year by year, to all his farmer tenants' satisfaction and advantage, seeing, after the lapse of time, that it was possible to do a great deal of good with his huge income, and to leave his young family of a girl and two stalwart boys in a better position than even his father's father's father had been, when Falconer's Court was at its zenith. But the added wing, and the beautiful grounds, and well-preserved shooting and fishing, with the meet of the county hounds at the front door, upheld its fame, even if times were more modern. But about the same time, far away in another land, a faded and broken girl, Dora Martin, would sometimes wander through the sunny precincts of the Sydney Domain, and rest awhile in shady spots under the honeysuckles, perchance gazing also wistfully over the blue expanse of the lovely harbour, past Garden Island down towards the "Heads," or watching the myriad small fast ferry steamers scudding to and fro. She was never even suspected of being a cause of trouble, but her conscience, although she had never thought that Dick could have plotted anything so awful as the preceding events have shown, was never at ease, and brought such a varied load of tribulation with it, that she sank, and a stone in the metropolitan cemetery now alone marks the sad record of her wasted life, with the fact that her age was only twenty-four!

MUZZLEM'S

> Will you walk into my parlour ? said the spider to the fly.
> —*Nursery Rhyme.*

THE name was enough. It was also enough for the enlightened wayfarer to know that "Muzzlem's" was at the end of his day's travel.

"Muzzlem's" was an infinity, a Paradise, a heavenly haven. There, after the weary turmoils of a long scorching ride, through a day of never-ending patches of mulga and gidyah scrub, one's hunger and thirst might be appeased. Here, after repletion, one might repose on a bench, outside the curious old dwelling—an excrescence in the middle of the little green plain—and watch the innocent twinkling stars, whilst puffing satisfaction and contentment from the peaceful dudheen. "Muzzlem" himself, would generally contrive to be present, and would enliven the conversation.

I must confess that I entertained suspicions that "Muzzlem" was a broken-down gentleman of fortune. The air with which he would hand you a glass of rum (there was no other beverage: but it was perfect) was gentility itself. He would affably join you in the funny little parlour, with its pine-logged sides, impossible "what-nots," bush-made tables, knick-knacks, and spoils of the chase.

Here might be seen a stuffed scrub turkey (in the skin, alas!), there a "gallar," there a "paddy melon," and blackfellows' "womeras," and "hielamans," and "waddies," and spears figured in odd corners, and, in conjunction with "boomerangs," were displayed as trophies on the walls. And gorgeous feather mats, made out of parrots, parrakeets, and lyre birds, adorned the corners and tables. And 'possum rugs graced the sofas and easy armchairs.

No one would have suspected "Muzzlem's" of being a sly grog shop. But it was so—and many wayfarers knew it. But they breathed it not in Gath, and Muzzlem—may every hair of his head be preserved—flourished and grew apace. There was a pervading friendliness in the way he clasped your hand in silence; a gentlemanly, persuasive, and secret way, which spoke volumes, although the owner never opened his lips. That hand-shake said, "Make yourselves at home, gentlemen; you are tired, fatigued. Outside, you will perceive, there is lush-green grass for your quadrupeds; inside I have that lush which will refresh the inner man. It is smuggled— I know that—it comes up the river. It never paid any duty, and I don't charge you for it. I annex it to your bill under the item of 'curios'.

"A fossil kangaroo tail, two pounds ten shillings—nothing, surely, for a night at *my* Paradise! And I win a little from you at euchre during the evening, say a five-pound note, but what of that? You are coming from the station where you have been working hard and earning money, and it is but just that I—'Muzzlem'—should have a little of your spare cash.

"I am only a wary old outside spider, but I am such a pleasant, gentlemanly dog, that you could not pass me, and your horses will be taken care of, and you will not be pressed to stay on the morrow. You will have an excellent breakfast in the morning, and sundry glasses of rum punch to carry you to the first *bonâ fide* 'pub' at the ferry. And on the other side of the river is the town—and 'nobblers'—and dissipation in a mild bush form." That is what the hand-shake said; and we were taken in, hospitably treated, and relieved of surplus cash.

And it was done in such a devilish gentlemanly manner that we liked it.

. . . .

"Muzzlem" was a pariah on the outskirts of civilisation, but we shall never see his like again; for alas, the old thatched rambling cabin is no more!

The trains whistle loud at Muzzlemville, where formerly the wild dog howled in the adjacent scrub, but near by the old spot is a neat iron railing, erected by subscription among many sorrowing friends. Inside that railing is a marble slab, at the head of a green grassy mound. On the slab is this inscription :—

MUZZLEM
OF
MUZZLEM'S.

He was generally "on"
Until he was taken "off".

L'ENVOI.

The old Gold-Reef's location—for I have ne'er forgot
The springing gum-tree saplings which grew about the spot,
Where parrots flashed and whistled, where bell birds hailed the dawn,
And I sometimes gladly greet you, and by you sometimes mourn.

For æons bush-fires swept you, coloured your " cap " like rust,
You kept the secret bravely deep down in the red, red dust ;
But the ages kept progressing, and the new white races came—
To some you left a fortune, and some you helped to fame.

But the glamour still keeps by you, visions of hidden wealth ;
In the old time you meant riches, in the present merely health ;
You bring me phantom " nuggets " to work to golden grain,
Wealth to the passing fancies still stirring in my brain.

And if there's good in asking, or "yes" to answered prayer,
I'd have those "nuggets" precious, bright idylls pure and fair ;
I'd let them work and fashion fresh stories in my mind,
And weld the gold in merit from out the years behind.

Whether in early morning, when thought is clear and bright,
Or in the noonday's splendour, or by the lamp alight,
Or in a dream of old days, when I see our camp again,
You and our merry party bring either joy or pain :

Pain to look back on lost friends, joy for the hither touch,
Of thoughts like little "nuggets" which mean to me so much,
"Nuggets" of recollection, from which I fashion tales,
And I long for those yellow gleamings, fresh from your golden vales.

Where the "Gully" sang of spring time, with its bubbling brooks and trees,
Where Nature's breast was wooing, where softly kissed the breeze,
 Mid scent of burning resin, from grass-trees on the range,
With perfume of bush-blossoms, and hues of glorious change.

Where tasselled wattles quiver, where all the herbs beneath
Bring back on Thought's fair pinions the west wind's bridal wreath;
So I pray her bring me henceforth some " nugget " from the reef,
For I fain would keep and treasure my fancy and belief.

For the " hitherto " kept me anchored, and I yearn for a golden gleam
From the bright good gold of the old reef to fashion a nobler theme,
With the " colour " of better merit, with the " mullock " washed away,
So that I leave behind me some " tribute " of my day.

www.ingramcontent.com/pod-product-compliance
Lightning Source LLC
Chambersburg PA
CBHW032108220426
43664CB00008B/1183